Business Park and Industrial Development Handbook

ULI Development Handbook Series

**Urban Land
Institute**

About ULI–the Urban Land Institute

ULI–the Urban Land Institute is a nonprofit education and research institute that is supported by its members. Its mission is to provide responsible leadership in the use of land in order to enhance the total environment.

ULI sponsors education programs and forums to encourage an open international exchange of ideas and sharing of experiences; initiates research that anticipates emerging land use trends and issues and proposes creative solutions based on that research; provides advisory services; and publishes a wide variety of materials to disseminate information on land use and development. Established in 1936, the Institute today has more than 17,000 members and associates from more than 60 countries representing the entire spectrum of the land use and development disciplines.

Richard M. Rosan
President

For more information about ULI and the resources that it offers related to business parks and a variety of other real estate and urban development issues, visit ULI's Web site at www.uli.org.

Cover photo: Stockley Park. Andrew Putler, Photography/Courtesy Arup Associates.

Project Staff

Rachelle L. Levitt
Senior Vice President, Policy and Practice
Publisher

Gayle Berens
Vice President, Real Estate Development Practice

Anne Frej
Director, Office and Industrial Development

Jo Allen Gause
Senior Director, Residential Development

Nancy Stewart
Director, Book Program

Leslie Holst
Senior Associate

Barbara M. Fishel/Editech
Manuscript Editor

Libby Howland
Case Study Editor

Helene Y. Redmond/HYR Graphics
Book Design/Layout

Meg Batdorff
Cover Design

Diann Stanley-Austin
Director, Publishing Operations

Recommended bibliographic listing:

Frej, Anne, et al. *Business Park and Industrial Development Handbook.* Washington, D.C.: ULI–the Urban Land Institute, 2001.

ULI Catalog Number: B30
International Standard Book Number: 0-87420-876-9
Library of Congress Control Number: 2001091816

**Books in the ULI Development Handbook Series
(formerly Community Builders Handbook Series)**
Downtown Development Handbook, Second Edition, 1992
Mixed-Use Development Handbook, 1987
Multifamily Housing Development Handbook, 2000
Office Development Handbook, Second Edition, 1998
Residential Development Handbook, Second Edition, 1990
Resort Development Handbook, 1997
Shopping Center Development Handbook, Third Edition, 1999

Authors

Project Director

Anne Frej
ULI–the Urban Land Institute
Washington, D.C.

Primary Contributing Authors

Marvin F. Christensen
Vice President
RREEF
San Francisco, California

William D'Elia
Principal
EDAW, Inc.
San Francisco, California

Mark J. Eppli, Ph.D.
Associate Professor of Finance and Real Estate
Department of Finance
The George Washington University
Washington, D.C.

Libby Howland
Writer/Editor
Takoma Park, Maryland

James R. Musbach
Managing Principal
Economic & Planning Systems, Inc.
Berkeley, California

Frank H. Spink
Principal
Spink Consultancy
Annandale, Virginia

Dorothy J. Verdon
Principal
Verdon Consulting
Alexandria, Virginia

Acknowledgments

The ULI Foundation, as part of its commitment to support ULI's core research program, provides funding for the new and revised editions of the ULI Development Handbook Series. The *Business Park and Industrial Development Handbook* was funded in part by grants from the Foundation. The Urban Land Institute gratefully acknowledges these contributions.

The *Business Park and Industrial Development Handbook* is the result of a collaborative effort on the part of ULI staff members and practitioners in the field of industrial development. Although it is impossible to mention everyone who participated in this effort, a number of individuals and organizations deserve special acknowledgment and thanks.

Special recognition goes to the authors of chapters or major portions of chapters. Chris Christensen and James Musbach put considerable time and effort into the text and case studies for Chapter 2. Ashley Powell and Pamela Stein of RREEF provided text on financial feasibility analysis, and Asieh Mansour provided an explanation of demand calculation. Mark Eppli, an active ULI contributor, wrote most of Chapter 3, portions of which were based on earlier work by James Burck of the Martin Group. Chapter 4 was produced by William D'Elia, Dorothy Verdon, Rick Bernhardt, and longtime ULI author Frank Spink. Libby Howland wrote Chapters 5 and 6 after in-depth research.

The individuals who reviewed the manuscript or portions of it deserve thanks for taking time from busy professional schedules to read the manuscript and make suggestions that improved the text. This real-life perspective is one of the factors that make ULI handbooks practical and usable. Luis Belmonte and Steve Chamberlin offered valuable insights from a developer's point of view. Brian Burrough, Donna Batchelor, and Karen Thorp added a hands-on perspective to business park operations and management. Architects Rick Donnally and Dell DeRevere answered countless questions on issues ranging from roofing materials to zoning. Deborah Brett gave substantive comments on project feasibility more than once. Three real estate brokers specializing in industrial properties—Rick Latini, Mike Elardo, and Jim Bohar—offered valuable insights into the marketing and leasing process. Molly Badgett served as a reviewer as well as a valuable source for photographs of industrial projects.

Other individuals furnished useful insights into the business park development process. Bob Barker provided background and comments on lease negotiations. John Worthington of DEGW Architects gave his insights into future trends in the industrial market. Robert Harris of Holland and Knight, L.L.C., offered updated information on zoning. John Rushton of the Small Back Room supplied graphics and background on how to establish the identity of a business park development.

Thanks go to the many organizations and individuals that contributed data, photographs, graphics, and other materials. Providing photographs to illustrate the book were IDI; DeRevere Associates; Julie Snow Architects; Arup Associates; Donnally, Lederer, and Vujcic; and others. Lend Lease and PricewaterhouseCoopers allowed ULI to reproduce a number of graphics from their publication, *Emerging Trends in Real Estate: 2001.* The Roulac Group and Real Estate Research Corporation provided useful data that were used to create exhibits in the chapter on finance and investment.

Much effort went into the presentation of each of the 14 case studies included in this book. The authors of the case studies deserve recognition for their thorough research—Michael Baker, André Bald, Tom Black, Ken Braverman, Ben Cornish, Steve Fader, David Fansler, Charles Lockwood, David Mulvihill, Dean Schwanke, Ginnie Sharkawy, and M. Atef Sharkawy. We also would like to thank the developers, investors, architects, landscape architects, and others associated with the projects described in the case studies for providing detailed information, photographs, and site plans.

Many Urban Land Institute staff members were instrumental in the book's publication. Considerable credit goes to Jo Allen Gause for initiating this project and carrying it through to the draft manuscript stage before it was handed over to me. Rachelle Levitt and Gayle Berens provided direction and encouragement throughout the production process. Leslie Holst contributed in countless ways, from writing text and captions to selecting photographs. Steve Blank reviewed the chapter on financing and investment to ensure that it was up to date. Joan Campbell and Rick Davis responded to numerous requests for information.

Michael Beyard, author of the first edition of this handbook, provided a foundation for this book; much core information, including the history of industrial and business park development, was drawn from that edition and from the earlier *Industrial Development Handbook* and updated to reflect current market practices. André Bald and Oliver Jerschow deserve credit for selecting case studies and feature boxes and obtaining photographs. Ryan Komppa tracked down and confirmed a wide variety of pieces of information.

Many thanks also go to the editorial and design team managed by Nancy Stewart. Barbara Fishel ensured that the text was clearly written and consistent. Helene Redmond took pieces of text, photos, and tables and created the final design. Meg Batdorff created the cover design, and Diann Stanley-Austin managed the printing production.

To all of these individuals and to others who inadvertently may have been overlooked, thank you for playing a role in the creation and production of this book.

Anne Frej
Project Director

Contents

Foreword

This handbook is part of the ULI Development Handbook Series, a set of volumes on real estate development that traces its roots back to 1947, when ULI published the *Community Builders Handbook*, the first book in the series. That edition was revised and updated several times over the following 25 years, and a replica of the original edition was issued in 2000. In 1975, ULI initiated the Community Builders Handbook Series. A number of titles were published in this series over a period of years, covering industrial, residential, shopping center, office, mixed-use, downtown, and recreational development. In 1997, the handbook series was completely redesigned and renamed the ULI Development Handbook Series.

This handbook was preceded by two publications dealing with the topic of business and industrial parks. *Industrial Development Handbook* was published in 1975. The second handbook on this topic, *Business and Industrial Park Development Handbook*, was published in 1988. Its new title was a reflection of the changes that had taken place in industrial development and the increasing focus on master-planned business parks. Another name change in this latest edition reflects the continuing evolution of business parks as integrated work settings that accommodate a range of activities from light manufacturing and distribution to office and service functions.

The objective of this and all handbooks in the ULI Development Handbook Series is to provide a practical overview of each sector of development for a broad audience. As such, this book systematically covers the range of issues to be addressed in the implementation of a major industrial or business park development from project feasibility analysis and financing to marketing, leasing, operations, and management.

Case studies give real-life examples of 14 diverse business parks and industrial facilities around the world, describing the development process, experience gained, and detailed project data, including rental rates and cost breakdowns. The projects documented range from new projects constructed on greenfield sites to renovated historic industrial complexes.

The creation of a successful industrial development, whether a standalone building or a multiphase business park, demands expertise in assessing market conditions, obtaining financing, creating an appropriate design, marketing, and managing the finished product.

It must achieve a balance between the goals of the local community and those of the project's sponsors. Although the process is not always simple, with a clear vision on the part of all parties it is possible to create a product that is an asset to the community and a profitable venture for the developer. It is hoped that this handbook can assist those involved in the development process to achieve their goals.

Anne Frej
Project Director

Business Park and Industrial Development Handbook

1. Introduction

The business parks of today are the product of an evolutionary process. From their antecedents in the manufacturing-oriented industrial estates and parks of the early 20th century, they have become dynamic workplace settings for business, incubators for new technologies, and employment centers that contribute to the economic life of many communities.

Flexibility is key to their success. Business parks not only accommodate a mix of activities such as storage, light manufacturing, research, and office functions, all in a planned and controlled setting; they also can be adapted in form and function to meet changes in the market. This attribute has been critical in recent years, as rapid technological innovation has created new requirements for the industrial sector. The growth of e-commerce and just-in-time distribution systems has led to the transformation of warehouses into sophisticated logistics centers. The need for flexible work spaces that can house office and industrial activities under one roof has resulted in new hybrid buildings known as *flex space*. The growth of employee-intensive operations such as call centers and data processing centers at business parks has increased population densities there and resulted in requirements for more parking and better on-site amenities and services.

For occupiers, business parks offer the capacity to grow and expand at the same location. With multiple buildings of different types, sizes, and prices to choose from, all in one business park, startup companies can begin operations in small-scale incubator space and eventually move to more prestigious headquarters without ever changing their address. Established companies can centralize their operations, from high-visibility corporate headquarters to inexpensive back-office or flex space. Leasing space, buying a facility, or having it built to specifications are also possible options for occupiers in modern multiphase business parks.

For developers, business parks offer flexibility as well. Despite business parks' being long-term investments with large budgets because of their size and infrastructure requirements, developers have the benefit of deciding whether to sell unimproved land parcels or completed buildings in a business park. Risk is also minimized by the opportunity to phase development, relying on positive market conditions or formal lease or sale agreements before proceeding with construction. Many developers will not initiate a project until a formal commitment has been received to lease or buy a major portion of the project.

Communities reap potential benefits from business parks. In an era of increasing competition to attract new businesses and jobs, many governments see business parks as a tool to stimulate economic development. In some cases, the argument is strong enough to warrant the public sector's active participation in the formation of business parks and the provision of tax incentives or financing assistance to developers.

Origen Center, Phillips Plastic Corporation, Menomonie, Wisconsin.

A characterization of submarket rents and lease terms was obtained through a survey of brokers and a review of comparable leased properties. Because the subject property can accommodate various sizes of tenants, warehouse rents in three size categories were analyzed. Discussions with brokers also allowed for a breakdown of industrial tenants in Valwood by industry group (see Figure 2-1).

The review of existing market conditions indicated that Dallas and the Valwood submarket were in the growth phases of their market cycles. Market conditions were typified by a growing warehouse inventory as a result of new development and low vacancy rates. Leasing trends, however, showed that warehouse spaces greater than 75,000 square feet (6,970 m²) were leasing more slowly, in part because larger distribution firms were moving to other submarkets outside Valwood. Meanwhile, users of spaces smaller than 40,000 square feet (3,720 m²) con-

tinued to locate in Valwood because of its functional space and centralized location.

Rents remained at attractive levels and were unencumbered by concessions or high tenant improvement allowances. Monthly rents for spaces of 100,000 square feet (9,300 m²) or more ranged from $.28 to $.30 per square foot ($3 to $3.25/m²), net, while rents for spaces of 20,000 to 40,000 square feet (1,860 to 3,720 m²) ranged from $.30 to $.34 per square foot ($3.25 to $3.65/m²), net. Spaces under 20,000 square feet (1,860 m²) garnered the highest monthly rents, $.32 to $.36 per square foot ($3.45 to $3.90/m²), net. Rent escalations for longer-term leases (five years or more) offered further evidence of a healthy market. The team also found the subject property to be typical of the submarket in terms of its spatial/functional characteristics and its lease terms. ■

Warehouse Rents and Lease Terms
Valwood Submarket

	Single Tenant 100,000 Square Feet (9,300 m²) or More	Multitenant 20,000–40,000 Square Feet (1,860–3,720 m²)	Multitenant Less Than 20,000 Square Feet (1,860 m²)
Monthly Rent (per square foot, net net)	$.28–.30	$.30–.34	$.32–.36
Term	5–10 years	3–5 years	3–5 years
Escalation	Flat for 3 years, mid-term increase for 5-year terms or longer		
Free Rent	1–2 months per lease term		
Tenant Improvements (per square foot)	Overall: $.50–1.00 Office: $2.00–3.00		
Expenses (per square foot)	$.85–1.20		

Note: Rents and terms for "new" warehouse properties with minimum 24-foot (7-m) clear heights and office buildout of 15 to 20 percent (under 10 percent for single-tenant building).
Source: RREEF Research.

spatial configurations, physical improvements, and economic performance. A related issue, with so many businesses today requiring flexible space to accommodate a wide range of activities, is the blurring of differences between the types of office and industrial spaces.

Realistically, few market data sources adequately segment industrial space into subtypes. Most secondary market data are lumped into a single category labeled "industrial," making it difficult to assess the performance of individual subtypes. One method of getting a rough picture of the various property types, however, is to segment properties by size categories, such as "under 5,000 square feet," "10,000 to 25,000 square feet," and "larger than 25,000 square feet" (or "under 500 square meters," "1,000 to 2,500 square meters," and "larger than 2,500 square meters"). For example, industrial properties under 10,000 square feet (930 m²) are more likely to be office/

warehouse facilities or showrooms than traditional bulk warehouses.

Another issue regarding industrial inventory data is that they typically do not include owner-occupied space, which in the future could be vacated and once again enter the rental market.

Industrial leasing brokers and others involved in land transactions are excellent sources of primary market data. A telephone survey of active local industrial brokers is one method of uncovering information on a submarket's tenant base, effective rents, and overall leasing terms. Property appraisers also have data on comparable lease transactions, but their data should be considered "lagging indicators" as they focus on past leasing and sales activities. Other survey candidates include industrial property managers and other developers active in the submarket. In some cases, these profes-

figure 2-1

Industrial Tenants by Industry

Valwood Submarket

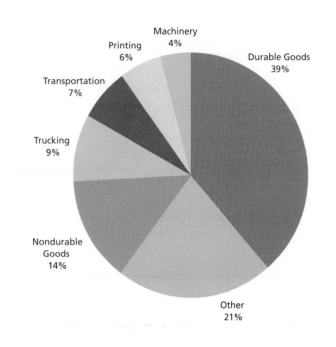

Sources: Cognetics Real Estate, Inc.; RREEF Research.

sionals may be willing to share information, particularly if it is somewhat general in scope. In other cases, it may be necessary to pay for the most up-to-date and detailed data available.

Information should be collected on leasing trends, rental rates for the pertinent industrial property sub-type, and available concessions. Additional questions may address leasing terms (including tenant improvement allowances), lease types (net or gross) and duration, rent escalations, utility costs, operational expenses (taxes, insurance, common area maintenance), and turnover. Other more general questions should address issues related to tenants in the submarket, such as expansion, moving in, and departure.

In conducting the survey, it is especially important to obtain data on effective rents, rather than asking or contract rents. Asking rents are those rents a landlord advertises and would like to obtain, contract rents are those rents recorded in the lease, and effective rents are contract rents minus any rent concessions. Contract and effective rents tend to be the same when market conditions are healthy, but *effective* rents may be considerably lower than contract rents in a weak market.

It is important to remember that although most brokers provide helpful insights into the workings of the market, some may tend to overstate the positives and understate the negatives. Because brokers are in the business of leasing and selling real estate, they tend to put a positive spin on market conditions.

As a follow-up to the more general market analysis, a competitive analysis or marketability analysis should be undertaken to assess the strengths of the proposed project in comparison with its competition. This step involves the collection of more detailed data on direct competitors, both existing and proposed. Again, a good place to start is with real estate brokers or management companies involved in the marketing of industrial developments who may be willing to provide plans or brochures and marketing materials on individual properties. Plans and project summaries are likely to provide more detail on the spatial configuration and technical features of buildings. Brochures, which are more oriented toward marketing efforts, generally contain less detail on specifications. Although they typically have general site and building plans as well as data on areas and general technical features, it may be necessary to follow up with calls to obtain more detailed information. Useful data on competing projects include:

- site sizes;
- building and lot sizes;
- building description;
- schedule, including when marketing was initiated and the status of leasing;
- quoted and effective rents;
- service charges;
- parking ratios;
- major tenants;
- typical lease terms;
- vacancy and absorption rates; and
- developer or current owner.

The most useful data about the building include ceiling height, column spacing, depth, the number of dock-/ground-level doors, and percentage of space in offices. Attention should be directed to those components that might give the development an advantage in the market. Air conditioning and oversized parking lots are physical components that might garner premium rents.

Industrial Space Demand Analysis

Demand analysis attempts to determine the level of demand for industrial facilities (by type if possible) in the market area. With this information as background, the analysis assesses the attractiveness of the proposed project in relation to its competition to determine the pace of leasing and rents the development can achieve.

Econometric models used to project absorption can be powerful analytical tools, but they do have serious limitations. To develop a properly specified econometric model, sufficient time-series data must be available. Without adequate data, the problems of misspecification and omitted variables can reduce the value of econometric forecasting. Moreover, it is difficult to forecast with econometric models because the relationship between variables can change as a result of factors not fully captured by the model.

In practice, demand models for industrial space often emulate office demand models, where a change in employ-

The demand for industrial space depends on economic and demographic factors. In the modeling framework, demand is estimated as a function of GMP and population using the following functional specification:

$$LOG(OSTOCK) = A + B \times LOG(GMP) + C \times LOG(NR) + E$$

where
OSTOCK = occupied stock in square feet,
GMP = gross metropolitan product in constant dollars, and
NR = population.

A double logarithmic functional form is adopted in the specification. Because the dependent and independent variables are in activity levels, the use of a double logarithmic functional form is most appropriate for at least two reasons. First, the use of logs enables the analyst to pick up any nonlinear relationship between the variables, which would not be possible if the variables were estimated in level form. Second, the use of logs reduces inefficiency of the estimated parameters resulting from the presence of heteroskedasticity.

The use of a log specification changes parameters B and D into simple proportionality relationships or "elasticities." An elasticity (in this case B and D) measures the effect of a 1 percent change in the independent variable (in this case GMP and NR) on the dependent variable (OSTOCK). The elasticity of OSTOCK with respect to GMP, for example, is the percentage change in OSTOCK divided by the percentage change in GMP (which is equal to B in this example). Elasticities are useful because they are unit-free; that is, their values are independent of the units in which the variables are measured.

In the Tradeport case study, for example,

OSTOCK@DALLAS =
EXP(9.7 + 0.28 × LOG(GMP@DALLAS)
+ 0.18 × LOG(NR@DALLAS).

The results of estimation show that B = 0.28 and D = 0.18, implying that for every 1 percent increase in GMP, occupied space increases by 0.28 percent. A 1 percent increase in population results in an 0.18 percent increase in occupied stock.

Before solving this equation for forecasting purposes, we determine the goodness of fit by solving the equation over history. The difference between the actual history of occupied stock and the estimated occupied stock is the adjustment term, which is added to the projections. In this manner, the adjustment term tells by how much the equation over- or underestimates occupied stock. In addition, it ensures that there are no major takeoff problems during the first year of the forecast horizon. ∎

Demand Calculation

Year	(A) Annual Percentage Change in GMP	(B) Demand Parameter	A x B	A x B x OSTOCK = Net Absorption	(C) Annual Percentage Change in Population	(D) Demand Parameter	C x D	C x D x OSTOCK = Net Absorption	Constant + Adjustment Term	Projected Total Net Absorption (000)
1999	0.016	0.28	0.00448	1,276	0.017	0.18	0.00306	871	4,702	6,850
2000	0.020	0.28	0.00560	1,622	0.015	0.18	0.00270	781	2,369	4,772
2001	0.023	0.28	0.00644	1,899	0.014	0.18	0.00252	743	2,701	5,343
2002	0.024	0.28	0.00672	2,020	0.015	0.18	0.00270	811	2,914	5,747
2003	0.026	0.28	0.00728	2,232	0.016	0.18	0.00288	882	2,820	5,935
2004	0.026	0.28	0.00728	2,276	0.016	0.18	0.00288	900	2,854	6,031
2005	0.026	0.28	0.00728	2,322	0.016	0.18	0.00288	918	3,079	6,320
2006	0.027	0.28	0.00756	2,461	0.016	0.18	0.00288	937	3,168	6,567
2007	0.027	0.28	0.00756	2,513	0.017	0.18	0.00306	1,017	3,341	6,871
2008	0.027	0.28	0.00756	2,567	0.017	0.18	0.00306	1,039	3,571	7,177

Nortel Networks renovated existing office space in Research Triangle Park, Raleigh/Durham, North Carolina, without disrupting the lives of 8,500 workers, resulting in new 100,000-square-foot (9,300-m²) office buildings.

ment is a prime determinant of potential space absorption. The connection between industrial employment and industrial space demand is not clear-cut, however, because space allocated per employee varies greatly among the different industrial subtypes. Research on similar industrial projects and interviews with architects and others involved in the design or construction of industrial buildings will help to establish an estimate. Multiplying the space per employee by the estimated number of new employees provides an estimate of future space requirements. It is also important to focus on the types of jobs that are most likely to make up demand for industrial space. Analysts tend to focus on manufacturing and export-oriented industries.

Equally important, a prime determinant of space demand in industrial analysis, especially for a warehouse property, is inventory flow, not jobs.[2] This approach to modeling warehouse space demand assumes that warehouse demand originates more from the volume of

inventories stored than from the workers used to move the material around. In the past, the lack of reliable regional or local data on freight inventories hindered the use of this methodology; however, the Reebie TRANSEARCH database has been found to be a useful source for information on freight activity across regions of the United States and Canada.[3] The data are disaggregated down to the county, business economic area, five-digit zip code, metropolitan area, state, and province (for Canada). Goods are defined by commodity across all regions, with volumes in terms of loads, tonnage, or value.[4]

Analysts conducting industrial warehouse analyses should also review other measures of metropolitan growth such as gross metropolitan product (GMP) or changes in total population or households. Growth in GMP is arguably one of the best indicators of absorption of warehouse space because GMP is a measure of the output of a local economy. Warehouse/distribution properties store much of this output during product manufacturing or during shipment to consumers.

Metropolitan Area Absorption Calculation. Calculating net absorption for the metropolitan area involves multiplying the annual percentage change in GMP and the annual percentage change in metropolitan area population (or households) by the appropriate space demand parameter. In its simplest form, a proportionality relationship is derived between the change in occupied stock (net absorption) and percentage changes in GMP and population.

Submarket Capture Rate. After space demand is calculated for a metropolitan area, a final step is to estimate what share of metropolitan absorption will be captured by the submarket. Often, analysts simply calculate a submarket capture rate by using a "fair share" approach. A fair share capture rate is simply the proportion of metropolitan space inventory located in a submarket. For example, if a submarket holds 9 percent of a metropolitan area's industrial space inventory, then its capture rate is 9 percent. It is important to note, however, that this

TechPark was developed by the city of Rock Hill, South Carolina, and the Rock Hill Economic Development Corporation as a high-amenity business park with a million dollar civic monument that symbolizes the city's history, spirit, and aspirations for the future.

Projections for absorption of warehouse space in the Dallas metropolitan area were calculated based on changes in GMP and population. Total employment growth as an indicator of demand in the market was also reviewed. The data, obtained from a national forecasting and economic consulting firm, indicated that growth in Dallas would slow during 1999 before expanding more rapidly in the long term.

The projections for GMP and population were used in modeling metropolitan area warehouse space absorption in Dallas. The model indicated that for every 1 percent increase in GMP, occupied space would increase by 0.26 percent. A 1 percent increase in population resulted in a 0.24 percent increase. Metropolitan net absorption was expected to average approximately 6.1 million square feet (567,000 m²) annually through 2008.

Absorption in the submarket was calculated for each year of the forecast period by applying a capture rate to metropolitan area absorption. Valwood captured from 15 to 20 percent of metropolitan absorption between 1990 and 1998. Submarket absorption during this period was buoyed by Valwood's strategic location adjacent to the Dallas/Fort Worth airport, its centralized location in the metropolitan area, and a substantial increase in warehouse construction since 1994.

Valwood's locational advantages were expected to remain in place over the long term. The submarket was expected to continue to witness further warehouse development, although construction volumes were expected to be more modest in the near term because of increasing vacancies. These factors, along with the general desirability of Valwood as a distribution location for small tenants, suggested a capture rate of between 10 percent and 15 percent in the near term, and between 15 percent and 20 percent in the long term. Net absorption in Valwood was expected to equal between 9 million and 10 million square feet (836,400 and 930,000 m²) over the next ten years. ∎

Economic Activity Trends
Dallas/Fort Worth CMSA

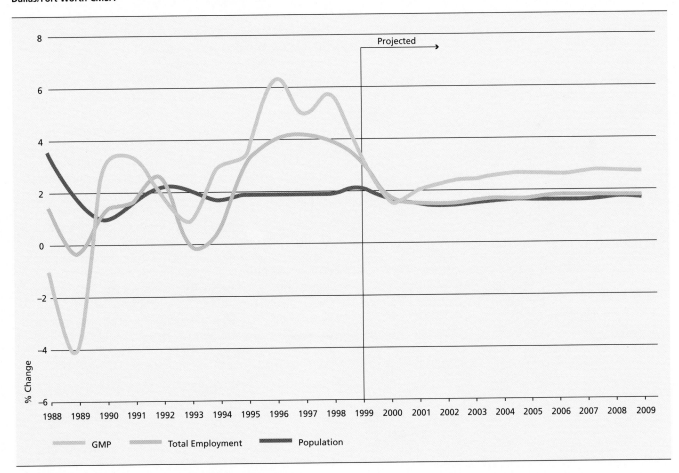

Sources: Regional Financial Associates, Inc.; RREEF Research.

percentage could change in the future if land inventory shrinks, if land becomes overpriced, or if the existing industrial product becomes obsolete.

Other methods of determining absorption in the submarket are largely subjective and are accomplished by examining the historical share of net absorption in the submarket in relation to metropolitan are net absorption over time. Observing the submarket's share of annual absorption should provide the analyst with an idea of how well the area stacks up against other locations. It

Tradeport Distribution Center: Supply Analysis

Warehouse space was being constructed in Dallas in numerous submarkets, including Valwood. Six projects totaling approximately 1.5 million square feet (139,400 m²) were anticipated to be completed in 1998, three of them early in the year. Another 2 million to 3 million square feet (186,000 to 278,800 m²) was expected to enter the market during 1999 to 2001.

Market conditions, including the availability of land, development costs, and public policy, were highly supportive of warehouse construction. Discussions with local developers and investment brokers revealed that, to be feasible, new warehouse properties require monthly rents of $.32 to $.35 per square foot ($3.45 to $3.75/m²), net. ∎

Warehouse Construction Pipeline
Valwood Submarket

Building	Size in Square Feet (square meters)	
Completed Early 1999		
2500 Harp Road	36,000	(3,345)
1800 Monetary Drive	67,200	(6,245)
Speculative Project	75,000	(6,970)
	178,200	(16,560)
Under Construction		
Bilko Trade Center #6	709,920	(66,000)
Bryan Distribution Center III	260,000	(24,200)
Bryan Distribution Center IV	260,000	(24,200)
	1,229,920	(114,300)
Planned		
Forbes Center 1-14	2,433,774	(226,200)
Bryan Distribution Center II	250,000	(23,200)
	2,683,774	(249,400)

Source: RREEF Research.

is likely that the amount of industrial space absorption captured by a single submarket will vary from year to year. The analyst must be careful not to exaggerate absorption levels during strong markets or underestimate absorption during slow periods. An understanding of where the broad metropolitan market and the submarket are in their respective property cycles can help the analyst determine the best capture rate for each year of the forecast period.

In estimating absorption, the analyst should be careful to ensure that figures are for actual industrial uses. Industrial facilities tend to house a variety of uses, from manufacturing to low-rent back offices to big-box retail or showroom operations. Nonindustrial uses such as offices are often tempted to move back into higher-image offices when markets are soft, so they should be separated from industrial uses when assessing demand.

A comparison of the current rate of net absorption of office or industrial space with the existing and planned supply represents an expedient way of gauging the market's short-term balance between supply and demand, but such a snapshot should never be relied on to predict future trends. For a forecast to be of any real value, the market analyst must look for factors that could affect absorption of space in the future and interpret current market conditions accordingly.

Industrial Space Supply Analysis. The first task in analyzing future supply is to identify properties that are currently under development or construction, and the easiest way to accomplish it is to drive through the submarket and record competing projects being built and their locations. Follow-up calls with brokers and sponsoring developers can then be made to obtain information on project sizes, completion dates, costs, and rents.

Proposed projects that have not broken ground may already have received development approvals from the local municipality. These "entitled projects" can be identified through a review of local planning and building department records or conversations with staff. Other proposed or announced projects that have not yet received development approval can be identified through discussions with local brokers or developers. Local business newspapers can be a good source for identifying industrial development announcements. Not all proposed projects are actually built, so once a project has been identified, it should be assigned a probability of actual implementation based on factors such as permit status and the development experience and financial strength of its backers. Doing so helps calculate the amount of competing space that is likely to enter the market in the near term. Comparing annual supply estimates with demand projections leads to an assessment of future vacancy levels and market rental rates.

Projecting additions to the supply of industrial space beyond two or three years becomes more uncertain. Because industrial space is low rise and simply constructed, warehouse buildings take much less time to

These two-story flex buildings in Koll Pacific Park, Aliso Viejo, California, are currently used as offices but could be adapted to other uses, such as light manufacturing.

Courtesy DeRevere and Associates

construct than offices. As a result, smaller warehouse markets can quickly become imbalanced. Aside from using an econometric model to project submarket construction, the analyst can take a more practical approach involving an assessment of factors that influence development. The following information can be helpful in establishing how much industrial development is likely to occur in the future:

- the amount of land available for development;
- an estimate of the number of years before the available land supply is exhausted, given the likely pace of development;
- construction costs versus the rent required to support new industrial development;
- public policy initiatives such as economic development incentives, zoning, and tax abatements that encourage, preclude, or limit industrial development in the submarket;
- the availability of utilities;
- the time needed to gain the necessary entitlements for an industrial project.

Clarification of these points does not reveal precisely how much space will be built in the latter years of a forecast period, but it will provide a framework for making a more credible long-term projection of the supply of industrial space.

The Outlook

A final step in the analysis is to present an outlook for the submarket and a projection of rents. To derive a projection of submarket rents, the analyst must identify both the direction and magnitude of rent changes during each year of the forecast period.

Annual absorption and construction of industrial space must be compared to determine future vacancy rates. Vacancy rates provide a general assessment of the future health of the submarket and an indication of whether

or not rents will change. A useful convention for industrial analyses is to assume that a submarket with a vacancy rate between 6 percent and 8 percent is in equilibrium. A market in equilibrium is often a market that will witness stable rents or some upward movement in rents. When vacancy rates go up, property owners begin to offer concessions to lure tenants and fill space, and effective rents decline.

A review of historical rent changes can be helpful in trying to sort out a credible rent projection. Looking at past increases or decreases in submarket rents relative to demand and supply may give some impression of how rents move in a particular submarket.

The extent to which rates can increase is also tied to the difference between market rents and economic rents. Economic rents are the rent levels needed to support new construction for competitive space. A submarket is more apt to see stronger rent increases when market rents are well below economic rents. This situation typically exists in the recovery stage of the market cycle when vacancy rates are falling and the gap between market and economic rents is wide, allowing for significant rent spikes.

Projecting rents is a complicated task. Rent changes are influenced not only by market fundamentals related to demand and supply but also by market perceptions.[5] A well-formulated market analysis assesses and measures the market fundamentals that influence rent. Conversely, market perceptions are not readily measured and therefore less easily addressed by market analysis, even though they may influence changes in rent as much as a change in market vacancy.

Given the complexities associated with projecting rents, care must be taken not to simply crank through a model and derive a point forecast of future rents. Point forecasts convey the impression of a high degree of accuracy that is not attainable in market analysis. More credible forecasts are those structured as a range, offering a best and worst projection for any single year.

Projections for warehouse space net absorption and supply (noted as completions) showed an upward trend in submarket vacancies after 1998. The supply-side analysis indicated that warehouse construction in Valwood would outpace absorption, even though the Dallas economy was expected to continue to expand at a healthy rate. The imbalance in supply was expected to correct itself by 2000 as development activity eased and absorption remained positive. Nonetheless, the threat of continued additions to supply in Dallas and Valwood was a long-term concern.

In light of these trends, submarket rents in Valwood were expected to experience only modest growth (see Figure 2-2). In fact, larger properties of 100,000 square feet (9,300 m²) or more were not anticipated to realize any increase in rates in the short term, given that much of the submarket's increase in supply was occurring in this property segment. Anecdotal evidence from discussions with local brokers suggested that as much as 80 to 90 percent of Valwood's warehouse vacancies were in larger buildings.

The near-term prognosis for warehouse space of 20,000 to 40,000 square feet (1,860 to 3,720 m²) was more positive. A lack of supply in this property segment was expected to allow modest increases in rent of up to 5 percent. This size space was considered well suited to Valwood's expanding base of small- and medium-sized users and to the tenant sizes proposed for Tradeport.

Spaces smaller than 20,000 square feet (1,860 m²) were projected to witness the strongest rent gains in the short term. At that time, a minimal amount of inventory in Valwood catered to users in this segment of the market. Cost constraints on building and steady demand were expected to allow rents to move up during each year of the forecast period.

Rent projections for Valwood could reasonably be applied to the proposed Tradeport Distribution Center, given its similarity with other competitive warehouse facilities in the submarket. The subject property's proposed smaller spaces appeared to have good prospects for garnering future rent increases, larger spaces less so. The market analysis showed that large users were leaving Valwood, pushing up vacancy rates. It may have been difficult to lease the Tradeport buildings to single-tenant users in light of market trends at that time. Configuring the Tradeport buildings to accommodate smaller tenants appeared to make the most economic sense in the long term. ■

Completions, Absorption, and Vacancy Rates for Warehouse Space
Valwood Submarket

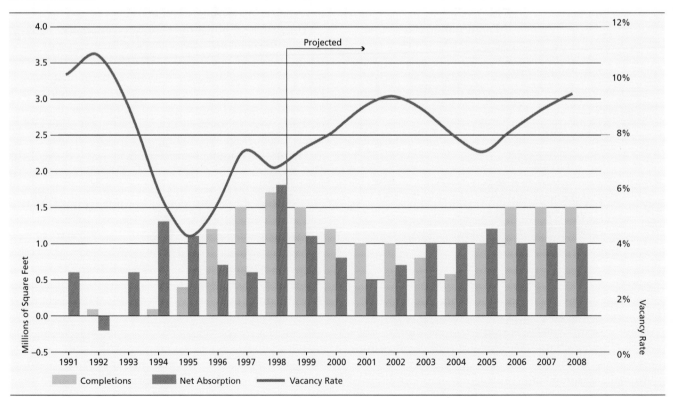

Sources: M/PF Research; RREEF Research.

figure 2-2

Projected Change in Warehouse Rents

Valwood Submarket

	Single Tenant 100,000 Square Feet (9,300 m²) or More		Multitenant 20,000–40,000 Square Feet (1,860 to 3,720 m²)		Multitenant Less Than 20,000 Square Feet (1,860 m²)	
	Rent Range (Per Square Foot)	Percent Change	Rent Range (Per Square Foot)	Percent Change	Rent Range (Per Square Foot)	Percent Change
2000	$3.00–3.25	0%	$3.25–3.50	0%	$3.65–4.40	3%–5%
2001	$3.05–3.30	0%–2%	$3.30–3.55	0%–2%	$3.80–4.60	3%–5%
2002	$3.15–3.40	2%–4%	$3.45–3.70	3%–5%	$3.90–4.75	2%–4%
2003	$3.30–3.55	3%–5%	$3.60–3.85	3%–5%	$4.00–4.90	2%–4%
2004	$3.45–3.70	3%–5%	$3.75–4.00	3%–5%	$4.10–5.05	2%–4%

Note: Net net rents are calculated using the mid-point of the forecast range. Changes in rent after 2004 will depend on future levels of construction and absorption.

Source: RREEF Research.

Financial Feasibility Analysis

With a completed market analysis in hand, the development team is ready to assess the project's financial feasibility. Feasibility analysis is a systematic approach to determining the profitability of a proposed real estate investment. It allows the team to ascertain whether the development will generate enough cash flow to pay the debt service and provide an adequate return to its investors. The major decision-making tool is a ten-year discounted cash flow (DCF) analysis showing property operations from the completion of construction to sale. It is not unusual for some developers/investors to revise the DCF analyses over the course of a development project as new information is obtained and as changes are made to underlying assumptions. A DCF analysis is often prepared before land is under option and again after the signing of an earnest money contract but before closing on the land.

Financial analyses for two case studies are presented below. The example for the Tradeport Distribution Center focuses on the acquisition and development of a single land parcel in a larger industrial park. The second case study is presented as a land development DCF for the Highlands Industrial Park.

Development Budget

Financial feasibility analysis begins with a review of a project's development budget.

As shown in the hypothetical development budget for the Tradeport case study, the development budget includes all potential costs related to the development of the proposed project, including land, site improvements, construction (shell costs), engineering, marketing, financing, and general project administration. A general contingency factor is also included.

An experienced developer should have a wealth of cost data from previous projects, but for those new to industrial development, preliminary cost data can be obtained from project architects, consulting engineers, professional cost estimators, or general contractors.

A separate construction cost report is often included in the analysis of project feasibility. It provides a monthly breakdown of the cost of various categories of construction work and a time line showing the percentage of total cost in each category that should be completed in any given month. The construction categories for which sep-

At Apple Computer's R&D campus in Cupertino, California, one building provides a cafeteria, auditorium, library, and conference facilities, all at a cost of only 5 percent of total campus space.

Tradeport's development budget shows approximately $9.5 million required to buy the land and construct the proposed two-building project. Land costs totaled more than $1.1 million, while building construction amounted to more than $6.7 million. The total cost per square foot of the project was $37.81. At this cost, monthly rents of $.43 per square foot gross and $.33 net were needed to support the project, assuming a 10 percent minimum return on equity, operating costs of $1.20 per square foot, and a 5 percent vacancy rate.

Referring to the market analysis, the development team concluded that the current market should support the proposed costs of Tradeport. Monthly net rents for multitenant warehouse properties reached as high as $.36 per square foot, excluding escalations on five-year leases. This amount compared well with the required monthly net rent of $.33 per square foot. ∎

Development Budget

Development Budget	251,200 Square Feet (23,345 m²)		Values	Amount per Square Foot
Land				
Site/Acquistion Cost			1,113,100	$4.43
Site Utilities (allowance)			0	$0.00
Closing/Miscellaneous			2,000	$0.01
Wetlands/Environmental Studies			2,000	$0.01
Subtotal Land			**1,117,100**	**$4.45**
Construction				
Base Building				
Sitework/Paving			1,199,563	$4.78
Shell, Building 1	100,400	(9,330)	1,451,901	$5.78
Shell, Building 2	150,800	(14,015)	1,941,929	$7.73
Subtotal Base Building			**4,593,393**	**$18.29**
Finishes/Allowances				
Building 1, Office Space			518,797	$2.07
Building 1, Warehouse/Distribution Space			118,014	$0.47
Building 2, Office Space			584,421	$2.33
Building 2, Warehouse/Distribution Space			177,997	$0.71
Select Alternates			640,990	$0.00
Signage and Graphics (allowance)			7,500	$1.59
Landscaping (allowance)			69,900	$0.03
Subtotal Construction			**2,117,619**	**$26.70**
Marketing				
Air Travel/Mileage			0	$0.00
Advertising/Marketing			5,500	$0.02
Brokerage/Commissions			300,000	$1.19
Renderings and Photos			1,200	$0.00
Site Signage (temporary)			600	$0.00
Subtotal Marketing			**307,300**	**$1.22**

Development Budget *continued*

Development Budget	251,200 Square Feet (23,345 m²)	Values	Amount per Square Foot
Architechtural/Engineering			
Architectural Fees		149,145	$0.50
A&E Support/Other A&E		13,200	$0.05
Platting/Replatting		4,000	$0.02
Soils Engineering		4,000	$0.02
Boundary Survey		3,500	$0.01
Topographic Survey		6,500	$0.03
As-Built Survey		5,000	$0.02
M/E/P Engineering		13,100	$0.05
Structural Engineering		50,700	$0.20
Civil Engineering		15,500	$0.06
Site Plan Review		1,000	$0.00
Subtotal Architectural/Engineering		**265,645**	**$0.97**
Financing			
Project Attorney		15,000	$0.06
Lender's Attorneys		15,000	$0.06
Other Legal		5,000	$0.02
Financing Fees (lender)		125,100	$0.50
Net Interest Reserve (12 months)		400,022	$1.59
Title Checkdown and Escrow Fees		1,500	$0.01
Title Insurance		39,700	$0.16
Subtotal Financing		**601,322**	**$2.39**
General Administration			
Project Development and Management		129,400	$0.52
Express and Delivery		500	$0.00
Reproduction		2,500	$0.01
Independent Inspector		7,700	$0.03
Testing Fees		40,200	$0.16
General Overhead		32,500	$0.13
Progress Photos/Video		1,200	$0.00
Taxes during Construction (2.5%)		28,533	$0.11
Appraisal		3,200	$0.01
Subtotal General Administration		**245,733**	**$0.98**
General Contingency (Allowance)		**250,000**	**$0.52**
Net Budget		**9,498**	**$37.81**

This two-story R&D building in Cypress, California, features a distinctive entrance in front with loading, services, and employee parking in back.

figure 2-3

Tradeport Distribution Center: Before-Tax Cash Flow from Normalized Operations

Stabilized Occupancy at End of Year 2

	Total (000)	Per Square Foot of Net Rentable Area[1]
Income		
Base Rent[2]	$1,055	$4.20
Reimbursements	296	1.18
Gross Potential Income	$1,351	$5.38
Credit Loss and Vacancy Allowance	54	0.21
Effective Gross Income	$1,297	$5.16
Expenses		
Operating Expenses	$72	$0.29
Real Estate Taxes	192	0.76
Other Expenses	3	0.01
Management Fees	32	0.13
Total Expenses	$299	$1.19
Net Operating Income	$998	$3.97
Annual Debt Service[3]	$551	$2.19
Before-Tax Cash Flow	$419	$1.67

1. Net rentable area = 251,200 square feet (23,345 m²).

2. $.35 per square foot per month × 12 months × 251,200 square feet (23,345 m²).

3. Project is assumed to be financed with a $5.7 million first mortgage (7.5%, 20 years) and an equity investment of $3,799,000.

arate budgets and schedules are provided include site improvements (grading, utility extensions), off-site improvements (roads, utility extensions), foundation, framework, facade, building systems, and interior finishes for common areas and tenant spaces.

Project Pro Forma

With cost and revenue data available, the development team can prepare a pro forma statement of before-tax cash flow from normalized operations. It includes a forecast of income and expenses, usually during the first year of stabilized operations. Like the development budget, the before-tax pro forma is a planning tool. It shows a one-time picture of the results of a development, based on the findings of the market analysis, actual operating results of similar projects, and the developer's general expectations. Tradeport's pro forma is shown in Figure 2-3.

Cash Flow Analysis

Once the development team establishes the development budget and Year 1 stabilized income and expenses, the next step is to extend this short-term view of the project over a long-term period through a DCF analysis.

The calculation of internal rate of return (IRR) is similar to the calculation of present value and can produce the same result. The main difference in the two is that the calculation of present value is based on a preselected discount rate, while the calculation of IRR searches for the discount rate that reduces future cash flows and the reversion to the original equity investment. The IRR results in a discount rate that can be compared with the yields offered by other projects and other investment opportunities.

Key Financial Ratios

Participants in the development process use different financial ratios to assess the anticipated risks and returns

Pacific Point is a high-profile commercial park with three two-story office and R&D buildings in San Diego, California. The contemporary buildings have views of the canyon and flexible design that combines office and manufacturing space with grade-level doors for easy truck access.

Courtesy Spieker Properties

of individual projects. Comparing financial ratios with accepted industry standards and investors' requirements for return can provide a picture of a project's general feasibility. As shown in the case study, three financial ratios are typically used to assess financial feasibility—debt coverage ratio, return on cost, and break-even occupancy.

Debt Coverage Ratio. In addition to projected returns, investors and lenders are concerned with the risks of development. One simple determinant of risk is the debt coverage ratio (DCR), which illustrates the capacity of a property to generate sufficient revenue to cover mortgage payments. Lenders generally require a minimum DCR when evaluating a loan application, but this minimum ratio can change over time. It can move up as the perceived risks of the project or market increase or down as lending institutions compete for borrowers.

Net Present Value and Internal Rate of Return

Calculation of *net present value* provides a way of comparing the present value of the cash investment in a real estate development project with the present value of the cash receipts from it.

Present value analysis equalizes the "time value" of money. For example, because one can earn interest on money, $100 today will be worth $110 in one year at 10 percent interest and $121 in two years with annual compounding. Ten percent interest represents the "opportunity cost" if one receives the money in, say, two years rather than now.

The present value of $121, received in two years, is $100. That is, the "discounted value at a 10 percent discount rate" of $121, received in two years, is $100 today. If the discount rate (opportunity cost rate) is 10 percent, then it makes no difference whether one receives $100 today or $121 in two years.

The formula for calculating present value is as follows:

$$PV = \frac{FV \times 1}{(1 + r)^n}$$

where
PV = present value,
FV = future value,
r = the discount rate, and
n = the number of years.

Calculation of *internal rate of return* allows an investor to determine the discount rate that reduces a future stream of cash flow to the initial cash investment. In other words, the internal rate is the rate that makes the present value of all the future cash flows equal to the initial cash outlay. If the rate equals or exceeds a minimum desired rate of return, then the project is acceptable. The generalized equation for the internal rate of return is as follows:

$$Cost = \sum_{t=1}^{n} (CF)_t \frac{1}{(1 + K)^t}$$

where
CF = cash flow,
Cost = initial cash investment, and
K = the discount rate (the internal rate of return). ∎

The DCF analysis covers Tradeport's first ten years of operation. The gross revenue stream (the rent per unit multiplied by the number of occupied units) together with the development team's estimate of development costs and long-term operating and financing costs was used to project the cash flows that Tradeport is expected to generate over time. This example excludes income taxes. Anticipated rent increases, as specified in leases, were factored into the income estimates when appropriate. Allowance was made for vacated space if and when tenants leave when the lease expires.

Year 0 represents the starting period for the project, with land acquisition costs totaling $1.1 million. A construction loan was obtained for the total cost of the project, with interest calculated at $304,000. Year 1 specifies the initial 12-month construction period, with some minimal leasing occurring after construction of the shell was complete and marketing began. Income and operating expenses were low at that time. Shell construction was complete in Year 2, and leasing began. Net operating income grew significantly, to $863,000, as more space was leased. Operating expenses also rose once tenants were in the buildings. Capital costs remained somewhat high because of the cost of outlays for tenant improvements, marketing, and leasing commissions. Tradeport was projected to reach 100 percent stabilized occupancy at the end of Year 2. The construction loan was retired at that time by a permanent loan of $5,699,000 (a 60 percent loan-to-value ratio).

Once stabilized, Tradeport was projected to generate positive cash flows based on monthly rents of $.35 per square foot and acceptable operating costs and debt service assumptions. The result is a 10.2 percent cash-on-cash rate of return, unleveraged, at the end of the first stabilized year (Year 3). The property was expected to generate stable returns during the fourth and fifth years, with income rising slightly because of increased operating expense reimbursements. Operating expenses also were expected to rise, often in line with the rate of inflation as defined by the consumer price index.

Base rent was assumed to decline in Year 6 as a result of tenant turnover. The volatility of cash flow during tenant turnover was defined by a list of assumptions regarding the percentage of tenants renewing leases, the length of leases, required tenant improvements on renewed leases, lease-up time, the dollar value of rent concessions and leasing commissions, and market rents at the time of rollover. In the case of Tradeport, base rent was projected to increase after Year 6 as the project's leases were renewed at higher market rents, as specified in the market analysis.

While expectations of positive cash flow contributed to Tradeport's overall profitability, they did not consider the timing of the project's income and appreciation upon sale at the end of the holding period. The return from a real estate investment takes the form of a series of annual cash flows and a reversion at the end of the holding period when a project is sold. The standard method for calculating a development's profitability is to use a discount rate equal to the required rate of return that converts all future revenues and the proceeds from the sale of the property into their present value.

Assuming a long-term hold, Tradeport's expected gross residual value, or sale price, in Year 10 was calculated at $13.1 million. The accepted method for indicating property value involves dividing net operating income by the overall capitalization rate. Tradeport's sale price, $13.1 million, was determined by dividing its Year 10 net operating income of $1.18 million by a 9 percent residual cap rate—assuming that the risks associated with the project would be lower in Year 10 than they were at the time of investment.

Subtracting selling costs such as brokers' commissions and legal fees as well as the payment of the loan balance from the proceeds of the sale left $8.5 million in before-tax net income. The present worth of the before-tax net sale proceeds was $2.73 million when discounted at the owner's required minimum before-tax annual rate of return of 12 percent. The sum of the present value of the annual before-tax cash flows, $2.57 million, and the net proceeds from the sale was $5.3 million. This amount exceeded the original equity investment of $3.8 million for Tradeport and suggested that, as proposed, the project would be financially feasible.

As noted in the project summary, Tradeport investors required at least a 12 percent return before income taxes. The DCF analysis shows that the project was expected to generate a before-tax unleveraged internal rate of return of 12.9 percent in Year 10 of the holding period. A leveraged internal rate of return of 16.8 percent was expected to be realized in the same year, easily exceeding the project's required return performance. ∎

Discounted Cash Flow Analysis

Returns

Unleveraged IRR	12.16%
Equity IRR	15.47%

Assumptions

Loan Amount	$5,970		Amortization (years)	20
Loan to Value (cost)	60%		Residual Cap Rate	9.00%
Interest Rate	7.50%		Cost of Sale	2.00%

Year	Land Acquisition 0	Devel- opment Period 1	Lease- Up 2	Stabili- zation 3	4	5	6	7	8	9	10	11
Income												
Base Rent		152	943	1,055	1,055	1,055	989	1,115	1,250	1,250	1,250	1,250
Expense Reimbursements		19	252	296	306	318	302	311	359	372	386	400
Gross Potential Income		171	1,196	1,351	1,362	1,373	1,291	1,426	1,609	1,622	1,635	1,650
Credit Loss		(7)	(48)	(54)	(54)	(55)	(52)	(57)	(64)	(65)	(65)	(66)
Effective Gross Income		164	1,148	1,297	1,307	1,318	1,239	1,369	1,544	1,557	1,570	1,584
Expenses												
Operating Expenses		(56)	(69)	(72)	(75)	(78)	(81)	(84)	(87)	(91)	(94)	(98)
Real Estate Taxes			(185)	(192)	(200)	(208)	(216)	(225)	(234)	(243)	(253)	(263)
Other Expenses		(2)	(3)	(3)	(3)	(3)	(3)	(3)	(3)	(4)	(4)	(4)
Management Fees		(4)	(29)	(32)	(33)	(33)	(31)	(34)	(39)	(39)	(39)	(40)
Total Expenses		(62)	(285)	(299)	(310)	(321)	(331)	(346)	(363)	(376)	(390)	(405)
Net Operating Income		$102	$863	$998	$997	$996	$908	$1,023	$1,181	$1,180	$1,180	$1,179
Capital			(27)	(28)	(29)	(30)	(31)	(32)	(33)	(34)	(35)	
Acquisition/ Development Cost	(1,117)	(6,724)	(2,109)									
Cash Flow before Debt Service	($1,117)	($6,622)	($1,274)	$970	$968	$966	$877	$991	$1,148	$1,146	$1,145	
Interest				(443)	(433)	(422)	(410)	(397)	(383)	(367)	(351)	
Principal				(134)	(144)	(156)	(168)	(181)	(195)	(210)	(226)	
Cash Flow after Debt Service	($1,117)	($6,622)	($1,274)	$392	$391	$389	$300	$414	$571	$569	$568	
Loan Proceeds			5,970									
Gross Residual Value											$13,100	
Cost of Sale											(262)	
Net Residual Value											$12,838	
Loan Outstanding											(4,766)	
Net Residual Proceeds											$8,072	

Note: All dollar figures in thousands (000).

For Tradeport, the minimum DCR was 1.25, while the actual ratio of annual net operating income to debt was 1.81.

$$DCR = \frac{\text{Net Operating Income}}{\text{Annual Debt Service}}$$

$$\frac{\$998,000}{\$551,000} = 1.81$$

Tradeport's ROC was 10.5 percent. Assuming a 9 percent reversion cap rate produced a spread of 150 basis points, an acceptable spread in light of the competitiveness of the project.

$$ROC = \frac{\text{Net Operating Income}}{\text{Total Development Cost}}$$

$$\frac{\$998,000}{\$9,498,000} = 10.5 \text{ percent}$$

Tradeport's BEO was just under 63 percent, compared with an 85 percent BEO allowed by most lenders.

$$BEO = \frac{\text{Operating Expenses} + \text{Debt Service}}{\text{Gross Potential Income}}$$

$$\frac{\$299,000 + 551,000}{\$1,351,000} = 62.9 \text{ percent}$$

These financial ratios show that Tradeport met or exceeded the feasibility requirements established by lenders and investors. Based on these calculations, the development team was generally confident that Tradeport would successfully meet its requirements for return on investment. ∎

The results of five sensitivity analyses were compared with the unleveraged IRR in Year 10 of the DCF analysis.

1. Downside: The building is leased at $.31 per square foot per month versus the projected $.35.

Downside IRR	Expected IRR
11.3 percent	12.9 percent

2. Downside: Lease-up is extended an additional 12 months, for a total of 24 months after completion.

Downside IRR	Expected IRR
11.2 percent	12.9 percent

3. Downside: The project is $500,000 over budget because of cost overruns.

Downside IRR	Expected IRR
11.1 percent	12.9 percent

4. Upside: Sell immediately upon stabilization using an 8.75 percent residual capitalization rate.

Upside IRR	Expected IRR
18.7 percent	12.9 percent

5. Upside: Base case with a nine-year holding period, leveraged 50 percent at an 8 percent interest rate.

Upside IRR	Expected IRR
16.1 percent	12.9 percent

∎

Return on Cost. Developers and investors anticipating a short-term hold often look at a project's return on cost (ROC), calculated by dividing net operating income by total development cost, which includes land costs, construction costs (building shell, architecture and engineering, and so on), soft costs (legal, insurance, and other items), and financing. A project's ROC is most often compared with the reversion cap rate. The difference or spread between ROC and the reversion cap rate reflects the amount of risk in the transaction. A spread of 125 to 150 basis point is generally acceptable for most industrial developments with no preleasing.

Break-Even Occupancy. Lenders and investors sometimes structure a development transaction based on its break-even occupancy (BEO) as measured by income and expenses. While helpful to know, industrial development projects undertaken in the current market have low levels of debt compared with projects built in the 1980s. BEO, as a result, is less meaningful as a measure of feasibility than it once was.

Conditions affecting financial feasibility change over time: development occurs in a dynamic environment, and market conditions must be monitored to assess their impact on a project's financial feasibility. One method for making such an assessment is sensitivity analysis.

Sensitivity Analysis

Sensitivity analysis allows the development team to assess the financial implications of changes to a project's underlying assumptions. Will spending more on office buildout improve the project's profitability? Will providing higher ceiling heights allow the development team to raise rents, shorten the lease-up period, and improve the financial feasibility of Tradeport? Sensitivity analysis is most often used

Highlands Industrial Park comprises 400 acres (162 ha) of land that will accommodate 5 million square feet (465,000 m²) of building space at buildout. The site has been divided into four subareas for purposes of infrastructure phasing and marketing. The areas will be marketed for development as the sequencing of infrastructure allows, with construction occurring in multiple areas simultaneously as the project progresses.

The development team must prepare a land development DCF to compare the relationship between revenues from the sale of improved land with the cost of acquiring a site and providing infrastructure improvements necessary to prepare the land for construction of buildings.

The price that a buyer will pay for the improved land is directly related to the economic characteristics of the building to be developed. The vertical development pro forma calculates revenues from sale or lease of the building minus construction and development costs, any applicable operating costs, and requirements for profit or return. The remaining proceeds constitute the residual value of the land. This land sale price determines the revenue to the land developer.

Land Sale Revenues

The Highlands Industrial Park DCF analysis shows revenues from land sales by area in each year. Land sales start in Area 1 in Year 1 as the first increments of infrastructure are installed. Area 2 comes on line in Year 3, followed by Areas 3 and 4 in subsequent years. Land sale revenues increase from about $3 million in Years 1 and 2 to a peak of $14 million in Year 5, when property from all four areas is being sold. All land sales are completed by Year 10.

Sale revenues for Highlands are shown in constant 2000 dollars. The totals by year are then inflated. Costs are treated in a similar manner so that a total project cash flow can be shown in inflated dollars. The discount rate used to evaluate feasibility reflects inflation as well as the cost of money and risk. For this reason, it is important that the calculation of IRR be based on nominal (future dollar) values. Land sale revenues total $79 million in constant dollars, $100 million with inflation taken into account.

Land Development Costs

The anticipated magnitude and timing of costs required to develop the industrial park are detailed in the DCF analysis. Preacquisition/predevelopment costs include the cost of the market studies, site due diligence, and other activities that need to be carried out by the development team before acquisition and development of the

site. In this case, those costs total $800,000. The cost of acquiring the unimproved land is $4.5 million.

Infrastructure costs typically are the most expensive investments for land developers, and phasing and financing these costs are critical to the project's financial feasibility. The developer seeks to spread the cost of infrastructure over buildout to the extent possible to generate maximum revenues relative to required capital outlays. Frequently, developers also use tax exempt financing from assessment districts or similar vehicles to lower the cost of these improvements.

Infrastructure improvements for this business park include on-site streets, water and wastewater utilities, stormwater retention ponds, public open space, telecommunications and electrical systems, and off-site traffic improvements. Costs total $40.7 million in 2000 dollars. More than 30 percent of these costs, $13.1 million, is incurred in the first year of development. The remainder of the improvements are phased over the first five years of development.

The next category of costs, typically termed "developer operations," includes planning and entitlements, property maintenance, asset management, project management (developer's general and administrative costs), closing costs for land sale transactions, sales, marketing, and commissions. These costs relate to the various functions performed by the land developer during project development and disposition from which the developer needs to receive a required financial return. Total costs of project development amount to $56.6 million in constant dollars and $60.1 million in inflated dollars.

Public Financing

The pro forma illustrates the impact of public financing on Highlands Industrial Park. Through the example shown, an assessment bond can be issued every three years based on the value of the land to be sold during a given year and the two years that follow. In the case study, the value of the land must hold a ratio of 3:1 over the value of the debt issued (value-to-lien ratio). Through this financing mechanism, the development team can receive near-term infusions of cash, to be repaid at relatively low (tax-exempt) interest rates over the coming years. With the time-value of money placing a premium on near-term cash, this arrangement benefits the developer, despite the fact that a balloon payment of the remaining principal on the debt will be due at the completion of land sales in the business park.

Cash Flow and Return on Investment

Because of the high upfront costs for predevelopment and infrastructure, the revenues in the first years of Highlands are well below the costs incurred. As a result, the

Discounted Cash Flow Analysis

Returns		Assumptions						
Internal Rate of Return	25.4%	Value to Lien	3:1	Planning and Entitlement	3.0%	Property Maintenance	0.5%	
		Interest Rate	6.0%	Project Management	5.5%	Closing Costs	1.0%	
		Amortization (years)	10	Asset Management	1.5%	Sales, Marketing & Commissions	6.5%	

Item	Total	Year 1	Year 2	Year 3	Year 4	Year 5	Year 6	Year 7	Year 8	Year 9	Year 10
Revenues											
Sale of Land											
Area 1	$27,059,285	$2,846,250	$2,846,250	$2,846,250	$2,846,250	$2,612,381	$2,612,381	$2,612,381	$2,612,381	$2,612,381	$2,612,381
Area 2	$16,187,737	$0	$0	$6,543,961	$5,164,801	$4,478,975	$0	$0	$0	$0	$0
Area 3	$20,419,942	$0	$0	$0	$0	$5,824,506	$5,824,506	$5,715,187	$3,055,742	$0	$0
Area 4	$15,342,199	$0	$0	$0	$1,746,444	$1,287,062	$1,287,062	$3,526,395	$2,803,108	$1,972,842	$2,719,286
Total Land Sale Revenues	$79,009,163	$2,846,250	$2,846,250	$9,390,211	$9,757,496	$14,202,924	$9,723,949	$11,853,962	$8,471,231	$4,585,223	$5,331,667
Total Land Revenues, Inflated at 5%	$100,008,225	$2,846,250	$2,988,563	$10,352,708	$11,295,521	$17,263,743	$12,410,497	$15,885,443	$11,919,872	$6,774,462	$8,271,165
Costs											
Predevelopment											
Preacquisition/ Predevelopment	$800,000	$800,000	$0	$0	$0	$0	$0	$0	$0	$0	$0
Land	$4,500,000	$4,500,000	$0	$0	$0	$0	$0	$0	$0	$0	$0
Subtotal	$5,300,000	$5,300,000	$0	$0	$0	$0	$0	$0	$0	$0	$0
Infrastructure											
On-Site Streets	$12,580,834	$3,451,355	$3,670,000	$2,700,000	$2,000,000	$759,478	$0	$0	$0	$0	$0
Water Utilities	$4,807,975	$1,764,081	$1,100,000	$908,769	$683,183	$351,943	$0	$0	$0	$0	$0
Wastewater Utilities	$1,749,688	$1,154,794	$594,894	$0	$0	$0	$0	$0	$0	$0	$0
Retention Ponds	$8,978,366	$3,061,820	$1,100,000	$1,577,301	$2,137,902	$1,101,343	$0	$0	$0	$0	$0
Public Open Space	$8,771,800	$2,586,078	$2,500,000	$1,332,222	$1,553,310	$800,190	$0	$0	$0	$0	$0
Telecom/Electrical	$3,100,000	$800,000	$800,000	$750,000	$750,000	$0	$0	$0	$0	$0	$0
Offsite Traffic Improvements	$750,000	$330,000	$0	$170,000	$165,000	$85,000	$0	$0	$0	$0	$0
Subtotal	$40,738,663	$13,148,128	$9,764,894	$7,438,292	$7,289,394	$3,097,954	$0	$0	$0	$0	$0
Developer Operations											
Planning and Entitlement	$814,773	$81,477	$81,477	$81,477	$81,477	$81,477	$81,477	$81,477	$81,477	$81,477	$81,477
Property Maintenance	$263,364	$26,336	$26,336	$26,336	$26,336	$26,336	$26,336	$26,336	$26,336	$26,336	$26,336
Asset Management	$407,387	$40,739	$40,739	$40,739	$40,739	$40,739	$40,739	$40,739	$40,739	$40,739	$40,739
Project Management	$2,897,003	$289,700	$289,700	$289,700	$289,700	$289,700	$289,700	$289,700	$289,700	$289,700	$289,700
Closing Costs	$846,775	$28,463	$28,463	$93,902	$97,575	$142,029	$97,239	$118,540	$84,712	$45,852	$110,000
Sales, Marketing, and Commissions	$5,360,998	$185,006	$185,006	$610,364	$634,237	$923,190	$632,057	$770,508	$550,630	$450,000	$420,000
Subtotal	$10,590,299	$651,721	$651,721	$1,142,519	$1,170,065	$1,503,472	$1,167,549	$1,327,300	$1,073,595	$934,105	$968,253
Total Costs	$56,628,962	$19,099,850	$10,416,615	$8,580,811	$8,459,459	$4,601,426	$1,167,549	$1,327,300	$1,073,595	$934,105	$968,253
Total Costs, Inflated at 3%	$60,060,577	$19,099,850	$10,729,114	$9,103,382	$9,243,879	$5,178,946	$1,353,509	$1,584,865	$1,320,386	$1,183,296	$1,263,350
Public Financing											
Assessment Bond Net Proceeds	$20,491,946	$3,385,611	$0	$0	$9,103,942	$0	$0	$8,002,393	$0	$0	$0
(Less) Debt Service	($25,264,986)	$0	($522,723)	($522,723)	($522,723)	($1,928,330)	($1,928,330)	($1,928,330)	($3,163,862)	($3,163,862)	($11,584,104)
Total Financing	($4,773,040)	$3,385,611	($522,723)	($522,723)	$8,581,219	($1,928,330)	($1,928,330)	$6,074,063	($3,163,862)	($3,163,862)	($11,584,104)
Cash Flow	$35,174,607	($12,867,988)	($8,263,274)	$726,603	$10,632,860	$10,156,467	$9,128,658	$20,374,641	$7,435,624	$2,427,304	($4,576,289)
Cumulative		($12,867,988)	($21,131,261)	($20,404,658)	($9,771,798)	$384,670	$9,513,328	$29,887,969	$37,323,592	$39,750,896	$35,174,607
NPV @ 15%	$7,764,583										

development team must provide the cash required to cover such initial shortfalls. The development team incurs a cumulative debt of as much as $21.1 million, shown in Year 2 of the cumulative cash flow. This substantial near-term cash outlay contributes to the need for a significant return on the developer's investment later.

The IRR approximates the average yearly return on the developer's investment over the entire ten-year buildout and sales period. In the pro forma, the IRR is 25.4 percent—a rate that makes it attractive for the team to pursue the Highlands development despite the large upfront costs.

The calculation of net present value (NPV) reflects the residual value of the land to the development team. The NPV reflects a discount rate of 15 percent, which accounts for inflation, the time-value of money, and the perceived risk. The NPV of $7.8 million means, in effect, that the development team would be willing to pay $7.8 million for the land to receive the expected cumulative cash flow of $35.1 million, given the team's assessment of risk and other financial considerations related to Highlands Industrial Park. Thus, the calculation of NPV is an approximation of the value of the land in its unimproved state. ∎

to examine a project's upside and downside potentials, accomplished by examining the effects of using both optimistic and pessimistic assumptions for key variables.

Summing Up

The process for successfully positioning an industrial project is determined, in part, by two interrelated steps: market analysis and financial feasibility analysis. The market analysis explores and forecasts underlying demand and supply conditions and current and future rents. Incorporating different levels of analysis from market screening to site selection and submarket analysis, market analysis helps determine the marketability of a proposed industrial project. It also provides the basic assumptions needed to carry out financial projections.

Financial feasibility analysis is the crux of the investment decision. It estimates how much profit will be made from a real estate development, and it is a valuable aid to investors in determining whether or not to proceed with a development project.

Market and financial feasibility analyses combine quantitative techniques and qualitative approaches, market knowledge and experience, and judgment and intuition. No foolproof methods exist, and no one can expect to foretell future market conditions or project profitability with complete certainty. Nonetheless, the combined benefits of market analysis and financial feasibility analysis can help investors identify investment opportunities, market risks, and the profit potential of individual real estate investments in light of realistic underwriting.

Notes

1. Pension Real Estate Association, National Association of Real Estate Investment Managers, and National Council of Real Estate Investment Fiduciaries, *Real Estate Information Standards* (Washington, D.C.: Author, 1996).

2. Glenn R. Miller and Steven Loposa, "The Path of Goods Movement," *Real Estate Finance*, Summer 1994, pp. 42–50.

3. More information on the Reebie TRANSEARCH database can be found at www.reebie.com.

4. Asieh Mansour and Marvin C. Christensen, "An Alternative Determinant of Warehouse Space Demand: A Case Study," *Journal of Real Estate Research*, January–April 2001, pp. 77–88.

5. Richard J. Buttimer, Jr., Ronald C. Rutherford, and Ron Witten, "Industrial Warehouse Rent Determinants in the Dallas/Fort Worth Area," *Journal of Real Estate Research* (Vol. 13, No. 1), 1997, pp. 47–55.

3. Financing and Investment

Industrial development, like real estate development in general, is a capital-intensive business. Significant capital is needed to develop almost any project—from single prefab buildings to a multiphase business park. Funds from outside parties are necessary—unless the developer can generate the necessary funds internally or is connected with an insurance company, pension fund, real estate investment trust (REIT), or other well-capitalized organization in the development business. Even when a developer has a solid relationship with a capital provider or has access to internal funds, it is necessary to understand the requirements of financing institutions and investors.

The funds to develop industrial buildings come in two primary forms: debt and equity. Debt and equity funds for real estate are raised in a variety of capital markets, where conditions are always in flux and competition is often intense. Historically, the capital market for the development of business parks and buildings has depended on local financial institutions and investors. A typical scenario for the development of a building for a thinly capitalized developer was, first, to solicit wealthy individuals in the community to invest in its ownership (equity investment) and, after a sufficiently large portion of the total cost was accumulated (say 20 to 30 percent), to approach a local bank for a development/construction loan.

At the same time, the developer would secure long-term, usually fixed-rate financing (known as permanent financing) from an insurance company, which would be funded after the building was completed and fully leased.

While the incentives for investors in the real estate development process have remained basically the same over time, the real estate capital markets now offer a greater variety of funding sources, many of which involve securitization. The securitization of real estate debt and equity provides greater liquidity—an enhanced flow of funds—for real estate investment.

The most common form of securitized commercial real estate debt is commercial mortgage–backed securities (CMBSs), which are put together by banks, mortgage companies, insurance companies, and investment banks. The sale of bonds that use real estate mortgages as collateral has increased the flow of funds into real estate debt. Securitization in the form of REITs has also broadened the sources of equity capital for industrial as well as other types of properties.

This chapter begins by looking at the capital markets for industrial investment and development. Within this market, the sources of debt and equity capital constantly change. The chapter turns next to a discussion of the forms of ownership for industrial development ventures to help developers and investors understand the legal and tax implications of different ownership structures. Sections follow on the basic requirements and expectations of lenders and investors in industrial projects: why

Chickasaw Distribution Center, Memphis, Tennessee.

figure 3-1

Capital Flows to Real Estate, 1990–1999

Annual

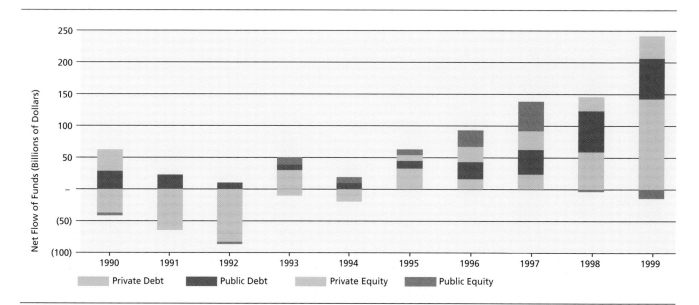

Private debt: life insurance companies, banks and mortgage companies, S&Ls and mutual savings banks, pension funds.

Public debt: government credit agencies, commercial mortgage securities, mortgage REITs, public real estate limited partnerships.

Private equity: pension funds, foreign investors, private financial institutions, life insurance companies, private investors (larger properties).

Public equity: equity and hybrid REITs, public real estate limited partnerships.

Source: The Roulac Group.

lenders lend and investors invest. The focus then turns to the primary sources of financing at different stages of development—predevelopment and land acquisition, construction, and operations. Finally, elements of the financing package are discussed.

The Capital Market for Industrial Development

While the benefits of investing in industrial development have changed little over the last decade, the sources of debt and equity funds have changed dramatically. The role of local banks as the primary source of construction loans has been largely taken over by well-capitalized banks with a regional, national, or international base. The local partnerships that were once a significant source of equity investment for industrial developments are now overshadowed by REITs, pension funds, and public property companies operating nationally and globally.

The shift from private to public sources of capital for real estate development began in the early 1990s, when lending from banks, savings and loan institutions (S&Ls), and other traditional sources of capital was severely curtailed and developers started going to the public markets to raise capital. While public markets have supplied real estate debt and equity for many years, their role since 1992 has expanded quickly in the wake of the real estate recession and capital shortage of the late 1980s. In the

1980s, private sources of debt and equity provided most of the capital that went into real estate. By 1999, public equity and debt markets accounted for more than 30 percent of the year's total net flow of capital into real estate. Property investment by pension funds has grown in recent years, although their current share is down from its high in 1990.

The emergence of the CMBS market has defined a totally new dimension in the financing of commercial real estate. A mortgage-backed security has as its collateral a pool of commercial mortgages—from a single mortgage to several hundred. Bonds backed by these mortgages are structured in tranches having varying risk and maturity profiles based on the characteristics of the underlying loans and the investment appetites and preferences of buyers of CMBSs.

The Resolution Trust Corporation (RTC) was a catalyst for the creation of the CMBS market. The agency found itself owning large portfolios of real estate following widespread S&L failures in the late 1980s. At first, the RTC tried to sell individual loans. But the market for them was limited because of the temporary withdrawal from the market of traditional investors in commercial mortgages—banks and life insurance companies. When the RTC was forced to turn to the public capital market, it found that the disposition proceeds it could realize from the sale of interests in CMBSs exceeded what it could realize from sales to private purchasers of whole loans or small whole-loan portfolios. Thus, the foundation

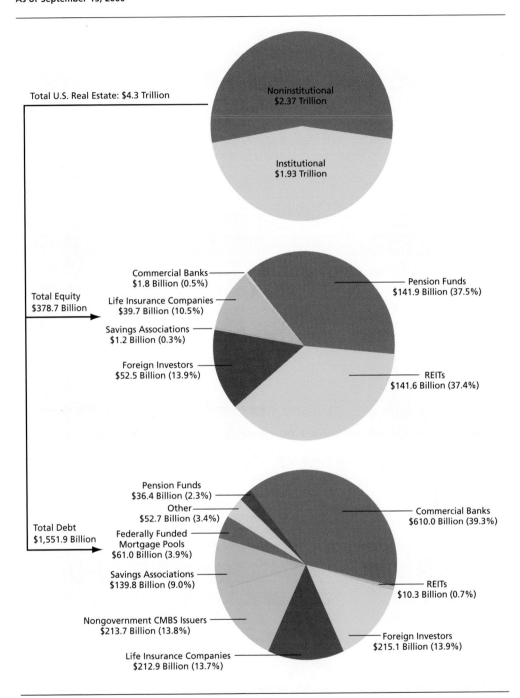

figure 3-2

Capital Sources

As of September 15, 2000

Total U.S. Real Estate: $4.3 Trillion

Noninstitutional
$2.37 Trillion

Institutional
$1.93 Trillion

Total Equity
$378.7 Billion

Commercial Banks
$1.8 Billion (0.5%)

Life Insurance Companies
$39.7 Billion (10.5%)

Savings Associations
$1.2 Billion (0.3%)

Foreign Investors
$52.5 Billion (13.9%)

Pension Funds
$141.9 Billion (37.5%)

REITs
$141.6 Billion (37.4%)

Total Debt
$1,551.9 Billion

Pension Funds
$36.4 Billion (2.3%)

Other
$52.7 Billion (3.4%)

Federally Funded
Mortgage Pools
$61.0 Billion (3.9%)

Savings Associations
$139.8 Billion (9.0%)

Nongovernment CMBS Issuers
$213.7 Billion (13.8%)

Life Insurance Companies
$212.9 Billion (13.7%)

Commercial Banks
$610.0 Billion (39.3%)

REITs
$10.3 Billion (0.7%)

Foreign Investors
$215.1 Billion (13.9%)

Source: Lend Lease Real Estate Investments, *Emerging Trends in Real Estate, 2001.*

was laid for a public market in commercial mortgage–backed securities.

The CMBS market has continued to gain share in overall holdings of real estate debt—from less than 0.5 percent of the value of outstanding commercial real estate mortgages in 1989 to roughly 8 percent ($81 billion) in 1996 to almost 14 percent in 2000 (see Figure 3-2).

This shift of real estate debt holdings into public capital markets has been paralleled by a similar and dramatic shift in the basic sources of public equity funds since the late 1980s. The annual market capitalization raised from REITs, the principal public source of equity funds, grew from just under $9 billion in 1990 to more than $138.7 billion by 2000 (see Figure 3-3). Institutional investors such as life insurance companies, mutual funds, and public pension funds that are attracted to the liquidity and diversification benefits of holding commercial real estate in a REIT are helping to drive the growth of public real

figure 3-3
Market Capitalization of U.S. Real Estate Investment Trusts, 1990–2000

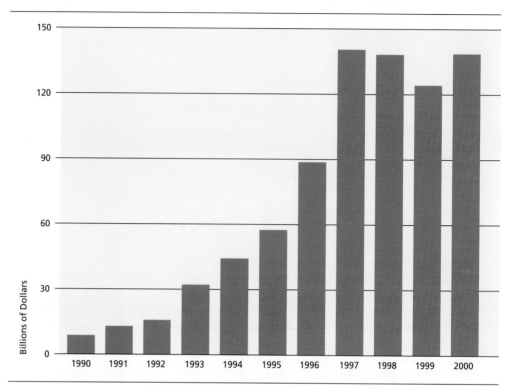

Source: National Association of Real Estate Investment Trusts.

figure 3-4
Features of Selected Ownership Forms

Ownership Form	Ease of Formation	Ability to Raise Funds	Management
Individual	Simple and inexpensive	Limited	Flexible, independent, may lack expertise
Tenancy in Common	Simple and inexpensive	Limited but superior to individual ownership	Depends on owners, may be cumbersome
General Partnership	Moderately easy	Limited but superior to individual ownership	Generally by designated partner(s)
Limited Partnership	Moderately difficult and expensive	Limited but superior to general partnership	Good, by general partners or agents
Ordinary Corporation (C corporation)	Complex and expensive	No problem if closely held; if public, depends on investment	Continuous and centralized
S Corporation	Complex and expensive	Limited, unsuited for income property	Determined by relative share of ownership
Real Estate Investment Trust	Complex and expensive	Good	Centralized, by advisory group
Limited Liability Corporation	Moderately easy	Limited but superior to individual ownership	Generally by designated member(s)

Source: Adapted from James H. Boykin and Richard L. Haney, Jr., *Financing Real Estate,* 2nd ed. (Englewood Cliffs, New Jersey: Prentice-Hall, 1993), p. 288.

Year 6	Year 7	Year 8	Year 9	Year 10	Year 11	Year 12
3,178,981	3,258,456	3,339,917	3,423,415	3,509,000	3,596,725	3,686,643
621,200	638,097	655,458	673,295	691,622	710,452	729,798
39,737	40,731	41,749	42,793	43,863	44,959	46,083
3,839,918	3,937,284	4,037,124	4,139,503	4,244,485	4,352,136	4,462,525
(230,395)	(236,237)	(242,227)	(248,370)	(254,669)	(261,128)	(267,751)
3,609,523	3,701,047	3,794,897	3,891,133	3,989,816	4,091,008	4,194,773
347,701	356,394	365,303	374,436	383,797	393,392	403,227
273,499	281,704	290,155	298,859	307,825	317,060	326,572
121,555	125,202	128,958	132,826	136,811	140,916	145,143
742,755	763,299	784,416	806,122	828,433	851,367	874,941
2,866,768	2,937,748	3,010,481	3,085,011	3,161,383	3,239,641	3,319,832
2,866,768	2,937,748	3,010,481	3,085,011	3,161,383	3,239,641	3,319,832
2,132,375	2,132,375	2,132,375	2,132,375	2,132,375	2,132,375	2,132,375
734,394	805,373	878,106	952,636	1,029,008	1,107,266	1,187,457
13.35%	14.64%	15.97%	17.32%	18.71%	20.13%	21.59%
					35,890,076	
					717,802	
					35,172,275	
					19,723,502	
					15,448,773	
734,394	805,373	878,106	952,636	1,029,008	16,556,039	
2,866,768	2,937,748	3,010,481	3,085,011	3,161,383	38,411,916	

ceeds remains from the takeout or permanent loan. This amount is entered as cash inflow during Year 2 on line (s) in Figure 3-16.

Year 3 through Year 12 of the cash flow analysis indicate that the equity investor's cash available for debt service in Figure 3-16 is equivalent to the cash available for debt service in Years 1 through 10 in the permanent lender's DCF analysis (Figure 3-14). Figure 3-16, however, also includes an analysis of the equity investor's returns.

Similarly, assumptions about the sale in both analyses are the same, except that in the investor's analysis, the outstanding loan balance of $19,723,502 must be repaid. (The loan for Meadow View was for nine years, with a 30-year amortization schedule.) After nine years, the outstanding permanent loan balance is reduced by $1,876,498. Subtracting the cost of selling the building and the outstanding loan balance from the reversion sale price of $35,890,076 (based on a 9.25 percent cap rate on Year 12 NOI) leaves the equity investor with $15,448,773 in cash. The equity investor's before-tax cash flow shown on line (y) represents an IRR of 17.13 percent over the 11-year holding period. The investor must determine whether this return is sufficient to compensate for the risk involved in undertaking this development.

Joint Venture Build-to-Own Development

Joint ventures are a common method of raising capital for industrial developments. Usually structured as a limited partnership or a limited liability corporation, a joint venture often pairs a developer (the "knowledge" partner) and a source of capital (the "money" partner). The developer contributes experience, reputation, and possibly equity capital, while the money partner brings capital to the table.

The terms and conditions of a joint venture are completely negotiable. At the insistence of the money partner, they often include financial incentives for the developer to bring the project in on time and on budget. To compensate for bearing most or all of the financial risk in the project, the money partner usually requires a preferred return; that is, the money partner will receive its share of the cash flow before the knowledge partner receives its share. The joint venture cash flow analysis shown in Figure 3-17 reveals that the equity investor raises the capital for the $5,500,000 purchase of the land. Cash flows to the joint venture begin with the cash flows to the equity investor (Figure 3-16). The remaining two sections of Figure 3-17 outline the returns to the two joint venture partners, the equity investor and the developer.

For investing $5,500,000 in the land, the equity investor receives 85 percent of the cash flow from the investment until he obtains a 12 percent preferred return. Thereafter, the cash flows are split 60/40, with the equity investor receiving 60 percent of cash flows over the 12 percent preferred return. Finally, the equity investor receives 80 percent of the sale proceeds in excess of the $5,500,000 investment. Additionally, the equity investor receives 75 percent of the proceeds of the takeout loan (the permanent loan) that exceed the construction loan.

Three financial incentives appear in lines (o) through (t) (the developer's return): a completion incentive for completion of the project on time and on budget; a property management incentive for efficient operation of the property; and a sale incentive for enhancing the value (sale price) of the property.

The completion incentive is a 75/25 split of the net proceeds from the takeout loan (line (o)). The partnership's split of these proceeds encourages the developer to complete the project on time, because if it is delivered late, construction interest will continue to accrue and reduce the net proceeds from the takeout loan. Similarly, if the property is delivered over budget, the added construction costs will reduce net proceeds from the takeout loan.

The property management incentive is a participation agreement that encourages the developer to maximize operational returns. The partners have agreed to split the property cash flow as follows: the annual cash flow will be split 85/15 between the equity investor and the developer until the money partner has received a cash flow return equal to 12 percent of his $5,500,000 investment ($660,000), and the cash flow above that point will be split 60/40. As can be seen on lines (p) and (q), the developer receives a relatively small cash flow return in the early years of operation. By Year 7, however, the developer begins receiving a larger share of the cash flow. The money partner should be pleased with this arrangement: he receives a 12 percent preferred return plus half of all net operating income above $660,000. The developer partner is clearly motivated to exceed the 12 percent cash flow performance level to participate more fully in the property cash flow.

The sale incentive (line (r)) is structured to encourage the developer to design and build the property well and maintain it in a manner that preserves its physical facilities so that its value increases over the 11-year holding period. After the $5,500,000 equity investment has been returned to the money partner and the selling cost has been deducted and the outstanding loan balance paid off, the partners split the proceeds from the sale of the building 80/20. The developer's 20 percent share gives him much to gain from a significant increase in the building's value.

For the money partner in a joint venture project, the primary measure of investment performance is the internal rate of return. For Meadow View, the investor's IRR is 14.85 percent.

The developer invested no money on which a rate of return can be calculated, but the present value of the cash flow return can be stated. Applying a 20 percent discount rate to the developer's cash flows (line (s)) throughout the holding period returns a present value of $706,749, suggesting that if the developer were to sell his interest in the development, it would be worth $706,749. In joint venture projects, the developer also is paid a fee for construction and development services (costs plus a small profit margin). The developer's big payoff comes, however, if the industrial building is a financial success.

Huntwood Business Center is a multitenant industrial park south of Hayward, California, with convenient access to Silicon Valley.

Financing the Stages of Development

Predevelopment Financing
Industrial development typically involves a series of financing arrangements—predevelopment financing, short-term construction financing, interim financing, and permanent financing—depending on the project's stage in the development process. As a project progresses through the process, its investment risk generally diminishes. Therefore, the interest rates and rates of return required by lenders and equity investors decrease as development proceeds. Predevelopment debt and equity carry the most risk and the highest expected returns. Financing the purchase of well-designed and -located industrial buildings with creditworthy tenants carries very low risk and correspondingly low investment yields. For the developer, it is critical to understand the risk/return orientation of various sources of debt and equity when deciding where to go for financing at each stage of development.

Lenders are concerned primarily about two loan risks involving projects: loss of loan principal and default or nonpayment of interest. Lenders try to mitigate the risk of losing the principal by establishing a safe LTV ratio. Risk involving interest payments is mitigated by lenders' setting a reasonable debt coverage ratio. More broadly, lenders are also concerned with matching the maturities of their loan assets with the maturities of their liabilities (such as bank deposits for banks, life insurance claims

for life insurance companies, and retirement payments for pension funds). Equity investors, on the other hand, are motivated by cash flow, appreciation of value, and/or tax shelter benefits.

Debt and equity investors differ in the amount of risk they will accept. Consequently, they require different rates of return. Permanent debt investors generally are the most risk averse, preferring to finance completed developments that have creditworthy tenants secured on long-term leases. With the rental income stream in place and backed by creditworthy tenants, such properties are low risk. Equity investors invest in riskier projects or in the risky portions of projects, but they require a higher rate of return for such investments.

In general, industrial projects in the predevelopment stage are the riskiest investments for two reasons. First, any positive cash flow is one or more years in the future. The value of industrial developments is in their income streams, and the more distant the stream of income, the riskier the investment. Second, the probability that any project in the predevelopment stage will be completed and occupied is smaller than the probability that projects in more advanced stages will be completed. At the predevelopment stage, it is difficult to obtain equity financing and next to impossible to obtain debt financing without more collateral than that provided by the site.

A number of predevelopment tasks pose substantial completion risk. Some of these high-risk tasks, which may require front-end capital, are the rezoning of property to

figure 3-17

Meadow View Business Park

Joint Venture Build-to-Own Analysis

	Year 0	Year 1	Year 2	Year 3	Year 4
Joint Venture Return					
(a) Property Cash Flow		0	0	531,561	597,529
(b) Net Proceeds from Takeout		0	550,000		
(c) Reversion Sale Price					
(d) Selling Cost					
(e) Outstanding Loan Balance					
(f) Residual Sale Proceeds for Equity Investor					
(g) Equity Investment	(5,500,000)				
Equity Investor Return					
(h) Proceeds from Takeout Loan Split		0	412,500		
(i) Cash Flow Split		0	0	451,827	507,899
(j) Participation Cash Flow			0	0	0
(k) Return on Investment					
(l) Sale Proceeds Split					
(m) Equity Investor Cash Flow	(5,500,000)	0	412,500	451,827	507,899
(n) Investor Internal Rate of Return		14.85%			
Developer Return					
(o) Proceeds from Takeout Split		0	137,500		
(p) Cash Flow Split			0	79,734	89,629
(q) Participation Cash Flow Split			0	0	0
(r) Sale Proceeds Split					
(s) Developer Cash Flow	0	0	137,500	79,734	89,629
(t) Present Value of Developer Cash Flow		$706,749			

Assumptions

Splits/Return Rates	Investor	Developer
Takeout	75%	25%
Cash Flow	85%	15%
Cash Flow Participation	60%	40%
Sale Proceeds	80%	20%
Equity Hurdle Rate	12%	
Developer Discount Rate	20%	

Year 5	Year 6	Year 7	Year 8	Year 9	Year 10	Year 11
665,126	734,394	805,373	878,106	952,636	1,029,008	16,556,039
						35,890,076
						717,802
						19,723,502
						15,448,773
565,357	624,235	660,000	660,000	660,000	660,000	660,000
0	0	17,341	60,981	105,699	151,522	198,477
						5,500,000
						7,959,019
565,357	624,235	677,341	720,981	765,699	811,522	14,317,496
99,769	110,159	116,471	116,471	116,471	116,471	116,471
0	0	11,561	40,654	70,466	101,015	132,318
						1,989,755
99,769	110,159	128,032	157,125	186,937	217,486	2,238,543

At the New Mexico Business Technical Center in Rio Rancho, New Mexico, the developer created a one-stop fast-track program that can have a prospective tenant beginning operations in a new facility within 90 days from initial contact with AMREP Corporation.

Courtesy AMREP Corporation

industrial use, securing tenants, completing conceptual designs, and conducting engineering and other studies.

Typically, developers cover predevelopment costs with their own equity capital, but high-risk, high-return capital may be available, usually from a joint venture partner. The usual joint venture agreement for industrial development is a limited partnership or limited liability company involving a money partner as the limited partner and the developer as the general partner. Developers can also enter joint ventures with other kinds of equity partners, including, for example, a landowner, a public utility seeking to sell a brownfield site, a high-profile corporation wishing to demonstrate its commitment to the community, or the owner of a hard-to-sell building.

Investors in other development projects in the area are also a good potential source of equity in the early stages of a project. Whereas outside parties may view a particular neighborhood as risky, local residents or investors that have already committed development funds there may view the development site differently. Moreover, the proposed industrial development may provide some indirect benefit for adjacent or nearby property owners. By improving the image of the neighborhood, the proposed development could enhance the financial position of neighboring sites. For that reason, local investors may be willing to invest in the proposed development.

Obtaining control of the development site is a predevelopment task that can take many forms, from purchase to option to lease agreement. Whatever the approach, finding the funds to control the site is normally the developer's biggest financial hurdle in the predevelopment stage.

Land Acquisition. A variety of sources provide land acquisition funds for industrial development. Commercial banks are a preferred source of land loans, which they make mostly to borrowers with other collateral or strong credit histories. S&Ls provide loan funds, but they tend to concentrate on improved sites. Some REITs and financial service companies provide land acquisition fi-

nancing. Mortgage companies and life insurance companies infrequently finance land acquisition, and when they do, it is with the hope of becoming both construction lender and permanent lender. These companies sometimes charge penalties up to 2 percent and more of the land acquisition and development loan if they are not the subsequent permanent lender.

Banks, S&Ls, and other sources of debt financing for land acquisition and development invariably offer recourse loans, that is, loans requiring that other assets of the borrower be available as collateral for the loan. For the developer, this course of action is risky. By pledging other assets as collateral for a land acquisition or construction loan, the developer in essence places debt against the other collateral to raise capital for the development. A developer who personally signs a recourse loan is usually pledging all his personal net worth as collateral for the loan.

The seller can provide financing for the land. Such financing is typically in the form of a seller-financed loan (known as a purchase money mortgage) providing 70 to 90 percent of the sale price, with the developer contributing the balance in equity capital. The deed to the land is transferred to the developer if the developer meets specific conditions and makes the required periodic payments. Seller financing can be an attractive option for the seller, who can report the transaction as an installment sale and thus defer income taxes. Seller financing can also be an attractive alternative for the developer, who needs to raise only 10 to 30 percent of the land value to control the site for development.

In a purchase money mortgage, the seller/lender may agree to a subordination clause that makes the seller a second-lien holder on the property. By enabling a financial institution to take a first-lien position, the seller makes it possible for the developer to obtain construction financing. Almost without exception, construction lenders require that they have the first lien against the property, guaranteeing in most instances that they will receive all property liquidation proceeds until the construction loan is paid off in full. Only after the first lien is paid in full will the second-lien holder receive any proceeds. Subordination makes seller financing much riskier, and, to compensate, sellers usually require a higher price for the land or an interest-rate premium. Construction lenders and permanent lenders include the debt service payments on seller-financed loans in their calculation of the debt coverage ratio. And if seller financing is in place, construction lenders usually lower the amount of the loan they will approve.

Despite the problems it poses for construction lenders, seller financing can be one of the best alternatives for a cash-strapped developer because of the leverage—the use of borrowed funds to finance the development—that it offers. The confidence that land sellers have about the potential of their land is likely to translate into seller financing that provides a higher degree of leverage for the developer than any available alternative for financing land acquisition. A developer with few assets and little capital may find that seller financing is the only way to obtain title to the land. But, as the next two sections illustrate, ownership is not the only way the developer can gain control of the land. Other strategies for land control include land purchase options and ground leases.

Land Purchase Option. Under a land purchase option, a developer agrees to pay a landowner a nonrefundable cash payment to take the land off the market during a specified option period. The cash payment, which often ranges from 1 percent to 10 percent of the land value, can take a variety of forms. It may be a lump sum paid at the time the agreement is signed, or it may take the form of debt service payments to the landowner during the option period. Some land purchase options include bonus payments to the landowner if the property is rezoned successfully to accommodate the uses the developer proposes.

A land purchase option is a relatively low-risk method of controlling the site before committing significant resources to the project. As such, it gives a developer much needed flexibility during the entitlement process. A good time to exercise an option is after the building permit is obtained. Then the developer can work on other steps in the development process, such as further land assembly, government approvals, rezoning, environmental assessment, due diligence, the signing of anchor tenants, and project financing. If conditions do not favor proceeding with the project, the developer walks away from the option, leaving his nonrefundable deposit with the landowner. Some short-term option agreements may require a refund of the deposit according to provisions in the agreement (see Chapter 2 for more information about land purchase options).

Ground Lease. Ground leases are another method of financing the land component of an industrial project. Instead of purchasing the land, the developer rents it for a long period of time. A ground lease can protect the landowner's long-term financial interests while enabling the developer to begin the project with minimal capital.

It should be noted, however, that lenders do not like to take a subordinate position on ground leases.

In a typical ground lease, rental payments are based on the value of the land, not including improvements. (Lease agreements that cover land and improvements, such as some master leases, are not referred to as ground leases.) Lease terms are typically long (from 25 to 99 years), and the agreement usually contains a provision to extend the lease. A ground lease is usually structured as an absolute net lease, meaning that the lessee is responsible for all expenses associated with the property. Land rents usually escalate according to a predetermined schedule, an agreed-upon index such as the consumer price index, or changes in the property's rental income.

The use of a ground lease offers advantages and disadvantages for the developer. Among the advantages are that no downpayment on the land is needed, the developer's leverage is increased, the developer can sublease the land, and lease payments are deductible on federal income tax returns.

From the developer's perspective, ground leases have some disadvantages as well. A ground lease can be difficult to negotiate. It is possible for the escalations in ground rent to grow faster than the building's cash flow. The developer does not participate in future land appreciation. And when the lease term ends, the improvements revert to the landowner. (If the improvements are expected to have value at reversion, the ground lease frequently includes a provision that the developer be paid for the value of the improvements.)

From the landowner's perspective, a ground lease also offers advantages and disadvantages. Among the advantages are a possibly significant improvement in the value of the land over time, a stream of income that entails few management responsibilities, and ownership of the improvements at the end of the lease. Among the disadvantages to the landowner are the possibility of default by the lessee, less control over the land, and forgone development opportunities during the ground lease period.

Once the developer has secured control of the land, obtained any necessary zoning and planning changes, and met preleasing requirements, he is ready to begin construction—if construction financing has been arranged.

Construction Financing

Commercial banks traditionally have been the primary source of financing for industrial construction; however, alternatives to bank-financed construction loans are available. Developers can obtain construction loans from pension funds, life insurance companies, and other nonbank lenders that are more known for their role as providers of permanent financing. Larger, well-capitalized developers can even issue commercial paper (short-term, unsecured promissory notes usually backed by the full faith and credit of the corporation) to finance construction. A few well-capitalized developers use only equity to fund the construction of their industrial projects.

In their search for a construction loan, many industrial developers look first at local and regional banks. For large projects, national banks and consortiums of banks are likely sources. Construction lenders generally require some preconstruction leasing. The preleasing requirement can range from 30 to 70 percent of the building's space, depending on market conditions and the developer's experience.

While the real estate asset is typically offered as collateral for a construction loan, negotiations between the lender and the developer ultimately determine what secures the loan. An industrial development's collateral value is based on the cash flow that it is expected to generate upon completion. The collateral value of an unbuilt project may be only a fraction of its completed and fully leased value.

Nonrecourse construction loans put the lender in a risky position during construction and lease-up, because in a foreclosure, it has recourse only to the real estate that secures the loan and not to any other assets of the borrower. Ever since the real estate market crash of the early 1990s, however, construction lenders have routinely sought personal liability or recourse for loans. Permanent lenders also have sought partial recourse for takeout loans.

The major sources of construction financing for industrial developers are commercial banks, S&Ls, credit companies, corporate debt, and mortgage bankers and brokers.

Commercial Banks. The dominance of commercial banks in nonresidential real estate lending has grown in the last 15 years, and banks now hold about 40 percent of outstanding commercial mortgage debt in the United States. The large size of banks' real estate loan portfolios has been a matter of concern to investors, debt rating agencies, and government regulators since the late 1980s, when widespread problems in commercial real estate lending surfaced. Despite this concern, banks are likely to remain the dominant source of debt financing for commercial real estate in the near term. Banks are the only institution with extensive commercial lending experience with local projects and with ties to regional and national mortgage conduits and loan participation networks.

In their effort to match the generally short-term nature of their primary liabilities (checking account and savings deposits), banks traditionally have concentrated on assets with a short-term maturity, such as construction loans.

The interest rate on most short-term bank loans is tied to short-term interest rates. Developers should assess the variability in short-term interest rates (i.e., Treasury bill rates, the London interbank offered rate [LIBOR], money market rates, and so on) when they are estimating construction loan interest costs.

The terms of construction loans range generally from six months to three years. Developers of large or multiphase projects that require longer-term construction loans may obtain them from a consortium of lenders that may be formed to share the risk of a large loan or a loan with a long time horizon.

Reflecting the riskier nature of construction loans, interest rate risk spreads are usually higher than on permanent loans. Construction loan interest rate spreads usually range from 1.5 to 3 percentage points above LIBOR, but they may be as high as 6 percentage points above LIBOR, depending on market conditions and the bank's assessment of the credit risk posed by the project or the developer. Upfront loan fees (expressed as "points," with one point equivalent to 1 percent of the loan amount) also vary with the market and the perceived risk of the project or the developer. A charge of one-half to two points is common on most construction loans. An additional point frequently is charged to extend the loan to accommodate construction delays or a difficult lease-up period. The developer needs to factor in all these costs to assess the effective cost of the loan.

Most construction loan agreements call for interest to accrue through the construction period rather than being paid periodically. When construction is complete and the building is leased, the developer obtains a permanent loan or sells the project and, at that point, pays off the total loan amount, which includes the accrued interest and the principal balance.

Banks have changed their construction lending practices dramatically over the past decade. They have become much more concerned, during the underwriting process, about loan repayment. Thus, they have increased prelease requirements and required borrowers to invest more equity. Banks have become key participants in the growth of commercial mortgage conduits, entities that spe-

---

figure 3-18
Characteristics of Lending Sources

	Short-Term Lenders	Long-Term Lenders	Floating-Rate Lenders	Fixed-Rate Lenders
Commercial Banks	●	●	●	●
Savings & Loans	●	●	●	●
Insurance Companies		●		●
Pension Funds		●		●
Credit Companies		●	●	●
Securitized Lenders		●		●
Mortgage REITs		●		●
Government Agencies		●		●

The privately funded interchange at Tuttle Crossing in Columbus, Ohio, eases existing congestion and opens access to the freeway system for the business park.

cialize in mortgage pooling and the issuance of mortgage-backed securities. The relatively newfound ability of banks to sell the mortgages that they originate to investors frees them from having to focus on short-term loans to match their assets and therefore empowers them to provide a wider variety of loans, including interim and permanent loans. To date, very few construction loans have been placed in commercial mortgage–backed securities because of the short-term nature of construction loans and the fact that most construction loans require a draw schedule and not one-time funding like a permanent or takeout loan. Still, banks underwrite loans destined for commercial mortgage conduits in much the same way, if not exactly the same way, they underwrite loans that will be held in their own portfolios.

Savings and Loan Associations. The reputation of S&Ls as thrift institutions—places where thrifty individuals could safeguard their savings—took a beating in the late 1980s and early 1990s when scores of thrifts failed from the weight of poor lending decisions. Commercial real estate lending was a major culprit.

Savings and loans used to specialize in long-term home mortgages, using their depositors' passbook and other short-term accounts to fund them. In the late 1970s and early 1980s, however, interest rates rose to historically high levels, and short-term rates exceeded long-term rates. The profitability of S&Ls began sinking, and the federal government—which insured S&L deposits through the Federal Savings and Loan Insurance Corporation (FSLIC) —responded by allowing S&Ls to broaden their lending activities and removing interest rate ceilings on their deposits.

Emboldened by rising deposits, the removal of investment restrictions, and the safety net of federal insurance, many S&Ls moved into the commercial real estate business and made risky loans on industrial and other development projects. Arguably, they did not fully understand the risks. The deterioration of the commercial real estate market in the last half of the 1980s sparked that period's thrift crisis.

Because the federal government insured the deposits, U.S. taxpayers bore the brunt of the damage. The FSLIC was dismantled and its regulatory duties handed over to the Resolution Trust Corporation, a government corporation created by the Financial Institutions Reform, Recovery, and Enforcement Act of 1989 (FIRREA). New rules were promulgated for S&Ls. These institutions still can make land, construction, and permanent loans for industrial buildings, but the strict parameters imposed by FIRREA have reduced their participation in the commercial mortgage market.

Credit Companies. Some large U.S. corporations use their power in financial markets to establish entities known as credit companies that issue low-cost debt and relend the money to entrepreneurs. Some of these companies, such as GE Capital and General Motors Acceptance Corporation (GMAC), provide construction and redevelopment financing. Credit companies profit on the spread between the cost of their funds and the interest rate they charge on loans to developers.

Compared with bank and S&L financing, the lending activities of credit companies are less entangled in federal regulatory oversight. The federal government regulates the investments of banks and S&Ls to protect the safety of their (federally insured) deposits. Because credit companies' source of funds is not the deposits of individuals, they are not subject to this kind of regulation. Therefore, they often are willing to lend on projects that are too complex, too risky, or otherwise outside the lending parameters of banks and thrifts. Often, however, they charge higher interest rates and have stronger recourse measures.

Corporate Debt. In some cases, corporate debt is also available to finance development directly. Large construction and real estate development companies can issue rated corporate debt, which is debt that is secured by the full faith and credit of the company and is not collateralized by a single project. This money can be used to support land acquisition and development. Corporate

figure 3-19

Comparison of Construction Loans and Permanent Loans

	Construction Loans	Permanent Loans
Term	Short term (18 to 36 months)	Long term (10 to 30 years)
Interest Rate	Floating	Fixed or floating
Funding	As construction or renovation is completed	Upon closing (except for required holdbacks)
Security	Secured by property	Secured by property and income from property
Liability	Borrower may assume personal liability	Nonrecourse to borrower
Repayment	From proceeds of permanent loan	From sale of property or assumption by buyer

debt does not necessarily mature when the projects it supports are complete.

Corporate debt is a potentially longer-term source of funds than construction mortgages. Development companies can finance several projects with one debt issuance, thereby avoiding the points and fees they would have to pay for loans secured project by project. As a share of total debt financing for real estate development, the amount of debt issued by corporations for development purposes is quite small; however, the use of this type of financing is likely to grow as REITs and real estate companies become larger players in the development of industrial real estate.

Mortgage Bankers and Brokers. Mortgage bankers originate real estate loans, which they then sell to institutions or securities dealers. Mortgage bankers have been a major force behind the growth of the CMBS market. They have acted as deal makers in this market, both soliciting business from developers and issuing debt. To date, few construction loans have been pooled as CMBSs and sold on Wall Street. Many observers, however, think that once investors become comfortable with securities based on pools of permanent loans, the pooling of construction loans may be the next step in mortgage securitization.

Mortgage brokers do not lend money. They act as intermediaries or conduits between the lender and the developer. They often represent a variety of debt sources, to which they can shop a loan proposal to find the best fit. Brokers' fees are negotiable, typically ranging from 0.25 to 1.5 percent of the loan amount and decreasing as the amount of the loan increases. Mortgage brokers generally do not service the loan. Their involvement in the lending process usually ends with the loan's closing.

Interim Financing

Interim financing bridges the gap between construction loans and permanent loans—when such a gap exists. Most construction loans are for projects on which the developer has a commitment for a permanent loan (or takeout loan). If all construction loans included an unconditional takeout agreement, the need for interim financing would

disappear. But sometimes obtaining a forward permanent loan commitment is not possible or is too costly for the developer. Alternatively, it is possible that when the project is complete, the permanent lender will not fund the takeout loan commitment because certain conditions have not been met.

Broadly, permanent lenders require that two conditions be met before they will fund the takeout of the construction loan. The building must be built as specified in the architectural and engineering drawings so as not to compromise its collateral value or post a letter of credit. And NOI must be adequate to service the debt, which means that the building must be leased sufficiently to meet the lender's minimum debt coverage ratio.

Developers may have to arrange interim financing when no takeout exists or when the construction lender needs assurance that the funds to repay the construction loan will be available even if the requirements of the permanent lender are not met. Construction lenders usually provide interim financing when it is needed. Thus, some construction lenders—especially commercial banks—will commit to convert their construction loans, if necessary, to short-term permanent loans called miniperms, with three- to seven-year maturities.

Committing to interim financing can be a risky proposition. To compensate for the risk, the interim lender often exacts a fee at the time the construction loan is closed and also charges a high risk premium if the interim commitment needs to be funded. The interest rate is likely to be less than the rate on the construction loan and more than the rate on permanent loans on other industrial projects. From the developer's perspective, an interim loan buys time for the project in the marketplace.

Permanent Financing

Long-term loans on real estate are called permanent loans. Historically, the primary sources of long-term debt financing for industrial development have been life insurance companies and pension funds, with commercial banks playing a limited role. When real estate values dropped in the early 1990s, insurance companies withdrew from the permanent loan market, leaving developers, property owners, and the RTC without a reliable source of long-term property financing. This lack of capital pushed up the financial returns on long-term permanent loans, which lured Wall Street investors into the market. Now commercial mortgage–backed securities are an important source of funds for permanent financing.

Permanent loans generally are underwritten with an LTV of 65 to 85 percent and a DCR of 1.20 to 1.50, depending on the riskiness of the property's long-term value and cash flow. The permanent lender's LTV and debt coverage ratios are of critical importance to the construction lender, because if the completed project falls short of property value estimates or income streams from leasing, the permanent lender will be unwilling to take out the construction loan.

Developers usually arrange the permanent financing before they seek a construction loan. When a permanent financing commitment is in place, it is much easier to obtain a construction loan. In most instances, the construction loan's principal and accrued interest are paid from the takeout loan. Thus, a takeout commitment improves the construction lender's risk position. As noted, takeout commitments are conditioned on the adequacy of the construction and the success of the leasing. The interest rate spreads on construction loans are typically higher than on permanent loans, giving the developer an incentive to replace the construction loan as soon as possible.

By providing long-term capital, the permanent lender assumes some of the project's long-term market risks. Historically, permanent financing was expected to remain in place through more than one market cycle. The typical loan was a 30-year, fixed-rate, fully amortized mortgage. More recently, most permanent lenders have shortened their loan terms to five to ten years and use a 20- to 30-year amortization schedule with a balloon payment at maturity.

Long-term financing is commonly provided in the form of a mortgage or a trust deed, both of which involve the commitment of property as collateral for the repayment of the loan. Mortgages come in many forms:

- Fixed-Rate Mortgage—The interest rate is held constant during the loan term. Fixed-rate mortgages are the most common type of permanent loan.
- Variable-Rate Mortgage—The interest rate adjusts periodically and is tied to a published index. Also known as an adjustable-rate mortgage, this instrument protects lenders against rising interest rates and inflation.
- Blanket Mortgage—A single mortgage that includes multiple properties as collateral, a blanket mortgage usually includes a release provision that allows individual properties to be unmortgaged without retiring the whole mortgage.
- Package Mortgage—Personal (non–real estate) items may be included as collateral in the loan agreement.
- Open-End Mortgage—The borrower may obtain additional funds later.

The dominant sources of permanent financing are life insurance companies, Wall Street in the form of commercial mortgage–backed securities, and pension funds.

Life Insurance Companies. Life insurance companies are a principal source of permanent financing for industrial development. They are able to invest a large amount of capital in long-term mortgages because their cash flow is continuous and predictable. They receive a constant flow of funds from premium payments, and they can accurately predict their future outlays from actuarial tables.

Life insurance companies incurred significant losses along with other lenders and investors when the bubble burst from the overbuilding of the 1980s and the value of commercial real estate declined. Since then, government regulations, new industry standards, and pressure

figure 3-20
Sources of Debt Financing

Type of Financing	Commercial Banks	Savings & Loans	Insurance Companies	Pension Funds	Credit Companies	Securitized Lenders	Mortgage REITs	Government Agencies
Line of Credit	Y	Y	N	N	N	N	N	N
Letter of Credit	Y	N	N	N	N	N	N	Y
Planning/Predevelopment	Y	N	N	N	N	N	N	N
Land Acquisition	Y	Y	N	N	Y	N	N	N
Land Development	Y	Y	N	N	Y	N	N	N
Construction	Y	Y	Y	Y	Y	Y	N	Y
Bridge (gap) Financing	Y	N	N	N	Y	Y	N	N
Takeout Commitment	Y	Y	Y	Y	Y	Y	N	Y
Standby Commitment	N	N	N	N	Y	N	N	N
Permanent Mortgage	Y	Y	Y	Y	Y	Y	Y	Y

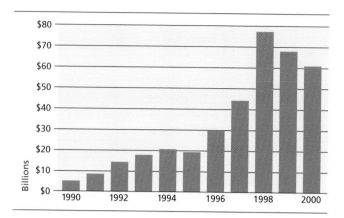

figure 3-21

CMBS Market Volume

Source: Lend Lease Real Estate Investments, *Emerging Trends in Real Estate, 2001.*

from investors have led life insurance companies to reduce the proportion of their assets held in mortgage loans. Life insurance companies once held one-third of their total assets in mortgages. In 1990, their total commercial mortgage holdings peaked at $255 billion and has declined since then—to about $182 million in 1999. Despite their recent pullback, life insurance companies remain the second largest institutional provider of commercial mortgages, after banks. They should continue to be a significant source of permanent loans for industrial development. Life insurance companies are also becoming major investors in CMBSs, a growing source of long-term debt financing for industrial development.

Commercial Mortgage–Backed Securities. The issuance of CMBSs—the sale of bondlike interests in portfolios of mortgage loans backed by commercial real estate and sold through the capital markets to individual and institutional buyers—has grown tremendously in recent years.

Loans securitized in CMBS pools are originated in a variety of ways. Traditional commercial real estate lenders such as banks and insurance companies may sell a portion of their existing portfolios by securitizing them. Or new loans can be originated strictly for the purpose of securitization. The process is known as the conduit process, and the loans are called conduit loans. Conduits are not like banks, as they do not rely on a base of deposits to fund loans; rather, they use short-term borrowings to fund loans that are held in inventory before securitization. Once the conduit has accumulated a portfolio of sufficient size, the loans are pooled and securitized and the resulting securities sold to investors.

The aggregate value of CMBS loans outstanding increased from $47.5 billion in 1993 to more than $200 billion in 2000.[2] Although CMBS issuers were consolidated in 1999 and offerings dropped, CMBS issuances in 2000 recovered to 1998 levels. They will continue to play an important role in financing real estate development by adding liquidity and depth to the commercial real estate market.

Pension Funds. Pension funds provide a significant source of equity for commercial real estate development. Like life insurance companies, pension funds have long-term and relatively predictable liabilities that correspond well with real estate assets. Their real estate investments include both debt and equity.

In the late 1970s and the 1980s, high inflation and the chance to diversify assets made real estate an attractive investment for pension funds. They hired advisers and moved into the real estate investment arena. After passage of the Employee Retirement Income Security Act of 1974, which required pension funds to diversify their investments (at that time mostly stocks and bonds), pension funds, often through advisers, began to invest in high-quality real estate assets, including industrial buildings. Investing continued until the early 1990s, when market values began plummeting and many funds tried unsuccessfully to divest themselves of poorly performing equity real estate. Although property investments doubled within the past decade to more than $140 billion in 2000, they are still less than 2 percent of total pension assets.

In addition to direct investment, some funds now invest in more liquid CMBSs. Moreover, recent changes in regulations for widely held REITs allow pension funds to invest in REIT stocks.

Other Sources. Among a variety of other sources of long-term industrial development financing are credit companies, foreign investors, REITs, and municipal bonds.

Developers often turn to credit companies for permanent financing for unusual or hard-to-underwrite projects. Because they are not subject to the kinds of federal and state regulations that restrict the investment policies of life insurance companies and banks, credit companies can be more flexible about the types of projects they lend to and the loan structures they establish.

Foreign investors are another source of long-term financing. U.S. property attracts foreign investment for a number of reasons: the large size of the market, the country's potential for long-term economic growth, U.S.

figure 3-22

Pension Fund Assets in Equity Real Estate

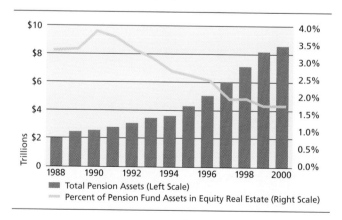

Source: Lend Lease Real Estate Investments, *Emerging Trends in Real Estate, 2001.*

figure 3-23
Foreign Investment in U.S. Real Estate
As of December 31, 1999

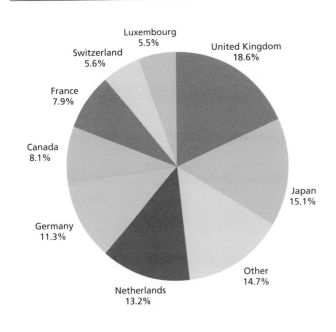

Luxembourg 5.5%
Switzerland 5.6%
France 7.9%
Canada 8.1%
Germany 11.3%
Netherlands 13.2%
Other 14.7%
Japan 15.1%
United Kingdom 18.6%

Source: Lend Lease Real Estate Investments, *Emerging Trends in Real Estate, 2001.*

political stability, the foreign trade deficit, and beneficial tax provisions. During the 1980s and 1990s, foreign trading partners with surplus dollars invested heavily in U.S. commercial real estate. In the late 1980s, for example, nearly two-thirds of the Class A industrial space in downtown Los Angeles was owned by foreigners. Foreign investors owned 20 percent of downtown industrial space in Chicago, 23 percent in Washington, D.C., and 21 percent in Manhattan.

Demand for U.S. real estate by foreign investors has varied significantly from year to year. Estimates suggest that foreign investment in U.S. real estate increased in the early 1980s, and moderated and then picked up again from 1983 to 1985. Foreign investment went through a number of cycles from 1985 until the early 1990s, when investment levels declined appreciably as the value of all U.S. real estate dropped and foreign investors sold off their U.S. holdings. In 1994, foreigners owned 2.5 percent of the value of U.S. real estate. The Japanese were the most active foreign investors in real estate during the 1980s. In fact, much of the growth in foreign ownership can be traced to the Japanese, whose investment positions in U.S. real estate rose from $744 million in 1984 to a high of $15.2 billion in 1990. Japanese investment activity in the 1980s was encouraged by the huge trade surplus Japan had with the United States, the relatively small size of its own real estate market, and the higher U.S. rates of return. In the 1990s, Japanese holdings of U.S. real estate decreased significantly, to about $8.8 billion in 1996,

largely as a result of low or even negative returns and steep drops in the value of Japanese property investments in the United States. From 1997 to 1999, the amount invested in U.S. real estate increased again, and Japan continues to be the largest foreign investor.

European investment in U.S. real estate has increased steadily since 1980. Europeans were particularly active from 1980 to 1986 and from 1989 to 1993. Dutch investors were typically in the number two or three position after Japan or Canada throughout the 1990s. German investors were also very active from 1995 to 2000.

A handful of mortgage REITs invest in debt vehicles unrelated to their own development projects. The lending policies of mortgage REITs vary, and they may provide short-term construction loans as well as long-term mortgages.

Municipalities also sometimes issue tax-exempt bonds to help finance the development of commercial real estate projects. Such public assistance is used when portions of a development are public uses or when the municipality wishes to encourage the development of a site, such as an urban brownfield site, or an area, such as a designated urban redevelopment district. This source of financing is limited by strict federal guidelines on how much of a tax-exempt municipal bond issuance can be used for private purposes.

The Financing Package

Industrial developers seeking financing for a project need to approach lenders or investors with an understanding of the money source's current requirements and policies, strong supporting evidence of the project's market feasibility, and a carefully prepared business plan. They would do well to anticipate the objections the lender or investor might raise and to consider beforehand alternatives that might deal with those objections.

To secure funds, developers need to compile a professionally organized financing package or hire a professional loan broker to assist in preparing the package before they contact investors and lenders. The financing package is typically a developer's first, and possibly only, chance to demonstrate his understanding of the project's market, investment criteria, relevant development issues, the lender's requirements, the financing process, and other critical issues.

The developer's financing package plays a significant role in the lender's assessment of the risk posed by both the borrower and the project. A cavalier attitude toward the financing process or an inexperienced reading of the lender's needs will impede the developer's efforts to secure funding.

The major elements of a good financing package include:

- table of contents;
- executive summary;
- overview of the proposed development;

A. General requirements for a loan submission package
1. Project information
   a. Project description—legal description of site, survey, photographs of site, renderings of building and any parking facilities, development strategy and timing
   b. Site and circulation plan, identification of any easements, availability of utilities, description of adjacent land uses, soil tests
   c. Plans for building improvements. Detailed list of amenities.
   d. Identification of architect, general contractor, principal subcontractors. Supporting financial data and past performance of parties. Copies of any agreements executed among parties. Description of construction and development procedures.
2. Market and financial data
   a. Full set of financial statements on the borrower and any other principal project sponsors, past development experience, list of previous project lenders
   b. Pro forma operating statement. Detail on proposed leasing terms to tenants, including base rent, escalations, expense stops, renewal options, common area expense allocation, overage (retail leases), finish-out allowances, other commitments.
   c. Detailed cost breakdowns including:
      • Any land acquisition costs
      • Any necessary land development costs
      • Any required demolition costs
      • Direct or hard costs with breakdowns for excavation, grading, foundation, masonry, steel work, drywall or plastering, HVAC, plumbing, electrical, elevator, and other mechanical, any special finish-out or fixtures
      • Indirect or soft costs, including architects, engineering fees, legal fees, property taxes, interest [during the] construction period, development fees, insurance and bonding fees, estimated contingency reserve, anticipated permanent loan fees

   d. Any executed lease commitments or letter of intent from tenants detailing all terms of leases
   e. Market study and appraisal, including all comparables and detached schedule of rents charged by competitors
   f. Loan request, terms, anticipated interest rate, amortization period, anticipated participation options
   g. Equity to be provided by developer and/or other sponsors (cash and/or land); anticipated financing of draws/repayment
3. Government and regulatory information
   a. Statement as to zoning status
   b. Ad valorem taxes, method of payment, reappraisal dates
   c. All necessary permits, evidence of approved zoning variances, etc.
4. Legal documentation
   a. Legal entity applying for loan (evidence of incorporation, partnership agreement)
   b. Statement of land costs or contract evidencing purchase
   c. Detail regarding deed restrictions, etc.
   d. Subordination agreements
   e. *Force majeur* provisions (events beyond the control of the developer such as an "act of God")

B. Additional information needed for interim loan package
1. A copy of the permanent or standby commitment from the permanent lender. Details on the amount, rate, term, fees, options relative to prepayment, calls, and participation. Details on contingencies that the developer must meet before the commitment is binding.
2. *Detailed* architectural plans and specifications
3. *Detailed* cost breakdown
4. All data relative to requirements list in Part A and *updated* as appropriate

Assuming that 1) upon review of all relevant materials in A and B, the interim lender makes a commitment and 2) the developer goes forward with the project, the next step [is] to close the interim loan.

• description and location of the project;
• design and construction details;
• schedule for the project;
• project economics;
• market analysis;
• regulatory approvals;
• the project team;
• sponsorship and financial details; and
• exhibits.

Most sections in the outline should include several subtopics, and all the topics in which the target lender (or equity investor) will be interested should be covered. When preparing the financing package, the developer should always keep in mind the audience, which is the specific lender (or equity investor) to which the project is being presented. The developer should be prepared to tailor the basic package for delivery to specific lenders or investors.

C. Interim lender closing requirements
  1. Project information: *final* drawings, cost estimates, site plan, etc.
  2. Market and financial information: statement that no adverse change in borrower's financial position has occurred since application date
  3. Government and regulatory information: all necessary permits, notification of any approved zoning variances, etc.
  4. Legal documentation
     a. Documentation indicating that the permanent lender has reviewed and approved all information in Part A and all updates in Part B
     b. All documentation relative to contracts for general contractors, architects, planners, subcontractors. Evidence of bonding, conditional assignment of all contracts to interim lender. Agreements of all contractors to perform for interim lender. Verification of property tax insurance contracts, etc.
     c. Inventory of all personal property that will serve as security for the interim loan . . .
     d. Any executed leases and approvals by permanent lender
     e. Copies of ground leases and verification of current payment status by the lessor/owner
     f. The interim lender will also insist on an assignment of all leases, rents, and other income in the event of default *and* a guarantee of loan payments by the borrower (personal liability). After review of all items indicated above, the interim lender will provide the borrower with a loan commitment detailing the terms of the loan, including amount, rate, term, fees, prepayment and call options, and any participations. However, the *permanent* lender may require certain agreements with the interim lender, including a buy-sell agreement or tri-party agreement.

D. Permanent lender closing requirements
  These requirements are necessary *if* the developer 1) completes construction and 2) satisfies all contingencies (including lease-up requirements) contained in the permanent loan commitment before the expiration date of the permanent commitment.
  1. Market and financial data
     a. Statement of no material changes in financial status of borrower, or
     b. A certified list of tenants, executed leases, and estoppel certificates indicating verification of rents currently being collected, any amounts owed, and any dispute relative to payments on finish-out costs agreement with the developer
  2. Project information
     a. Final appraisal of project value
     b. Final survey of building on site
  3. Government and regulatory information
     a. Updates on currency of property taxes
     b. Certificate of occupancy issued by building inspector
     c. Other permit requirements (fire, safety, health, etc.)
  4. Legal documentation
     a. Delivery of the construction loan mortgage (if assigned to the permanent lender)
     b. Architect's certificate of completion with detailed survey and final plans, etc.
     c. Endorsements of all casualty and hazard insurance policies indicating permanent lender as new loss payee
     d. Updated title insurance policy
     e. Updated verification on status of ground rents (if relevant)
     f. An exculpation agreement relieving the borrower of personal liability (if applicable)
     g. Lien releases from general subcontractors, verification of any payments outstanding, and proposed disposition ∎

Source: William B. Brueggeman and Jeffrey Fisher, *Real Estate Finance and Investments,* 10th ed. (New York: Irwin/McGraw-Hill, 1996), pp. 486–87. Reproduced by permission.

Graphics, including maps, site plans, building plans, photographs, and graphs, should be combined with narrative to make the points clearly, strongly, and concisely. Developers without experience in putting together financing packages should consider hiring a real estate consultant to help them create an informative and persuasive presentation.

The goal of successful loan submissions is to make it easy for the loan underwriter to make a case when presenting them to the loan committee. Lenders must be convinced that the loan will be secured by a high-quality asset and that repayment of principal and interest is ensured; therefore, it is important to highlight the project's positive aspects, identify risk areas, and clearly state the ways risks will be minimized. Developers should be prepared in advance to answer all difficult questions.

The assessment of risk is a paramount factor in the financing of industrial projects. Investment and loan cri-

Large recesses in the roof above the entry areas and the projected main entry portico accentuate the Flex Tech building at Avion in Chantilly, Virginia.

teria are established on the basis of the risks involved, with perceptions of risk being different for the developer, the lender, and the investor. Accurate risk assessment is important: too much optimism can advance a project that should not be developed, and too much caution can scuttle a project that would have served the market well.

Lenders are often characterized as "risk averse." A good financing package should identify various risks and specify ways in which the developer of the proposed project will seek to minimize them, as follows:

- Borrower—The developer's performance risk is usually measured by such factors as the composition of the development team, the strength of the developer's financial statement (its capacity to cover potential losses), the developer's track record and reputation, and the developer's collateral. Developers with large capital assets and a record of successful undertakings typically get better loan terms because they pose a smaller risk for the lender.
- Lender/Investor—The ability of the lender or investor to perform is measured by its financial capability and stability, its approach to business, and its management philosophy.
- Market—Supply and demand depend on factors like demographic shifts, changes in absorption rates, and development of competitive space.
- Political—Among the risks to a project's successful development are the developer's ability to navigate the

local approval process, shifts in regulatory or community attitudes, and changes in tax laws.
- Design and Construction—Industrial projects abound with risks related to design and construction, among them risks that the schedule will be delayed, contractors will not be able to obtain bonding or completion insurance, the budget will be exceeded, and contracts (especially contracts negotiated to achieve particular objectives, such as a maximum cost ceiling or a fast-track schedule) will not be met.
- Economic—Changing interest rates and the risk of recession are the chief economic risks confronting industrial developments. Industrial development typically is highly leveraged; thus, rising interest rates can increase development costs to a point where the trade-off between risks and return is unacceptable. Nevertheless, such risk is an external factor that the developer cannot control.
- Market Preferences—Shifts in consumers' preferences affecting the local business climate, and in location and design factors pose risks to industrial development.
- Operational Management—Management's performance can be assessed by reviewing the experience and attitude of the property manager, the management approach, and the operational budgets and schedules. Insurance is a related risk.

Once a top-quality financing package with professional content and appearance has been prepared, developers can directly contact funding sources. Or they can retain consultants or brokers with experience in real estate investment, development, and finance to locate likely lenders or investors.

Developers must allow sufficient time to gather and analyze data, prepare the submission, and complete the loan closing. A typical timetable for the process, beginning after the developer has completed the necessary research and analyses and obtained control of the site, includes:

Preparing loan submission package	2–4 weeks
Contacting lenders and establishing their interest in the project	2–4 weeks
Finalizing loan terms and beginning the formal application process	1–2 weeks
Undertaking due diligence, assessing outside reports, and preparing the loan commitment (lender)	4–6 weeks
Closing and funding	2–3 weeks

Preparing the loan submission package and establishing lenders' interest can take longer than four weeks if the project involves multiple phases, mixed uses, or other complicating factors. And while some lenders can close a loan in four weeks, it can take others up to six months.

Notes

1. Note that lenders often originate a loan for a set number of years, ten in the case of Meadow View, but amortize the loan over a 30-year term. By partially amortizing loans, lenders reduce the risk that the value of the property will not be sufficient to refinance the loan in ten years.
2. *Commercial Mortgage Alert* (Hoboken, New Jersey: Harrison Scott Publications).

4. Site Planning and Industrial Building Design

Once the feasibility of developing a business park or an industrial building has been determined and the decision made to proceed with the project, site planning and architectural and structural design can move beyond the preliminary stage. This chapter addresses the planning and design of both business parks (roughly the first half of the chapter) and individual buildings (beginning with "Industrial Building Design"). The intent is to provide a checklist rather than specific engineering and architectural design methods or criteria that can be applied to a parcel of land or a building under consideration for development.

Site Planning for Business Parks

Site Design

Site design for a business park must consider a variety of interrelated variables, from lot layout to street systems and landscaping plans. Developers are required to conform to local zoning and planning regulations, and, in addition, they may choose to adopt covenants, conditions, and restrictions to ensure the maintenance of a safe and aesthetically pleasing environment.

The Process. Site planning is the process of designing a development project and obtaining the necessary approvals to begin construction. It begins with the study of alternative sites and becomes more formalized and specific when a site has been selected. When used as a tool in decision making, the site planning process minimizes the developer's risk and maximizes the project's long-term benefits.

Site planning proceeds through three general stages: concept planning, preliminary planning, and final planning. Each stage involves the collection and analysis of information about the site, the identification and evaluation of alternatives, and public review. The activities are highly interdependent and are normally undertaken in several cycles during each stage. Developers typically go through preliminary and final planning for each phase of a multiphase project like a business park.

Concept planning deals with the broadest possible site-specific issues and is often conducted before committing to a site to explore its opportunities for and constraints on development. The product of concept planning is a schematic diagram of the major components of the project, such as proposed parcelization, building location and scale, occupancy type and orientation, site access and transportation links, surface or structured parking, amenity areas, landscaping, security issues, and parcels reserved for future development. During this stage, developers should attempt to obtain a clear understanding of the public sector's plans for providing roads, infrastructure, and other public services, as this information is integral to evaluating a project's economics.

During *preliminary planning*, the concept plan is refined through the identification and evaluation of alternative

Apple Computer R&D campus in Cupertino, California.

Technology is an increasingly important development tool. For the Chickasaw Distribution Center in Memphis, the Construction Management System software program provided instant access to information about the progress of a client's warehouse/distribution center via a secure extranet.

types and sizes of and locations for buildings, streets, parking areas, major elements of the pedestrian circulation network, and landscape features. One of the most informative products that can be prepared during preliminary planning is an illustrative site plan that schematically depicts how the site might appear after development. Illustrative plans are essentially a conceptual interpretation of the plan, and developers should not let them drive future decisions. Care must be taken to ensure that the illustrative plan does not result in images or conditions that the developer will be held to. The plan must be reviewed at this time for compliance with local codes and ordinances, park covenants, or design guidelines. Setbacks and easements, utility connections, stormwater management, and mitigation measures will also be determined.

If the project will be built in stages, the developer's phasing strategy must be incorporated as part of the preliminary planning process and documents. During design development, the phasing strategy will be applied to designing an infrastructure that enables future construction with minimum disruption to existing buildings, circulation, and services. At this stage, a construction manager is often brought in as part of the development team. Whether they have a stake in the final implementation of the plan or not, experienced construction managers can provide invaluable guidance on project cost and constructability. The schedule is then adjusted accordingly and a detailed and accurate cost estimate completed.

During *final planning*, the preliminary plan is refined, which for a single building site means the preparation of detailed design and construction drawings. For a business park, however, it means completing a final master plan; preparing the final subdivision map, CC&Rs, and design guidelines; and seeking final public approvals. After final approval is granted, minor changes can normally be made to the final plans through amendments. Construction documents contain all the information about the project that is necessary to obtain accurate, final bids from contractors. A complete set of specifications establishes

guidelines for the brand, quantity, size, and quality of materials and plants to be installed during construction. A list of add-ons or alternates—items that the developer may opt to include or not as part of the final contract— is also included. The tighter the specifications are written, the more realistic and dependable the construction bids will be, with no room for misinterpretation. With public approval, the construction and marketing phases can begin.

The developer and the project planning team should undertake site planning in consultation with representatives of public agencies and other interested parties. A concerted and proactive effort toward gaining consensus on the project should always be made. A meaningful dialogue with the jurisdictions involved in the project should take place early in the process, no later than during preliminary planning. Business parks can have widespread impact on local communities and do not always garner public acceptance. Municipal staff can be allies by assisting in compliance and facilitating public understanding and support of a project. Economic development agencies aim to promote economic and job development, and they may provide assistance to new industries or employers through funding, tax incentives, and assistance in gaining timely public approvals. In addition to working with government organizations, it is sometimes advisable to include abutting residential neighborhoods in preliminary discussions to uncover and respond to their concerns in the early phases of project development.

A realistic work program and schedule to guide site planning is essential. The work program and the schedule must reflect specific requirements for submitting materials and review periods that are necessary for the project's approval. Once the required approvals are identified, a realistic schedule for completing the approval process can be prepared. As new requirements are identified during planning, the work program and schedule will need to be revised. The length of time required for

In December 1997, developer IDI broke ground at Weston Business Center in Fort Lauderdale, Florida. Eighteen months and four buildings later, IDI won approval from the city for the site plan for Buildings E and F, the last of the six buildings planned for the park.

a proposed business park to receive all the approvals necessary for construction to begin varies widely among jurisdictions—from a matter of months to several years. The developer should be aware that many communities expect the developer to be in contact with adjacent residents early and often in the process. While this expectation can sometimes cause problems, it is better to deal with them early than to be surprised during a public approval hearing.

In the final analysis, the planning process for business parks involves primarily land planning, subdivision design and platting, establishing controls for the use and development of individual sites, the construction of street and utility improvements, and overall site landscaping. This process is followed by marketing individual sites for sale or lease and in some cases developing speculative buildings without signed leases in place. Actual building design occurs as sites are sold or leased to new owners or tenants, or designed and constructed under a build-to-suit agreement. At this stage, the requirements of the master developer and CC&Rs, if implemented, serve to control how an individual site is developed. Much of the long-term value of a business park is tied to the quality of overall development and what takes place on individual sites. It is the interplay among site controls, the community's zoning regulations, and building codes that helps to achieve the desired result—a successful business park with long-term value for all interested parties.

Platting. A preliminary plat indicating street and parcel layout is submitted to the appropriate public agencies during preliminary site development review and approval. A plat is a map showing actual or planned features such as streets and building lots. It also depicts the setbacks required by the municipality or city where the site is located as well as additional setbacks for any environmentally sensitive areas. The layout incorporates known public requirements and neighborhood concerns to the extent possible. Public agencies' review comments are incorporated formally or informally in the park's master plan as part of

a public/private agreement for developing the property. Although an estimate of cost can be made from the proposed master plan, accurate development cost estimates can be prepared only after the final plan is approved. Flexibility should be negotiated with the public agency so that the preliminary plan can be changed if market conditions change.

Lot Layout and Size. The site layout for the business park should be based on anticipated future development patterns and the results of the marketing, feasibility, planning, and engineering studies for the site. A range of parcel sizes and shapes must be provided to accommodate the planned uses.

Although lot sizes are not standard, lots of 200 to 300 feet (60 to 90 m) deep are popular for a range of uses. Several larger lots of 500 feet (150 m) deep or more may be useful because they can be subdivided in a future development phase if a large single user does not materialize. Larger lots can be improved by building a cul-de-sac

The design of the roadways at ConAgra Corporate Campus in Omaha, Nebraska, reflects the topography of the site and provides opportunities for future growth.

At Avion in Chantilly, Virginia, open space and retention ponds enhance the business park's attractive environment and connect to surrounding networks.

into the lot that facilitates access to the entire area. If used, culs-de-sac should end in a paved turnaround 100 feet (30 m) in diameter to accommodate larger trucks, including 45-foot (14-m) trailers, and to allow a 180-degree turn without backing up.

Individual lots should be laid out to take advantage of the site's natural features and views. In addition, lots should be compatible with the surrounding development pattern and the open spaces designed around them on land that may be unsuitable for development. This open space, which may include retention ponds, stands of trees, and recreation areas (tennis courts, exercise stations, jogging trails), should be planned to enhance the attractiveness of the platted lots and to provide connectivity to surrounding networks where possible. These features are known to increase marketability and value of business park developments.

Planning individual buildings and sites in business parks depends on the location and development strategy chosen. Features such as setback requirements, lot sizes and shapes, building coverage, floor/area ratios (FARs), relationships of different land and building uses, vehicular parking needs, truck loading and maneuvering depths, pedestrian connections, open space, and protected areas vary widely. For example, an urban business park that contains primarily office uses will have very different building and site design requirements from a suburban park geared toward manufacturing and warehouse uses or one geared toward flexible-use R&D space.

Building setbacks from the fronting street vary from none for buildings on a property line in a dense urban area to 50 feet (15 m) or more for those in some suburban areas. Large multiuse parks may have even greater setbacks as part of the design, particularly if major site features such as woodlands will be preserved. Side and rear setbacks often are less than front setbacks and can be 10 to 15 feet (3 to 4.5 m) or less.

The Fred Hutchinson Cancer Research Center is dedicated to the study of cancer and its cures. Its newest building at the South Lake Union Research Campus in Seattle, Washington, houses laboratory space, offices, and amenities such as a cafeteria and a lounge.

R&D buildings designed for laboratories, engineering, manufacturing, assembly, storage, and office space are configured differently from multitenant industrial buildings, and they typically require differently shaped lots. These types of facilities, often designed for a single tenant, generally require deeper lots with less emphasis on the length of frontage than do office and industrial facilities. Hybrid warehouse/R&D buildings require more parking spaces than bulk warehouses; spaces usually are accommodated around three sides of the buildings. Open space and landscaping requirements vary depending on the lot coverage required and the site planning concept. Adequate space must be provided for loading docks and truck/van turnaround areas.

Positioning Uses. A business park developer's goal is to position uses where they will bring the greatest value to the project. Grouping compatible uses results in cost savings and more efficient use of the land. With basic information on market factors, physical site characteristics, proposed building size, adjacent uses, and traffic patterns, an astute site planner or designer can begin to place each use according to its appropriateness for specific areas of the site.

Initially, the planner creates several rough site layouts that include lot layouts, access points, and internal circulation. Cost estimates are then provided for each alternative to help the owner and the team of advisers—the market analyst, financial analyst, civil engineer, traffic consultant—make the best decision for the most profitable, practical, and code-compliant use of the property. The same process can also be used to analyze sites for suitability for the project.

As a general rule, sites for building types that are the least industrial in appearance and function, such as offices and R&D and flex facilities, should be situated on the most visible part of the property, close to freeway interchanges, major arterials, commercial services, and residential areas. Often more industrial-looking buildings —manufacturing and assembly facilities and bulk warehouses—are placed in less prominent areas of the property. Office/warehouse combinations may fit into either category, depending on the design.

Beacon Centre (see the case study in Chapter 7), a 205-acre (83-ha) multiuse business park in Miami, effectively segregates uses, with retail space located on the front of the site at the southern end, warehouse uses in the center of the site, and office, showroom, and retail uses on the northern and western edges. The plan also pays special attention to the aesthetic treatment of the leading edge of the warehouse zone. By containing truck traffic, screening loading docks in the zone, and placing smaller build-to-suit buildings in front of the larger bulk storage structures, designers made this edge an effective transition zone that has sustained significantly higher land values per square foot for adjacent retail and office sites.

Warehouse/distribution facilities typically cover the largest amount of land of any building type in a park, although, as is the case for the other types of facilities, they vary widely in size. The percentage of lot covered is

generally high, more land is required for truck loading/unloading and turnaround than for other uses, and less land is needed for parking spaces. Warehouses typically are sited along the park's edge, with their backs facing other industrial uses outside the park. Truck access for these facilities is provided by secondary park entrances where practicable so that this activity does not conflict with employee and visitor traffic. If rail access is required, warehouses should be sited as close as possible to the ex-

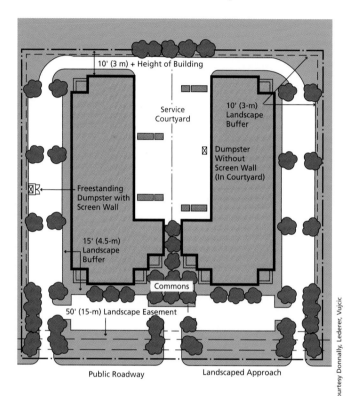

Typical multibuilding site concept.

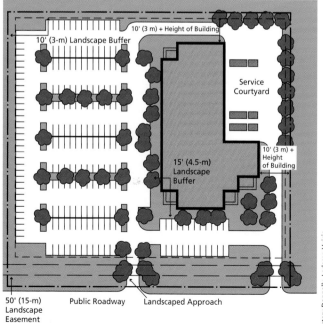

Typical single-building site concept.

isting rail line to avoid the cost of extending the line and to minimize intrusion in the park.

Access and Internal Streets

Access is fundamental to the success of modern business parks. The location of roads in the park depends on planning factors as well as the development concept for the site. Roads must be designed to permit maximum flexibility in shaping developable parcels, because changes in demand may require dividing planned parcels, either combining or reconfiguring them at some future date before buildout. In addition, truck traffic should be separated physically from other traffic in the park to the extent possible to avoid disrupting essential tenant operations.

Planners organize the site from the outside in when planning street systems. Existing public roadways that encircle, intersect, or lead to the parcel of land being developed are the launching pad for the site plan. The location of these roads and the volume of traffic they carry provide key planning criteria for site access points and on-site vehicular circulation. Based on the character of the roadways outside the site, the planner selects practical locations for the primary and secondary entrances, orients buildings' front doors for high visibility, and configures internal roadways.

Early field reconnaissance should uncover any problems that may affect the feasibility of road locations. Several factors influence the siting of new roads:

- location of existing roads and facilities on and near the site;
- expansion plans for the business park;
- the mix of desired lot layouts, including sizes, frontage, and depth;
- geological conditions, including soils, water, and drainage;
- grading and alignment relating to topography;
- clearing and grubbing;
- ground cover and foliage;

- maintenance considerations;
- rail service;
- local jurisdictional controls.

All types of business operations must be considered, including truck ingress and egress and employee and visitor vehicle access. Depending on the size of the development, roads can be designed to reflect a hierarchy of uses, such as a central parkway linking major sections of the park, secondary roads serving individual sections, and service roads.

Beacon Centre's plan is based on a simple framework of internal roads that connect with and blend into surrounding streets. By maintaining the fabric of the surrounding street grid, the plan makes locating internal building addresses easy. Moreover, by adhering to the property's rectilinear shape, the plan maximizes efficient land use and flexible parcel sizes. Five major entry points, each with entry and identity features, funnel truck traffic to its destination with minimal impact on office and retail areas.

Administrative and operational controls and procedures for planning, design, construction, and operation of streets and highways are the responsibility of authorized local, regional, state, or national public agencies. Streets, frontage roads, and intersections are designed and constructed at the developer's expense for dedication to the municipality, local transportation district, or state. Some of the road system in a business park may be private, depending on local regulations or the needs of users with special requirements for security and privacy.

Because a site plan has to satisfy the local jurisdiction's requirements, research must be conducted even before the first concept plan is drawn. Most planning departments have published guidelines that address off-site and on-site roadway requirements. They usually include information about connecting new roadways with existing intersections, and improving existing roadways, street widths, turning radii, access for emergency vehicles, culs-

The Wet Seal building in Lake Forest, California, is part of the larger 100-building Foothill Ranch Business Park.

Courtesy DeRevere and Associates

©John Gillan

de-sac, curbs, sidewalks, and landscaping. Every jurisdiction is different, and the potential to obtain approvals and variances improves with knowledge of its specific requirements and the amount of overall flexibility. If the site planner is not local, it is a good idea to enlist the services of a planning or engineering professional who has done substantial work in the jurisdiction.

Major public roadways that run through a business park must tie into the area's existing road pattern, link the park to nearby freeway systems and commercial services, and promote maximum flexibility for the developable parts of the park. Although roads constituting a substantial portion of a park's internal road system can enhance its value and increase the number of visible frontage sites, they can also create disadvantages that require mitigation during the design phase:

- Intersections of internal streets with a major thoroughfare may need to be controlled with traffic lights, stop signs, or overpasses to promote access and safety.
- Inappropriate traffic that passes through the development can cause congestion and detract from the appearance, order, and quiet environment characteristic of a well-planned business park.
- Highways can divide rather than unify a business park. They can also connect distinct sections, such as warehouse/distribution, R&D, and service areas.

Traffic Controls and Regulations. Zoning and subdivision regulations increasingly are used to regulate the design of on-site and off-site supporting roads in tandem with the type and intensity of land use in business parks. Different land uses generate variable amounts of traffic, traffic peaks, and directional movement. The multiple uses of many of today's business parks make it increasingly difficult to estimate traffic generation and potential street requirements.

Local jurisdictions consider many factors when determining requirements for on-site and off-site transporta-

tion improvements. They analyze the traffic that the new development will generate and its relation to street capacities, service levels on those streets, adequate provision for tenants' ingress and egress, parking, and internal circulation. The jurisdiction's subdivision regulations address road patterns, alignments, driveway separation, lot sizes, and configuration in relation to streets, drainage, grading, utilities, and access to external public roads.

Traffic Generation. Traffic generation is often a key issue for communities during the approval process for business parks. Therefore, it is essential to understand the nature and extent of traffic potentially generated by the uses envisioned for the business park.

In the United States, traffic generation rates are indicated in vehicular trips per acre and in vehicular trips per 1,000 square feet of gross floor area (GFA). In traffic generation studies for business parks, the principal measure of density is number of employees per acre, an inexact measure because of the mixing of industrial and office activities, often in the same building. Traffic plans should account for the highest density that can be accommodated in flexible-use buildings on the site. The operations with the lowest employee density are highly automated industries or data center warehouses supporting fewer than five employees per acre; the highest are call centers.

Because traffic planning is a complex endeavor, a traffic engineering consultant should be retained to ensure that the street design meets the park's and the jurisdiction's requirements. Transportation consultants, the local jurisdiction, or both normally predict the amount of traffic that will be generated. These calculations are typically based on methods presented in reference works such as the Institute of Transportation Engineers's *Trip Generation*, which outlines techniques and models that can be generated by different kinds of uses—office, R&D, warehouse, manufacturing, and support activities, for example.[1] The consultant or jurisdiction usually adapts these models to local conditions. They can be used to

figure 4-1

Vehicle Trips per Weekday

	Per 1,000 Square Feet of GFA	Per Developed Acre	Per Employee	Per Employee
	Average	Average	Average	Range
General Light Industry	6.97	51.8	3.02	1.53 –4.48
General Heavy Industry	1.5	6.75	0.82	.75 –1.81
Industrial Park	6.96	63.11	3.34	1.24 –8.80
Manufacturing	3.82	38.88	2.1	.60 –6.66
Warehousing	4.96	57.23	3.89	1.47 –15.71
Miniwarehouse	2.5	38.87	56.28	17 –194.0
Office Park	11.42	195.11	3.5	2.92 –3.85
R&D Center	8.11	79.61	2.77	.96 –10.63
Business Park	12.76	149.79	4.04	3.25 –8.19

Source: Institute of Transportation Engineers, *Trip Generation,* 6th ed. (Washington, D.C.: Author, 1997).

estimate not only the total volume of traffic but also use during the day.

As a general rule, one lane of pavement can handle 800 to 1,200 trips per hour in the development. The actual number of cars accommodated within these limits is a product of street layout, traffic control at intersections, and adequacy of highways serving the site.

Design Requirements. Contemporary suburban business parks typically are not designed around the grids common in earlier business parks. Today, streets are more likely to curve and follow land contours. The main entrance or entrances to the park receive special treatment, because the park's image has become more important to tenants. Special landscape treatments, including heavy plantings, water features, earth shaping, and custom signage, are common. On individual sites, parking areas, truck access roads, and loading/service areas are screened with landscaping, hidden by a planted berm, or located to the rear of the site.

A system of sidewalks or pedestrian pathways that links buildings or parcels to each other and to their parking areas, recreational areas, and transit stops is desirable. When plans include significant amounts of open space, commercial support uses within the project, and off-site commercial, office, or residential uses within convenient walking distance, a unified walkway system is more justifiable from a financial perspective.

When higher employment densities are planned, the value of bicycle paths should be considered using criteria similar to those suggested for sidewalks and walkway systems. Bicycle paths in street rights-of-way are one means of providing bicycle access, but because of the presence of heavy truck traffic, the design of bicycle facilities must be in accordance with recommended design standards, including appropriate width and other design criteria.

Design requirements for streets in business parks are based on the anticipated amount and type of traffic generated when the park is completed to its maximum allow-

able density, including not only internal traffic but also through-traffic expected to use the park's public streets. The character of buildings, land uses, and traffic generation in a business park may change over time. For example, a reduction in warehouse uses plus an increase in R&D or office uses will lead to less truck traffic and more automobile traffic; a demand for larger lots may mean that fewer access roads will be needed in the future. To encourage pedestrian and transit use, however, the interconnectedness of streets is very important to reduce travel distances.

In larger developments, particularly those built in phases, it is not necessary or desirable to design and build the entire road network in the first phases of development. Market demand may change before the development of additional sections, and streets would consequently have to be redesigned. Enough of the network should be constructed to connect essential roadways and give the section under development a finished appearance, however.

Successful modern business parks are part of the overall road network. An integrated road network provides multiple access points to local streets and individual building lots. A complete roadway network also provides options for travel, thus relieving congestion and encouraging alternative modes of travel. Many older parks have but one access point to a major street, resulting in congested traffic, especially at peak hours. Even transportation management programs that include staggered closing hours cannot prevent traffic jams within the development and on public arterials if there are too few entrances. Truck access often can be provided through secondary entrances and along the property lines where heavier industry or bulk warehouses usually are sited, or in screened or bermed areas between back-to-back buildings.

In some cases, existing road networks may no longer be suitable. It may then be necessary to upgrade existing streets to current standards for width, turning lanes, sur-

At Apple's R&D campus in Cupertino, California, a system of pedestrian pathways links buildings to the cafeteria and outdoor eating areas.

Courtesy ACI Real Properties

face quality, shoulders, and landscaping. In other cases, it may be necessary to realign certain streets or remove others to accommodate new uses, or to open new road access to the project.

Roadway reconstruction projects are often required by the local jurisdiction as part of site-related improvements. Local governments also often collect transportation impact fees to offset the cost associated with the provision of the additional road capacity. These fees are most often collected in areas of high growth where existing municipal revenues do not allow adequate expansion of the roadway system. The fees are based on nationally acknowledged trip generation rates for the type of development proposed. Because of the significant amount

of money involved, the developer should be certain the rates accurately reflect the type of development proposed. Local governments frequently allow an independent calculation that may lower the required fees. Developers should keep in mind that a variety of sources go into financing highway improvements, and they should not assume that a major roadway construction project will be implemented in a timely manner simply because they have paid an impact fee.

Layout and Planning Criteria. After existing roads serving the development have been inventoried, a preliminary street layout and cost estimate should be prepared as part of the master plan to evaluate its adequacy and cost. Street function, cross section elements, traffic con-

figure 4-2
Characteristics of Motor Vehicles Typically Used in Business Parks
Typical Dimensions in Feet (Meters)

Type of Motor Vehicle	Wheelbase	Front Overhang	Rear Overhang	Overall Length	Overall Width	Height	Minimum Outside Turning Radius[1]	Minimum Inside Turning Radius[2]
Passenger Car	11 (3.3)	3 (.9)	5 (1.5)	19 (5.8)	7.0 (2.1)	–	24 (7.3)	14.9 (4.5)
Single-Unit Truck	20 (6.1)	4 (1.2)	6 (1.8)	30 (9.1)	8.5 (2.5)	13.5 (4.1)	42 (12.8)	27.8 (8.5)
Intermediate-Size Semitrailer Combination	13 + 27 = 40 (12.2)	4 (1.2)	6 (1.8)	50 (15.2)	8.5 (2.5)	13.5 (4.1)	14 (4.3)	17.7 (5.4)
Large Semitrailer Combination	20 + 30 = 50 (15.2)	3 (.9)	2 (.6)	55 (16.8)	8.5 (2.5)	13.5 (4.1)	45 (13.7)	16.6 (5.0)
Semitrailer/Full Trailer Combination	9.7 + 20 + 9.4[3] + 20.9 = 60 (18.3)	2 (.6)	3 (.9)	65 (19.8)	8.5 (2.5)	13.5 (4.1)	45 (13.7)	21.4 (6.5)

Note: Dimensions may vary slightly, depending on the vehicle manufacturer.

[1]To the path of the left front wheel.

[2]To the path of the right rear wheel.

[3]Distance between rear wheels of front trailer and front wheels of rear trailer.

Sources: Wolfgang S. Homburger, ed., *Transportation and Traffic Engineering Handbook,* 2nd ed. (Englewood Cliffs, New Jersey: Prentice-Hall, 1982);

Patrick Meehan, "Industrial Park Guidelines," *Landscape Architecture,* November/December 1985, p. 90.

trol measures, road condition, and special features should be noted during field inspections. To expedite the process, municipalities, regional commissions, and state or federal governments provide the following information:

- plans, plats, and maps of existing and proposed streets and highways;
- traffic counts and traffic projections;
- intersecting traffic movements;
- trip generation studies;
- origin/destination studies;
- results of interviews and questionnaires conducted by official planning agencies.

The site's natural features and their effect on street planning should be analyzed by using topographical maps, geologic maps, aerial photographs, drainage and floodplain maps, and site photographs. If current information is not available from public sources, special engineering studies commissioned by the developer may be required.

Criteria and standards for streets have not been adopted universally; however, planning and design policies have been established by the American Association of State Highway Officials for urban and rural highways, local roads, and streets and highways other than freeways. State and local highway agencies have controls and procedures for roads within their jurisdiction; developers should check with the local jurisdiction's engineering or public works department for local street standards, which are based on standard reference documents such as the Transportation Research Board's *Highway Capacity Manual*.[2]

The jurisdiction will carefully investigate actual need for and width of collector and arterial roads for each development. Unlike traffic volumes for residential and multifamily developments, which are based on the number of trips generated per unit, a detailed traffic study normally is required for business park developments.

Widths of roadway rights-of-way are established by local jurisdictions and are sometimes subject to negotiation. In practice, a right-of-way width of no more than five feet (1.5 m) beyond the pavement edge may be adequate. Easements adjoining each side of the street can be provided for roadway maintenance, drainage and utilities, sidewalks, bicycle paths, and transit access facilities.

Engineering Standards. Because standards are subject to constant revisions and quickly become obsolete, developers should check with local authorities to see what engineering standards govern the design of the roads to be constructed. When no controls exist, roads should be designed in accordance with accepted practice to avoid both extra costs in upgrading underdesigned facilities and liabilities that result from operations on such roads.

Standard drawings, available through most agencies, include configurations and details for typical street sections, commercial entrances and private driveways, culs-de-sac and turnarounds, intersections, interchanges, medians, bridges and bridge approaches, guardrails, signals, signage, and lighting. Standard construction details are usually available for:

- drainage items;
- curbs and gutters;
- erosion control features;
- sidewalks and paved approaches;
- bicycle lanes;
- transit access facilities;
- pavement joints;
- traffic control equipment;
- lighting; and
- signage equipment.

The type of paving surface for streets in business parks may range from rigid pavement to flexible surfaces. Pavement type and thickness are usually the most rigid standards specified by local jurisdictions. Most street pavements are built to an arbitrary thickness determined entirely by past experience. Several structural design procedures have been developed for the different types of pavements and should be followed where standards are not established. Flexible pavements contain a flexible base with an asphalt surface; rigid pavements are made from Portland cement concrete. Structural design of rigid pavements generally follows the theoretical stress analysis method or soil classification methods, whereas that for flexible pavements generally follows empirical or soil classification methods.

Wheel loading, repetition of loads, subgrade soil conditions, frost action, and subgrade drainage are factors in pavement design. Information about soils should be obtained from existing data. Borings, soil profile maps, construction excavation information, and visual inspection are necessary to determine the nature and suitability of the on-site material for use in roadway fill.

Geometric requirements for road design include dimensional features such as alignment, sight distances, and clearances. Values for geometric standards range in accordance with the design speed, usually given in ten-mile-per-hour increments. Design speeds of 40 to 50 miles (65 to 80 km) per hour are typical for internal streets in office and business parks. Normally, the design speed is ten miles (15 km) per hour higher than the anticipated posted speed. This allowance can work to the developer's disadvantage: a street designed for higher than the posted speed usually encourages traffic to flow at the higher speed and discourages use by pedestrians and bicyclists. A design speed of 30 miles (50 km) per hour provides the optimum environment for a roadway system that accommodates and encourages pedestrians and bicycles together with automobile and truck traffic. Design speeds of greater than 40 miles (65 km) per hour should be avoided except in direct connections to interstate highways or expressway systems. Sight distance requirements include stopping sight, passing sight, and corner sight.

Other Design Considerations. Conformance with public policy, design criteria, and appropriate engineering

Originating in the automobile industry, just-in-time inventory has moved to other manufacturers as well as to wholesalers and retailers. Its purpose is to reduce inventories throughout the industrial pipeline by redesigning the way goods are manufactured and shipped. Inventory arrives in relatively precise quantities and at just the time it is needed rather than being stored in a warehouse. The traditional ship-stock-sell process is reduced to ship-sell. Production processes involve fewer steps, smaller lots, and quicker changeover. JIT shops make frequent but smaller purchases of materials and of finished goods. ■

Source: Marvin F. Christensen and Kenneth B. Ackerman, "Warehouse/ Distribution Facilities: Emerging Industry Trends and Future Market Implications," in *ULI on the Future: Creating Tomorrow's Competitive Advantage* (Washington, D.C.: ULI–the Urban Land Institute, 1996).

©1999 Gary Knight and Associates/Courtesy IDI

Today's warehouses and distribution centers are state-of-the-art facilities with accommodating clear heights, easy truck access and loading, advanced fire protection systems, above-standard column spacing, and other amenities.

These new office/distribution warehouses are being built with more flexible designs that give them a longer life and with structural systems and layouts that allow for large expanses of column-free space and high bays, a significant percentage of office space, and more glass in walls and roofs. With the advent of highly sophisticated computer-based inventory programs, quick response manufacturing, and JIT delivery strategies, for example, many warehouses will be used much more for rapid turnover than for long-term storage. The ultimate example of this phenomenon is cross-docking. On occasion, value-added services such as repackaging may be part of a cross-dock operation. In some situations, goods never leave a trailer until they are transferred to another vehicle for delivery.

At O'Hare Express Center at Chicago's O'Hare International Airport (see the case study in Chapter 7), containers are off-loaded from jumbo jets ferried to the cross-dock facility, broken down and reassembled into pallets, then reloaded on trucks for delivery throughout the central United States. The goods rarely stay in the warehouse more than 48 hours. This same procedure occurs in reverse, as goods coming in from various U.S. locations are reassembled into loads for air shipment throughout the world.

In an evolving market, even some conventional thinking about warehouses as "to-the-trade-only" is changing. For example, where zoning permits, many computer companies and other types of product lines are adding retail components to their industrial/warehouse facilities to become, in effect, factory outlets. After a customer places an order, the merchandise is taken off the warehouse shelves and, if required, custom assembled on the spot.

With all these new warehousing activities, the office functions that used to be conducted elsewhere are now frequently located at the warehouse. Thus, purchasing, accounting, and customer service departments that used to be located away from warehouse operations have become an integral part of new warehouse/distribution centers.

figure 4-3

Selected Building Attributes of Warehouse Distribution Facilities

	Ten Years Ago	Today	Ten Years from Now
Clear Height	24 Feet (7.3 m)	24–30 Feet (7.3–9.1 m)	24–30 Feet (7.3–9.1 m)
Sprinklers	0.33–0.45 GPM[1]	ESFR: 0.60 GPM[1]	ESFR: 0.60 GPM[1]
Dock Doors/Space Ratio	1.0/15,000 Square Feet (1,395 m²)	1.5/10,000 Square Feet (930 m²)	2.0/10,000 Square Feet (930 m²)
Truck Maneuvering	115–120 Feet (35–36.5 m)	120–150 Feet (36.5–45 m)	185 Feet (55 m)[2]
Bay Spacing	40 x 40 feet or 48 x 48 feet (12.2 x 12.2 m or 14.6 x 14.6 m)	48 x 48 feet or 52 x 52 feet (14.6 x 14.6 m or 15.8 x 15.8 m)	52 x 52 feet or 60 x 52 feet (15.8 x 15.8 m or 18.3 x 15.8 m)

1. GPM = gallons per minute; ESFR = early suppression, fast response.

2. Includes space for trailer parking.

Source: Fremont Development, Hill Pinckert Architects, and RREEF Research, *ULI on the Future: Creating Tomorrow's Competitive Advantage* (Washington, D.C.: ULI–the Urban Land Institute, 1996).

Many parts of the country saw the return of industrial development in the late 1990s. Rents for functional, modern, and well-located industrial space rose, and tenant concession packages were scaled back or eliminated. But before smart developers leaped on the construction bandwagon, they considered that many industrial building requirements and features had changed over the previous decade, among them location, site plans, building design, height clearances, building systems and technology, and workplace quality of life.

But that is not all. "Industrial users are no longer looking only at operating expenses and bottom-line rent, as most were ten to 15 years ago," explains Craig Peters, first vice president of CB Commercial in southern California. "Users are also looking to the future. They see their buildings as investments and keep one eye on what their exit strategy will be ten years from now."

Some ten- and 15-year-old industrial buildings already are functionally obsolete. Clearly, developers cannot keep building the same old products. Corporations constructing facilities for their own use should proceed with caution. Following are some key considerations before undertaking industrial development.

Location

Developers should not automatically rush back to the prime locations of the 1980s; today's markets—and tomorrow's—could well be somewhere else. To enhance the value of new facilities and help to recruit and retain employees who, understandably, do not want to work in rundown or dangerous areas, developers should find sites whose real estate value is steady or is appreciating, not stagnant or in decline.

The location should not only be convenient to highways and transit but also provide amenities for employees, such as nearby retail stores, dining, recreational facilities, daycare, and open space. A suburban or exurban location close to housing will save employees money and time spent commuting while saving companies money on commuting and parking expenses in compensation packages.

In weighing the pros and cons of different properties, "developers and corporations should pay close attention to a site's shape and topography," advises John Kriken, a partner at Skidmore, Owings & Merrill in San Francisco. "Do planned buildings and ancillary facilities fit on the property in an efficient, cost-effective layout? Does the site have one or two unique features like a stand of trees, body of water, or view that create workplace amenities and promote corporate identity? Is the site visible and accessible?

Site Plan

Elements of industrial site planning include roadways, entrances, building placement, parking, and open space. "Roadways are perhaps the single most important component in creating long-term property value," notes Kriken. "They don't merely provide circulation; they also create an overall sense of place, promote building identity through placement and highly visible frontage, and—when properly planned—make the property flexible enough to support expansion, contraction, or subdivision in the future."

Site entrances for visitors, employees, parking, and service vehicles should be clearly visible and distinctive. Usable, attractive open space should be left along the perimeter of the site and as contiguous areas within the

Parking areas tucked against the back and side of buildings and broken into several lots separated by landscaping ensure that lots do not physically or visually dominate a property. Open space left along the perimeter of a site can enhance a facility's value, as found at Weston in Raleigh/Durham, North Carolina.

Clearly visible and distinctive site entrances, such as those at the Miami International Corporate Center, are key elements of business park site planning.

site. Open space enhances corporate identity and facility value and provides recreation areas for employees, which, in turn, promotes productivity and loyalty among employees.

"Above all," says Kriken, "don't let parking physically or visually dominate the property as it does at shopping malls. Tuck parking in tight against the back and side of the building and break it into several lots, separated by landscaped buffers around the building. That way visitors and employees are greeted by a firm's corporate identity—its buildings—and that creates value."

Built-in flexibility can also create value. The site plan should easily accommodate new buildings, changes in traffic flow, and division into smaller parcels for new users. A warehouse, for example, does not need much parking. But down the road this same building could accommodate a manufacturing facility, which would require much more parking for workers. Allocating two parking places per 1,000 square feet of building space would provide for today's users—and tomorrow's. Additional parking can mean more potential users—and marketability—for a site.

Another important element of the site plan is vehicle maneuverability. "Much of the plan should be devoted to assuring the safe maneuverability of different size trucks," points out architect Bryon Pinckert of Hill Pinckert Architects in Newport Beach, California. "These days, most industrial facilities get their goods in and out by highway, not rail. The real art of industrial site planning is providing the most convenient truck maneuvering space on the least amount of land so the site isn't turned into one huge staging area.

"A good site plan also avoids congestion by creating efficient traffic flow around the building," adds Pinckert. "This includes minimizing interaction between trucks

and passenger vehicles by separating their roadways and parking areas."

Building Size, Shape, and Height

Generally, a rectangular building is the most flexible shape. Buildings that are L-shaped or have angles often impede traffic flow, truck maneuverability, and future adaptive uses. Because industrial racks and assembly lines usually are straight, L-shaped buildings can be inefficient. A clear separation of uses creates building value. A staging area should be set aside for shipping and receiving and a separate area for offices; the manufacturing or warehouse facility should then be planned within the framework.

The size of the building should be selected carefully. Warehouses have gotten much larger since the 1980s, when a building was considered large at 200,000 square feet (18,600 m²). Today, a building is considered large if it measures more than 1 million square feet (93,000 m²).

The trend in warehouse facilities today is consolidation. Nestlé, for example, is consolidating 37 warehouses around the United States into eight giant warehouses. "Fast-growing cities such as Phoenix, Dallas, Fort Worth, and Atlanta have fifth-generation cores emerging about 50 to 60 miles (80 to 95 km) outside their downtowns; those cores are generally being led by industrial development because the land is so cheap, it has easy freeway access, and it's less congested for now," says Christopher B. Leinberger, managing director of Robert Charles Lesser & Co., an international real estate consulting firm in Los Angeles. "That's where the new mega-warehouses, which run 1 to 2 million square feet (93,000 to 186,000 m²) each, are located. That's 25 acres (10 ha) under one roof."

Mezzanine office space should not automatically be included in the facility. Many users do not need a lot of mezzanine space, and some do not want it; it costs more, eats up valuable space, and reduces flexibility. When it comes to structural bay spacing, the columns should be built large enough to reduce their number and to avoid interference with future reconfiguration. Floorslabs should be built to accommodate the different weights of a wide variety of uses. The building's clearance heights should be carefully selected. Twenty years ago, the standard was an 18.6-foot (6-m) clearance from the floorslab to the lowest part of the roof structure. Today, the standard is a 28- to 30-foot (8.5- to 9.1-m) clearance, and it is still rising; 45-foot (13.7-m) clear buildings are not unheard of.

A number of reasons exist for this upward push in building height. First, today's higher land costs, particularly in desirable markets, are forcing developers and corporations to get maximum value out of each square foot, which can mean building higher. Second, with today's high-lift forklifts, users can stack higher than before. It is not uncommon to see the stacking, or racking, of five pallets rather than two. Third, most industrial space is sold or leased by square footage, not by volume. If a building can show a 10 to 20 percent increase in storage capacity for the same square footage costs, it is infinitely more desirable for tenants and buyers. Finally, construction costs are only slightly more for the added weight. Only above 30 feet (9.1 m) of clearance are new, expensive structural issues encountered. Though a lofty clear height is not important to most manufacturers, it does provide the flexibility to lease or sell the facility to different users in the future.

Power requirements have grown substantially—and are still growing—for all industrial uses. Warehousing and manufacturing are becoming more automated; as a result, more machinery and high-tech equipment are needed, entailing a greater need for electrical power. Five years

ago, few warehouse buildings had electronic information systems to track inventory. Today, the majority of new facilities have some sort of electronic systems management. In manufacturing, the change is even more dramatic. Whereas ten people previously assembled a product, now two people and a machine are doing the job.

To support today's power needs and ensure the flexibility to adapt to tomorrow's requirements, a building should be designed to accommodate both warehouse and manufacturing functions, which typically means 1,200 amps of 480/277-volt, three-phase, four-wire power. An underground conduit should be installed so that capacity can be increased to 2,000 to 2,400 amps in the future by changing the transformer, pulling in cable, and boosting power without major construction costs. Additional power should not be installed at the beginning of construction, however, for it is expensive. Only the space for future expansion should be provided so that new power can be added when needed.

Improvements in HVAC systems and their greater use are two reasons that electrical power needs have increased at industrial facilities. Today's HVAC systems must work harder than ever before. To maintain a healthy work environment, these systems must handle more heat and ventilate more airborne dust, oil, and off-gases generated by the greater use of machinery and high-tech equipment.

Facility needs have changed in other ways, too. Ten years ago, for example, air-conditioned manufacturing operations were rare. Today, more and more manufacturers want air conditioning or evaporative cooling, in part because today's systems are more efficient and affordable than a decade ago. Though most warehouse and distribution facilities still do not need air conditioning unless they are handling a product, such as food, that requires refrigeration, new buildings that serve warehouses may need to be air conditioned. Five or ten years in the future, when a warehouse tenant leaves, air conditioning may be needed to attract new tenants.

In recent years, lighting systems at many industrial facilities have changed dramatically. Ten years ago, most companies used warehouse-style fluorescent light. Today, metal halide lighting is increasingly popular. Though the fixtures are more expensive than fluorescent lights, they last longer, run more efficiently, and provide better illumination. Skylights—which were introduced in the early to mid-1980s—are also appearing in more industrial facilities, saving on electric costs and enhancing the work environment. According to several studies, workers are more productive in natural than in all-artificial lighting.

The biggest single change in life-safety systems is the introduction of early suppression, fast response (ESFR)

Courtesy Colliers, Bennett & Kahnweiler

A high ceiling in a warehouse at Goose Island Industrial Campus in Chicago, Illinois.

equipment. While traditional fire sprinkler systems react to a fire that is already burning and are designed to contain the blaze until the fire department arrives and puts it out, ESFR can put the fire out, fast. In conventional systems, sprinkler heads can be exposed to 280°F (138°C) temperatures for two minutes before going off. ESFR heads react when they are exposed to 150°F (66°C) for only 30 seconds. Then they pour up to six times more water on the fire than previous systems. ESFR systems have one drawback: adding the system to an existing building is quite expensive because the building structure and roof must be precisely configured to accommodate the spacing of sprinkler heads and to prevent interference with the water supply. An ESFR retrofit typically costs $4 per square foot ($43/m²), whereas designing ESFR into a building from the start costs only $.50 to $1.50 per square foot ($5.40 to $16.20/m²). If ESFR is not installed in the building at construction, the building should be designed to accommodate ESFR easily in the future.

Employees' productivity is crucial to the success of any business. To maintain and raise productivity, companies need to provide employees a high quality of life in the workplace. Properties should be landscaped with outdoor eating and recreational areas, have interior environments lit partially by natural light from skylights and operable windows, have HVAC systems that provide superior air quality, and be near amenities such as shops, restaurants, and child care facilities.

With more women in the workplace and more employees working late, security has become increasingly important. "If your facility is located in a dangerous area," says Scott Sheridan, senior vice president at the Hewson Company, a real estate development management firm in Sylmar,

Electronic security systems are commonly found in industrial buildings, such as this Hewlett-Packard facility in Bergamo, Italy.

California, "high-tech gadgets won't help. This is a crucial issue for every tenant. It's one thing to cope with graffiti, pilfered hubcaps, even stolen cars. But it's another matter if workers are held up or harmed," says Sheridan. "The trauma to the entire workforce is vast, and morale drops. The site owner and employer also face considerable liability."

In addition, companies can reduce internal theft through good design. For example, loading dock doors should be wide enough to accommodate only one truck, thus preventing hand-offs to the side, often a problem with small, high-value electronic products.

Building for success means cost-effective architectural design with an emphasis on efficient, flexible industrial buildings that can easily adapt to future technology and workplace requirements, take on new uses and configurations, and improve the quality of life in the workplace. ∎

Source: Adapted from James Brown, "Industrial Edge," *Urban Land,* June 1999, pp. 70–73.

Water features can help create recreation areas for employees and promote corporate identity.

Dock doors run the length of this industrial building at Rock Run Business Park in Joliet, Illinois.

Building Features. The traditional bulk warehouse has limited office space, a lunchroom, toilets for a small staff, and possibly a storage facility for flammable materials. Power required is primarily for warehouse lighting, space heating, charging fork lifts, and possibly some special purposes. In contrast, the new office distribution warehouse might have 25 percent of the building in offices, full HVAC in both the offices and throughout the warehouse, and a greater variety of materials-handling equipment.

Typical warehouse facilities in use today might measure 500 feet long by 300 feet wide (150 m by 90 m), but the warehouse of the future is more likely to be 1,000 feet long by 150 feet wide (305 m by 45 m). This longer and narrower structure will have dock doors throughout the length of the property. As many as one dock door for every 2,000 square feet (185 m²) of space may be needed, and because cross-dock operations will involve a high volume of truck traffic, more room will be required for maneuvering trucks.

A flexible design should have bay spacing as wide as possible to reduce the number of columns to a minimum to avoid interference with the installation of storage systems and to accommodate future reconfiguration of the building. Increasingly, large users are looking for bay spacing in excess of 50 feet by 50 feet (15 m by 15 m) to accommodate more efficient racking and storage systems. Bays as large as 60 feet by 60 feet (18 m by 18 m) are often required for staging areas in front of loading doors.

With ever-changing occupancy and thus unpredictable floor loading, a floorslab that will support 250 pounds per square foot (1,222 kg/m²) will allow the building to accommodate different weight loads and thus the widest variety of users over time. Floors are being leveled through the use of lasers to accommodate high-stacking units that will not behave satisfactorily on less than very level floors. A laser screed allows for larger areas of the floor to be finished simultaneously, thus reducing the number of construction joints. Using a laser screed to level floors can reduce variances in flatness from 0.75 inch to 0.25 inch (1.9 cm to 0.6 cm) over a length of 50 feet (15 m).

The standard for clear height is rising from 24 to 30 feet to 45 feet (7.3 to 9.1 m to 13.7 m)—even higher in some cases. Designing clear heights above 30 feet (9.1 m) presents additional and more expensive structural issues that need to be considered. While a lofty clear height sets a facility apart from its competition, many users may not find it valuable. If costs can otherwise be justified, however, the extra clear height does provide the flexibility to lease or sell the facility to different users a few years in the future.

Truck and Rail Access. Well-designed truck access, docks, and doors are critical to the operation of warehouse/distribution facilities. Minimizing on-site interaction between trucks and passenger vehicles by separating their roadways and parking areas is a desirable feature, usually achieved by separate entrances for cars and trucks and the location of employee/visitor parking on the front facade of the building and the truck dock on the opposite wall. If cross-docking is planned, then the employee/visitor parking would be on one of the sides with sets of truck doors opposite each other.

The distance of the truck apron from the truck dock affects the maneuverability of trucks in and out of the facility. The current maximum length for a tractor and semitrailer can be somewhat longer than 70 feet (21.3 m). Therefore, the current recommended standard for a truck apron is 120 feet (36.5 m) from the truck dock; some developers provide as much as 150 feet (45.7 m). If the building floor is at grade, then the apron must slope down so that a standard truck bed will be more or less at floor height. An alternative—used when rail access is also required—is to build the warehouse on compacted fill so that the rail car bed is level with the rail dock and the truck dock can thus be more or less at grade. Truck docks need to be four feet (1.2 m) above grade or served by a ramp with a maximum 5 percent slope. The installation of hydraulic levelers at truck docks—instead of a steel plate dragged by a forklift operator to bridge the gap between truck and dock—is becoming more common.

Opinions vary about the number of loading docks for a building of any given size, but the trend is toward more rather than fewer. The number of truck docks required has increased, as many business park properties have gone to cross-docking or putting truck doors on multiple sides of a building. When several distribution centers are consolidated into one large center, for example, the same amount of product is shipped though the new facility but at a faster pace, and the same number of trucks are involved but they use less building area. Additional dock doors are the only way to accommodate those demands. Clearly, the number of docks desired varies, based on the intended operation of the building. Because doors and docks are at the heart of inventory flow, the ratio of doors to building square footage is on the rise. And because it is difficult to predict how many additional dock doors an operator may require or where the doors will be located, developers often design one wall of a facility with depressed footers, thereby allowing for additional doors to be cut into the wall if needed. Having more doors or the ability to add more easily places a building in a more competitive position.

Truck doors are becoming larger to accommodate oversized freight, moving from nine feet by ten feet (2.7 by 3 m) or eight feet by eight feet (2.4 by 2.4 m) to ten feet by ten feet (3 by 3 m). These wider doors can be a security problem, however, as they can allow pilferage of high-value goods by side handling.

Parking. A bulk warehouse user does not need much employee parking, perhaps only one or two spaces per 1,000 square feet. When a traditional bulk warehouse is converted to a high-velocity distribution facility, however, required parking might increase to three to four spaces per 1,000 square feet. In this case, the volume of trucks and the demand for trailer storage space will also rise. If,

however, the use changes to a manufacturing/assembly facility, the demand for additional employee parking will likely be offset by a reduction of in-and-out truck traffic. In this event, some of the asphalt once used for trucks can be restriped for automobile parking.

Landscaping. Industrial warehouses are often thought of as big, plain—if not downright ugly—buildings surrounded by a sea of asphalt. While a certain segment of the market may still not care what the facilities look like, a building that is well landscaped with more than just the minimum of glass stands a better chance in the marketplace. Screening trailer parking and loading dock areas from adjacent streets and parcels goes a long way toward making warehouse uses compatible neighbors. As the building's function evolves from bulk warehouse to high-velocity distribution center, the quality of landscaping should rise to appeal to the greater number of employees and visitors. Landscape design elements like fountains and sculptures and well-designed signage can be used judiciously and very effectively to create an upscale image without elaborate plantings. Employee satisfaction can also be improved if outdoor eating and exercise areas are provided for individual buildings or on a shared basis.

Building Systems and Technology. As late as the mid-1990s, few warehouse buildings had sophisticated electronic information systems to track inventory. Today, the majority of new facilities offer some sort of electronic systems management. Innovations in materials-handling equipment—bigger forklifts, narrow-aisle racking equipment, and sophisticated computer-operated conveyor belt systems—have prompted the evolution of modern warehouse buildings and thus business park infrastructure and design.

All-glass walls in the office areas are being used more frequently as a simple design improvement over irregular wall surfaces. More glass is also being used in many warehouse buildings that would previously have been windowless.

Innovations in materials-handling equipment have prompted the evolution of modern warehouse buildings and thus business park infrastructure design. Innovations include sophisticated computer-operated conveyer belt systems and halide lighting, as seen at PFSweb in Memphis, Tennessee.

©Cotton Alston/Courtesy IDI

Defining exactly what a smart building is is difficult, as landlords offer a variety of definitions, ranging from any facility that leases quickly and makes a profit to buildings that are completely automated.

Since the 1980s, the term "smart buildings" has generally referred to the automation and integration of the hidden elements of construction and design, including HVAC, electrical, sprinkler, security, lighting, and telecommunications systems.

Today's smart buildings are evolving into something more than the facilities of the 1980s: modern buildings must provide sophisticated telecommunications systems for voice, data, and video transmission. In short, prospective tenants are demanding facilities that offer a combination of telecommunications and Internet services, because their businesses depend more on technology than ever before, particularly when it comes to Internet access.

Increasing in popularity are "shared tenant services," a central bank of telephone systems and services that can be used and shared by tenants much like a building's HVAC system. Although the service is not new, advanced technology has made it more appealing to landlords.

"It really started coming out in the 1980s with the smart buildings. Everybody thought it would be the next generation, but it didn't quite work out that way," says Nick Clark, a principal of Memphis-based office developer Clark & Clark. "Now, people like office developers are looking to outsource services that aren't part of their core services."

Those services—particularly Internet access—are becoming a necessity rather than an amenity. Businesses are finding it necessary to send and receive E-mail, communicate with clients and branch offices via the Internet, download valuable information, and create private networks with vendors and customers. Owners, asset managers, and property managers recognize that access to the Internet, like electricity, is rapidly becoming an essential service.

Granting access to companies that outsource telecommunications to buildings also gives landlords another source of revenue, because the contract often includes an agreement to share a percentage of the profits with the building owner. In return, the telecommunications firm has access to the buildings' tenants and receives marketing help from the landlord.

"Most important, it gives the landlord flexibility," Clark says. "There are vast improvements in technology occurring rapidly. The question is, How are you going to prepare for tomorrow? And shared services give tenants a choice and reduce the cost of communications. The bottom line is that it is an asset to the tenants." ■

Source: James Overstreet, www.bizjournals.com

Manufacturing/Assembly Facilities

While it is only a short leap from a warehouse/distribution facility to a manufacturing/assembly facility, there are differences. A typical manufacturing/assembly facility in a business park is smaller than most warehouse/distribution facilities, although it should have the capability for expansion. Many are as small as 25,000 to 30,000 square feet (2,325 to 2,790 m²), and few are more than 200,000 square feet (18,600 m²).

Employees are likely to be more skilled and therefore higher on the wage scale, with greater expectations for a high-quality workplace environment. The number of employees per building area is higher than for a typical warehouse/distribution operation, and the percentage of women is likely to be greater.

The demand for rail/truck access depends on the nature of the manufacturing/assembly activity. More than likely, the required truck dock area is smaller and fewer access doors are necessary; for assembly-to-customer products, incoming trucks might be semitrailers, while outgoing deliveries are by van.

Typical building characteristics are different as well. Clear heights rarely need to exceed 32 feet (9.8 m); however, clear spans are still preferred for maximum flexibility on the manufacturing floor.

The demand for power is higher, with loads from 2,000 to 6,000 amps of 270/480-volt power, not counting the power supply that might be needed for machinery. Building operations demand more power. Ten years ago, air-conditioned manufacturing operations were rare. Today, more and more manufacturers, particularly those of high-tech/high-value products, want or need air conditioning. Lighting levels need to be much higher in a manufacturing/assembly facility. While warehouse-style low-lumen fluorescent lighting might be acceptable for a distribution facility, metal halide lighting with higher lumens is the current preferred lighting for new facilities. These fixtures cost

An early suppression, fast response fire sprinkler system was the system of choice for Sony's build-to-suit facility in Turnberry Lakes International Business Park in Chicago, Illinois.

©1998 Gary Knight and Associates/Courtesy IDI

more but last longer, run more efficiently, and provide better illumination.

Higher fire protection/life safety standards may be necessary. A well-conceived new manufacturing/assembly building should be at least ESFR-ready. While ordinary wet-pipe systems may suffice for many manufacturing/assembly operations, ESFR is rapidly becoming the new standard.

More glass is required in manufacturing/assembly facilities, both for operations and for a livable workplace. Skylights not only save on electrical costs but also enhance the work environment. Facilities like employee lounges and locker rooms, and cafeterias and thus a commercial kitchen may be required. The site design might include outdoor eating and recreational areas for employees. The number of required toilet facilities is higher, with separate facilities for men and women.

Security requirements may be significantly higher, particularly if the product being assembled or manufactured

has a high street value. Some systems are quite sophisticated, including key-card access. In some instances, the site perimeter as well as the building must be secure. If operations go beyond a single daylight shift, better on-site night lighting and better areawide night security and lighting in the business park are required.

With typically higher numbers of employees, on-site parking requirements may increase dramatically, so the site should have the flexibility to provide four or more spaces per 1,000 square feet, most likely at grade. In some situations—for example, where a manufacturing/assembly facility would benefit from proximity to an airport and thus have to be accommodated on more expensive land—it may be possible to accommodate parking in a low-cost, one-level, above-grade parking structure.

A special feature that may make a site more attractive to a manufacture/assembly operator is the availability of a foreign trade zone (FTZ). The distribution networks required to handle the increasing volumes of world trade

Significant Differences between a Bulk Warehouse and a High-Velocity Distribution Facility

- Greater visibility of location within the overall development and from the surrounding area may be desired.
- With many more employees on site, parking ratios must rise from the minimum of one or two spaces per 1,000 square feet to three and perhaps more, depending on the size of the office component and level of automation in the warehouse.
- The volume of automobile use changes, with separation of truck and employee/visitor parking becoming more important.
- The movement of goods shifts from truck-to-truck to truck-to-van.
- The number of delivery service vehicles (UPS, FedEx, etc.) increases.
- As the need for rail access declines, truck volume and docking and door access could increase.

- Use shifts from eight hours per day to 12 to 24 hours per day.
- Security needs increase, for both employees and goods.
- Building appearance becomes more important—more glass in exterior walls, skylights, elevators in the office wing, better exterior wall treatments.
- The site's appearance also becomes more important—better landscaping and signage, outdoor recreation, eating, exercise, and play facilities.
- Nearby or on-site business and employee services become important—restaurants and fast food, banking, hotel/motel, post office, cleaners, barber, beauty shop, daycare, for example. ∎

are more sophisticated than those used for domestic commerce. Products moving across national borders require customs documentation, incur duties and port fees, and rely on multiple transit modes. Operators must be prepared to handle language barriers, multiple currencies, and other issues that distance may complicate. For example, a 2,000-acre (810-ha) foreign trade zone has been created at Alliance, a trade complex in Fort Worth, Texas, to stimulate economic development (see the case study in Chapter 7). A freeport tax abatement program has been adopted to give Alliance's manufacturers and distributors increased inventory and distribution flexibility for goods in transit.

Flex Space

Because of its ability to meet the needs of a variety of users, flex space is the most common speculative industrial building type. It can be used for offices, showrooms, distribution, light industry, and even heavy industry.

Although no clear-cut definition of flex space exists (some would define it as anything between offices and warehouses), it has a number of distinguishing characteristics. Flex buildings are typically one- or two-story buildings ranging from 20,000 to 100,000 square feet (1,860 to 9,295 m²). Clear heights have increased to 14 feet (4.3 m) or more to accommodate warehouse and industrial activities, as well as the current generation of building service systems, telecommunications cables, and electrical conduits.

Current external designs call for clean, rectangular shapes with an abundance of glass on the front facade. Building depths vary, so developers need to research the market to determine the best strategy. In some places, buildings have grown deeper, to as much as 125 feet (38 m), while in others they have grown narrower for more daylight. In all cases, generous column spacing is desirable for tenants who want maximum flexibility to accommodate open or subdivided space.

The pattern for internal uses has been about 25 percent office space and 75 percent warehouse space, but this proportion is changing in favor of more office space in many areas. In some markets, "flex tech" buildings are now entirely office in character with provisions for four or more different occupiers per building.

Flex buildings with limited warehouse or distribution uses may have truck doors at the rear drive-in level rather than elevated truck docks, because goods tend to be received by two-axle trucks and vans rather than by tractor semitrailers. Rear dock doors can be designed with glass for conversion to loading doors. Buildings used exclusively as office space include minimal or no provisions for loading.

For most flex tenants, telecommunications capacity is a critical factor in their location decision. The old real estate axiom, location, location, location, has become location, *bandwidth,* location. Available bandwidth is an important consideration for high-tech firms as well as for a host of other potential flex space occupants.

What Is a Foreign Trade Zone?

A foreign trade zone is a site in the United States in or near a U.S. Customs port of entry where foreign and domestic merchandise is generally considered to be in international commerce. Foreign or domestic merchandise may enter this enclave without a formal Customs entry or the payment of customs duties or government excise taxes. Merchandise entering a zone may be stored, tested, sampled, relabeled, repackaged, displayed, repaired, manipulated, mixed, cleaned, assembled, manufactured, salvaged, destroyed, or processed.

If the final product is exported from the United States, no U.S. customs duty or excise tax is levied. If, however, the final product is imported into the United States, customs duty and excise taxes are due only at the time of transfer from the FTZ and formal entry into the United States. The duty paid is the lower of that applicable to the product itself or its component parts. Thus, zones provide opportunities to realize customs duty savings by zone users. In addition, zone procedures provide one of the most flexible methods of handling domestic and imported merchandise.

Two types of foreign trade zones exist: general purpose zones (GPZs) and subzones. A GPZ is established for multiple activities by multiple users. It must be operated as a public utility and must be located within 60 statute miles (95 km) or 90 minutes driving time from the outer limits of a U.S. Customs port of entry. FTZ projects may consist of one or multiple sites, for example, a single building, a business park, a deep water port, or an international airport. While activities including storage, inspection, and distribution are permitted at all FTZs, other activities such as processing or manufacturing require special permission from the Foreign Trade Zones Board.

When a firm wants FTZ status for its own plant or facility or when an existing GPZ cannot accommodate the firm's proposed activity, the designation of subzone may be granted. No legal difference exists in the types of activity that may be undertaken in GPZs or subzones. Typically, subzones are designated for an individual company's manufacturing operations. Subzones can be located anywhere within a state so long as a sponsoring grantee of a GPZ exists in the state and the U.S. Customs Service can fulfill its proper oversight functions at the proposed location of the subzone. ∎

Source: National Association of Foreign-Trade Zones, www.naftz.org.

Current R&D designs call for clean, rectangular shapes with lots of glass on the front facade, as shown at Centerpark Plaza II in San Diego, California.

No rigid parking standards exist for flex buildings, but providing a generous amount has become a competitive strategy as companies using flex space have increased employee densities. Flex tenants frequently need four to five spaces per 1,000 square feet, compared with one or two for a bulk warehouse. If a potential tenant is a call or information service center, a parking ratio approaching seven or eight spaces per 1,000 square feet might be required. One strategy applicable when land is relatively expensive is to provide surface parking at three or three and one-half spaces per 1,000 square feet of office space, anticipating the addition of an inexpensive parking deck to boost the ratio to five spaces per 1,000 square feet if more spaces are needed. Another strategy is to allot three parking spaces per 1,000 square feet and a 120-foot-wide (36.6-m) loading area where two double rows of cars can be parked if the building is leased to an office tenant that requires four and one-half spaces per 1,000 square feet.

Flex space must able to respond to the requirements of changing markets and rapidly growing businesses. Thus, flexibility in tenant spaces and the flexibility for companies to expand or contract in their space as their business evolves are important. Because flex space refers not just to construction specifications but also to the way a tenant's changing day-to-day needs are supported, developers of this product type need to be creative in offering tenant improvements, opportunities for expansion or contraction, and even termination clauses.

A strategy of the Irvine Company at the Irvine Spectrum is to build incubator flex space with offices in the front and a truck door at the back in multitenant buildings, divisible to 500 square feet (45 m²). A total of about 400,000 square feet (37,200 m²) of this type of space is scattered throughout the development, and occupancy has generally been around 90 percent. Target tenants include startup businesses that previously have been operating out of a garage but may be candidates for a much larger space in a short time or, equally likely, disappear.

R&D Facilities

The R&D sector encompasses a wide variety of types of occupiers. According to the National Council of Real Estate Investment Fiduciaries, an R&D building is a one- or two-story building with ten- to 15-foot (3- to 4.5-m) ceilings, up to 50 percent office/dry lab space, and the remainder wet lab, workshop, storage, and other support space. Wet lab space offers sometimes very expensive special plumbing and mechanical services like gas, vacuum, deionized water, and fume hoods. Dry lab space does not require these extra features, which cannot necessarily be transferred to another tenant's area. Thus, a typical R&D user is probably looking for space to accommodate some combination of office space with generic flexible space for some other use such as laboratory, testing facility, manufacturing, storage, assembly, distribution, and, perhaps most important, future expansion.

R&D buildings designed for labs, engineering, manufacturing, assembly, storage, and offices are configured differently from multitenant flex buildings. An R&D building is typically designed for one or two users and does not have the capability of being subdivided like flex space. Building sizes cover a broader range than flex space, usually 30,000 to 100,000 square feet (2,800 to 9,300 m²). They typically have deeper floorplates, square rather than rectangular, and they often require special interior finishes peculiar to their activity.

While R&D users may want tight security, they also prefer good visibility from adjacent streets and highways. They often look for their own building or a multitenant building that can be expanded. Even with such unpredictable requirements, some features set this group apart.

Corporate identity and image are important, even for a startup company. A well-designed building with strong entrance treatment, good visitor access and parking, and an attractive lobby are preferred over a more generic design that might be acceptable for a speculative flex building. Attractive landscaping can be a cost-effective substitute for more expensive exterior building finishes

At TechPark in Rock Hill, South Carolina, the developer implemented a civic arts project that includes four 13-foot (4-m) bronze female statues entitled "Civitas."

©Nancy Bundt

or features. Open space elements like attractive outdoor eating and recreational areas for employees are a plus. One developer uses outdoor sculpture to establish a special identity.

Flexibility is still a key requirement for R&D tenants, because many are in a constant state of evolution. Rectangular or square buildings are the most adaptable; therefore, distinctive design must be achieved with entrance features, fenestration, and exterior finish materials.

Users may require a showroom or demonstration studio, and some may want to isolate their public areas from the labs. Special facilities like clean rooms and isolated rooms are often required. Who pays for such improvements—the developer or the tenant—is negotiable, because it is highly unlikely that the next tenant will find the specifications for special spaces to its liking. In any case, R&D tenants want more than just a box. They are on the lookout for amenities in their buildings, including architectural highlights and striking features.

R&D tenants also prefer locations that not only offer convenience to highways and transit but also provide important amenities for workers like on-site or nearby retail stores, recreation facilities, daycare, and open space. A campus setting is strongly preferred. R&D employees are likely to work irregular hours, often through the night; thus, a location near residential areas is also an advantage.

With 24-hour operations, exterior lighting on the site as well as in the business park is important. R&D firms are typically involved with highly proprietary work and thus want tight security for the workplace that goes well beyond key-card access, which may require special security features for buildings and the entire business park.

Power demand varies and planning for the ability to add supply at least cost is a competitive feature. The ability to control power fluctuations or outages may also be vital to some users, and thus the availability of standby power or cogeneration facilities may be desirable.

Parking at four spaces per 1,000 square feet may not always be adequate; some users may need as much as five or six spaces per 1,000 square feet. When the tenant requires parking greater than four spaces per 1,000 square feet, it may be appropriate to consider some form of structured parking if it can be built less expensively than land costs for this much surface parking. Another factor to consider is that parking at this ratio means that much of the parking will be farther away from the building than 350 feet (105 m), the maximum desirable distance that most people are willing to walk.

Truck service might be required for dock-height or floor-height loading, but usually it is needed only at grade. Truck traffic to R&D buildings is more likely to be small trucks and vans rather than tractor trailers; therefore, separating automobile and truck traffic is probably not necessary.

Multiuse Buildings

Multitenant buildings house small-scale offices, showrooms, and production and service businesses in what could be described as an industrial shopping center. The businesses could include building trade contractors, cabinet makers, equipment repair and maintenance services, specialty food and beverage suppliers, and a host of others. If allowed by zoning, some of these users sell retail as well as wholesale products. In many cases, tenants are interrelated; for example, a kitchen and bathroom remodeler might be located near a plumbing firm or an electrical firm.

A typical building contains one story, is 60 to 100 feet deep (18.3 to 30 m), and has 14 to 18 feet (4.3 to 5.5 m) of clear height. Space typically is divided into units 24 to 30 feet (7.3 to 9.1 m) wide, perhaps as many as ten modules along the building length. The front has glass and an entrance door, the rear a service door and an at-grade truck door. Such buildings might also be double-ended, with a drive-in door in the front for customer pickups and a four-foot (1.2-m) truck door in the rear for deliveries. They can also be built back to back, in which case the truck door must be in the front and the space left for glass and the entrance door is smaller, although the design can be modified according to tenants' needs.

A typical tenant has a small office/showroom in the front, with warehouse, assembly, manufacturing, and service operations in the rest of the building. Each unit is separately metered, with 200 amps per bay, HVAC in the office/showroom space, toilets for employees, and two to three parking spaces per 1,000 square feet. With some adjustments, space users as small as 500 square feet (46.5 m²) could be accommodated.

Internet use has propelled workers' productivity to new heights, powered by the ability to download or transmit data via the Internet. Broadband is a high-bandwidth technology that delivers high-speed Internet access or the ability to send data over cable lines, telephone lines, or dedicated connections. It is quickly becoming a necessity for businesses.

Internet speeds are measured in units called bits, with each bit representing a 1 or a 0. These speeds can range tremendously—from 56 kilobits per second (kbits/sec) for a standard modem to 1.5 megabits per second (Mbits/sec) for a T1 line. Previously, Internet access was obtained through a modem connection, which transferred data from telephone lines to computers using a dial-up connection. Because of FCC (Federal Communications Commission) restrictions on phone lines, the fastest modems can receive data at 56 kbits/sec but can send data at only 48 kbits/sec.

ComputerWorld lists three different options for broadband access, each suited to specific needs and all at rates up to 1.5 Mbits/sec or faster. Integrated cable modems provide Internet access through a specific frequency on television cable lines. This service is geared toward residential and small business use. The disadvantage of cable modem use is the possibility of slow service: if many people are trying to download information from the Internet using cable modems, the system slows down.

According to *PC Magazine,* digital subscriber service (DSL) uses a dedicated telephone line to deliver bandwidth. DSL is always "on" and is not affected by traffic caused by other users on the line at the same time. Currently, DSL is the preferred broadband for residences and small businesses.

T-carrier lines are the most common type of broadband available. *ComputerWorld* reports that T-carriers differ from cable and DSL because they do not use existing cable or telephone lines. Instead, T-carrier wires must be installed in a residence or office. T-carriers use four copper wires; one pair receives data and one pair transmits data. Of two types of T-carrier lines, T1 and T3, T1 lines are slower. T1 lines transmit data at 1.54 Mbits/sec, while T3 lines

transfer data at 44.76 Mbits/sec. Although T-carrier lines can be used in residences, their cost and speed make them more compatible with office buildings.

In response to the more mobile needs of the Internet economy, fixed wireless has emerged as a complement to DSL and T-carrier lines. According to *E-week,* "fixed wireless gives users within 35 miles (56 km) of a central broadcast tower [access to] high-speed Internet, voice, and video services with a small parabolic antenna, a low-end transmitter, and a beefed-up cable modem." The most promising possibility for fixed wireless use is its ability to bring the Internet to cities and rural areas that do not have reliable access. The next generation of broadband technologies may feature multimedia services such as full motion video, videoconferencing, and Internet access using wireless technologies.

In today's market, broadband access is no longer an extra amenity but an expected standard. Building Owners and Managers Association explored what property managers must know about providing information technology for their buildings. The survey found that tenants expect not only the infrastructure in place for high-speed access but also the ability to adapt their offices as new technologies are introduced.

In developing business parks, developers should consider the different types of broadband services and which services might fit the needs of the individual project. ULI's *Tech Trends* for October 1999 suggests ways to meet current technology needs and adapt to future capabilities: 1) include both wired and wireless bandwidth for continued adaptability, 2) work with local and regional telecommunications and cable companies to benefit from competition in prices and services, and 3) use high-capacity wiring such as Cat 5 extended (telecom) and RG-6 (cable) that can be used for many purposes.

Broadband technology is constantly changing. To stay on top requires foresight and flexibility to plan structures for potential technology services. ∎

Source: Leslie Holst, "Broadband Buzz," *Urban Land,* February 2000, p. 136.

Exterior designs vary. Some markets require a more upscale look, and higher construction costs can therefore be supported. Other markets define multiuse buildings as economy space that must use the most cost-effective combination of construction materials and structural systems.

Having several tenants in a building requires a plan for signage that allows for individuality while maintaining a coordinated appearance.

Web Hosting Facilities

A building type that has emerged recently is a highly secure, large-floorplate box that houses the transmission gear for phone, data, and Internet companies. "Web hosting facilities" describes them well, but they are also known as "mission critical facilities," "data centers," and "telco hotels."

Because of the mission-critical nature of these facilities and their typically small requirement for office space, the buildings generally have a very low ratio of glass to floor area. In existing structures adapted for this use, glass areas are typically closed off with block walls set inside the glass, or Kevlar bullet-resistant material is applied to the inside. Steel bollards, security cameras, and perimeter fencing are sometimes required.

One story is the most common form for such buildings because of slab-on-grade requirements, which vary from 150 pounds per square foot (735 kg/m²) for colocation/raised floor/server areas to 400 to 800 pounds per square foot (1,955 to 3,910 kg/m²) for battery backup/UPS rooms. These structures can be multistory in urban areas if they are provided with flooring that can withstand 150 pounds per square foot (735 kg/m²) live load. Clear heights of 18 to 24 feet (5.5 to 7.3 m) are most common, although this amount can be reduced for multistory urban centers that require at least 14 feet (4.3 m) of clear height. Floorplates range from 50,000 square feet up to 300,000 square feet (4,650 to 27,900 m²). Buildings can be as little as 100 feet (30 m) deep, although depths up to 200 or 300 feet (60 or 90 m) are desirable.

Column spacing at least 40 feet by 40 feet (12.2 by 12.2 m) is most desirable. Unlike for standard warehouses, this requirement is not dictated by movement of goods or equipment layout but is a response to the extremely high income per square foot such centers generate and the desire for maximum efficiency.

Data centers are sensitive to water damage and therefore require upgraded or even redundant roofing systems. A 60-mil adhered rubber single-ply to a four-ply built-up roof would be acceptable to most users. Roofs should drain to the exterior and at a minimum directly below to the slab or, preferably, through exterior scuppers or downspouts. The roof structure should be a higher clear span but also may have to support hanging loads of 10 to 50 pounds per square foot (50 to 245 kg/m²) for electric conduits or HVAC ducts.

These centers require up to ten times the electric and air-conditioning loads of a typical office building; they generally have backup systems for electric service, air conditioning, and telecommunications access. Air-conditioning units typically are installed on the site rather than mounted on the roof to avoid leakage. Air can then be moved overhead in very large ducts or under raised floor systems. Backup cooling towers or other systems may be required for redundancy.

Larger facilities require two truck-high docks plus two drive-in doors. The remainder of what would have been a typical warehouse loading area is used instead for emergency generators, fuel storage, ground-mounted cooling towers, and other equipment. Because of the noise and requirement for security, this space should be screened and fenced and located at the rear of the site.

Electricity demand in such facilities ranges from 70 to 120 watts per square foot, and users prefer separate, distinct power sources if possible (separate feeds from distinct substations or transformers in a substation, for example). If five diesel generators (the size of a locomotive) would accommodate total power failure, the engineer typically puts six in the design in case one fails. Fuel tanks and containing possible spills in fueling areas are a major concern; therefore, electric and fiber-optic services in the facility are run overhead in cable trays or conduits, in a raised floor area in a building adapted for this use, or under the slab in a build-to-suit facility.

While few developers want to risk building a structure whose only purpose is Web hosting, certain modifications to standard industrial facilities will assist in leasing such space to this type of user in the future. At a minimum, six-foot (1.8-m) concrete slabs, 18-foot to 24-foot (5.5- to 7.3-m) clear structures, roof drainage, and proper site layout will enable a structure to be adapted to this use. The typical user who is looking at a buildout cost of $200 to $400 a square foot will not balk at some cost to adapt a building to his requirements. A competitor with a more readily adaptable building may have an edge, however.

UPS Worldwide Logistics, a subsidiary of United Parcel Service of America, Inc., is a third party provider of global supply chain management solutions. This 710,400-square-foot (66,025-m²) build-to-suit warehouse and distribution center is located in Park West International Industrial Park in northern Kentucky, just outside Cincinnati, Ohio.

©1998 Gary Knight and Associates/Courtesy IDI

Build-to-Suit Facilities

Facilities that are built to fit a known client's clear requirements offer the least risky form of development for business park sites. The size of the parcel can be customized to fit the client's immediate and future space needs, and building design parameters can be based on the client's functional requirements and financial strength. Upon completion, ownership of the building may rest with the occupant or with the developer under a long-term lease whose terms both the client and the developer agree to.

For companies that can plan ahead, build-to-suit facilities may be the best way to accommodate their special requirements. A major disadvantage, however, is the relatively long lead time required for negotiating the terms of the agreement, and then designing and constructing the building. For developers, securing the commitment of an occupant before construction begins is desirable and sometimes necessary to obtain financing.

Development team members in a build-to-suit project include the developer, client, project architect, space planner, site planner or landscape architect, engineer, perhaps other specialists, and general contractor. Selection of team members is most likely a concern of both the developer and the client, and the client is likely to have its own group of advisers, including a broker and a specialist to monitor the construction process.

The full team's early involvement is important to eliminate as many unpleasant surprises and uncomfortable compromises as possible. In addition to avoiding problems, the team's early assembly and involvement can directly add value to the build-to-suit project. For example, even though the client has specific requirements, the issue of the facility's adaptability for other users in the future may be important to consider at the beginning.

Thus, the developer needs to understand in detail the client's long-term business vision and convey that vision to members of the team. Perhaps the greatest source of added value in the build-to-suit process is the ability to design features that meet the client's specialized needs.

Renovation and Adaptive Use
Redesigning, Renovating, and Repositioning Older Parks.

Older industrial parks can be rehabilitated into contemporary business parks with the introduction of new R&D, office, and flex uses to achieve a competitive repositioning. To effectively redesign older industrial properties and convert them to competitive business parks requires more than just the renovation of older buildings or the introduction of new building types, however. A process of reverse engineering is necessary that includes modifying the existing internal road networks, upgrading existing streets to current standards if necessary, and realigning or removing streets to accommodate new uses.

Utilities may need to be upgraded and reconfigured. Additional electrical capacity may be required. Telecommunications links may need to be installed. Internal configurations for water lines, storm and sanitary sewers, and electrical lines may need to be reverse-engineered. Other structural changes may be necessary. As with new devel-

Cummings Properties rehabilitated the abandoned United Shoe Machinery Corporation building in Beverly, Massachusetts, turning it into a $40 million office and R&D complex complete with a coffee shop and on-site elementary school.

opments, local jurisdictions and utility companies must be contacted early in the development process if new, previously unapproved utility connections are planned.

In site redevelopment, it is important to start with what already exists and try to minimize changes to the existing utility configuration to reduce construction costs—the reverse of the process followed in a completely new development. This "reengineering" can be expensive, but effectively applied, it determine the most efficient use of the existing utility systems while providing for the most efficient layout of new uses envisioned for the site over the long term.

A major shift in employment densities has also changed the parking demand for many industrial and business parks. R&D and office tenants require more parking spaces because employee per area ratios are higher. Thus, building sites that were planned with little or no parking and are at the maximum lot coverage allowed under local regulations must be modified to be competitive. One alternative is to demolish parts or all of buildings on adjacent sites so parking can be provided "on site." Another strategy is to provide remote or ancillary parking at the other underused parcels in the park and make it available to building owners who do not have room on their own parcels but would be willing to shuttle employees. The shuttle might be a service provided by the park itself. Shared parking, organized van and car pools, access to transit, and shuttles connecting activities inside and outside the park are additional options.

The new business parks place a greater emphasis on appearance. Thus, renovation invariably means that the entrance or entrances to the park will receive special treatment. Better landscape treatments, including heavy plantings, water features, earth shaping, and carefully designed signs, are common.

With overall image and particularly first impressions an objective, the removal or modification of "industrial"-looking buildings along the park's frontages and replacement by upscale buildings with a strong office component can result in a dramatic change in a project's image and better position it for a new market. Likewise, the use of plantings to screen borders, architectural fencing, and landscaped berms can conceal less attractive developed areas of a project and allow a shift in focus.

Building Rehabilitation and Adaptive Use. Suitability for rehabilitation depends on several factors other than demand: the building's structural soundness, the availability of space for additional parking, and the condition of utility systems and rooftop equipment, for example. But not every older industrial building is suitable for upgrading. In many locations, demand for low-tech, light industrial, and warehouse uses remains predominant, and existing facilities meet a demand for space where low cost is tenants' primary requirement. Nevertheless, industrial buildings are more and more often undergoing rehabilitation for adaptive use. This phenomenon takes many forms:

• upgrading building systems and the appearance of low-tech, light industrial/warehouse buildings to make them competitive;
• converting warehouse buildings to R&D and office use;
• adapting obsolete urban warehouse and manufacturing buildings for a myriad of what were previously considered nonindustrial uses but are now new industries.

The rehabilitated building must be given an identity to differentiate its present use from its previous ones.

Praxair Distribution's renovation of a warehouse in Ankeny, Iowa, is designed to house office, conference, and training facilities as well as warehousing and distribution. To unify operations, the building's structure and shell were left exposed throughout the facility, with the office structure, furniture, warehouse racking, and mechanical system organized to reinforce this relationship.

©Assassi Productions/Courtesy HLKB Architecture

As many features as possible should be retained to keep costs low, but new features will be required, such as an increased percentage of exterior glass, particularly along parking lots and entrances; a more impressive entrance; extensive landscaping around the building and parking area; removal of excess loading docks and storage areas; and replacement of outdated, unattractive portions of the building's facade. At some point, demolition becomes more cost-effective than renovation; it should always be kept in mind as an alternative.

Renovation of interior space depends on the type of user that will occupy the building. A typical older warehouse/manufacturing building has one floor with a 24-foot (7.3-m) ceiling, a small office/mezzanine area in front, and a large, windowless interior space. Upgrading the building for office or R&D uses might involve some or all of the following improvements:

• carving out a second floor and creating new interior offices, laboratories, or research areas;
• putting in skylights to provide interior light;
• raising the ceiling in the entranceway and adding glass and high-quality materials to form a more dramatic lobby;
• gutting the interior, because working around existing non-load-bearing walls may be less efficient than removing them;
• extending ductwork for the HVAC system, adding plumbing and restrooms, and upgrading electrical systems;
• installing additional telecommunications capacity, including T-carrier lines and fiber optics;
• reconfiguring interior spaces to meet tenants' specialized requirements; and
• removing asbestos.

Architectural and engineering firms specializing in the renovation of older facilities can help determine the most efficient and cost-effective way of upgrading a facility.

Other Opportunities for Reuse. Obsolete private or public institutional buildings and complexes, closed military bases, and shut-down manufacturing/heavy industry sites are often suitable for reuse as office and industrial facilities, incubators, and R&D facilities. Such facilities that are no longer in use often are well located in established neighborhoods and communities. They may offer several advantages:

• infrastructure already in place, including parking, roads, sidewalks, and street lights;
• utility services already in place, including electricity, water, sewage, HVAC, and telephone lines;
• construction quality and materials that cannot be duplicated economically;
• a one-of-a-kind architectural design that makes the project unique in the marketplace;
• access to arterials or freeways;
• proximity to high-quality housing and commercial services, sometimes in historic neighborhoods;

Industrial design is not just concrete and steel. This 45,000-square-foot (4,180-m²) office interior for hair care products manufacturer Graham Webb International is a plush part of the company's 180,000-square-foot (16,730-m²) distribution center in Carlsbad, California.

- an attractive purchase price;
- the availability of government-sponsored development incentives;
- a variety of spaces that can be leased or sold;
- mature landscaping; and
- proximity to educational services, including universities.

The redevelopment of old industrial or institutional buildings and complexes requires a major reengineering process of much greater complexity than that required for upgrading and repositioning an older business park, and it must be included in the calculation of development costs.

A major concern that must be addressed is cleaning up contaminated sites. In some instances—on military bases, for example—the location and degree of contamination may not be fully known. At the Union Seventy Center in St. Louis, site of a former GM plant with high clear heights and wide clear spaces suitable as warehousing, a major remediation program was required to deal with environmental problems to remove machinery, contaminated wood block floors, process piping, paint and grinding materials, asbestos, polychlorinated biphenyls (PCBs), and an underground storage tank before the building could be suitable for a new use (see the case study in Chapter 7).

The issues of who in the ownership chain is responsible for cleanup and what constitutes a suitable cleanup for various planned uses is still evolving. Many developers suggest that avoiding any site where a potential problem exists is the best course of action, while others see it merely as a potential obstacle to be overcome on the way to a successful and profitable development.[5]

With the basic infrastructure in place, it is essential that the site plan be designed around what exists. Engineering studies can determine which buildings can be adapted and which need to be demolished. As with the renovation of relatively new light industrial buildings, the need for additional parking may limit the types of suitable uses or may require a creative parking solution, such as a nearby shared parking lot or structured parking. At Starbucks Center in Seattle, for example, a warehouse building attached to one side of the 1.5 million-square-foot (139,400-m²) former Sears distribution center was converted to a six-level 605-stall parking garage to provide adequate parking for the new use (see the case study in Chapter 7). The carefully planned demolition of buildings can also free up well-located portions of the site for needed additional parking space.

Large institutional complexes or military bases frequently have central heating/cooling plants. Such a facility may be a great advantage or a disadvantage for adaptive use. The cost-effectiveness of its continued operation must be determined by a study. Abandoning the old system and introducing modern HVAC systems for individual buildings or tenants may be a better alternative.

Existing roads, rail, utilities, sidewalks, and landscaping may not meet the standards expected in a modern business park. Decisions regarding required improvements should be made in line with the development strategy. If startup, incubator tenants are targeted, the cost of significantly upgrading these features upfront may not be justified, but if office and high-tech/R&D firms are envisioned for the site, upgrading may be required so the development is competitive. Repaving or removing obsolete streets; landscaping parking areas and front setbacks and along building foundations; removing outdoor storage areas, outbuildings, and dilapidated site features; and providing curbs and organized curb cuts improve the site. In addition, the entrance to the rehabilitated complex and signage throughout must be installed to create a distinctive identity. If new construction to enhance the existing complex is contemplated, its location should minimize the cost of hookups to existing utility lines and the cost of providing access from existing streets (or rail).

Reengineering older and perhaps historic structures is a special challenge specific to the building.[6] Architectural features should be retained as much as possible, and additions and improvements should be sympathetic with the existing design. New roofing and insulation, new windows with energy-efficient double- or triple-paned glass (often with solar glazing to reflect the summer sun), the repair and cleaning of exterior wall surfaces, painting, and other cosmetic improvements are common exterior changes. Often the desire for a new look, which might include an improved entrance, has to take into account the historic design. When no mandate for historic preservation exists, the use of dramatically different but contextually appropriate contemporary additions can enhance rather than detract from the character of old buildings.

Period interior architectural details should be retained and incorporated into the new design to the extent possible. Because some existing interior walls will be load-bearing masonry, the new internal configuration must be designed around them.

A significant portion of the budget for internal redesign may be required to bring a building up to current fire and safety codes: enclosing stairways, adding sprinklers and fire alarm systems, installing or upgrading new wiring and plumbing, and overhauling or replacing the HVAC system. Installation of a central air-conditioning system can be a major expense if ductwork is not already in place. In seismically active areas, older structures need to be structurally reinforced to meet current building codes. And older buildings will most likely need modifications to provide access for handicapped individuals as required by the Americans with Disabilities Act.

Support Services

A business park may include services geared to on-site tenants as well as visitors. The type and scale of such uses depend on zoning regulations and demand. Where industrial zoning is cumulative—that is, where all the uses allowed in other zones are permitted by right or use permit in an industrial zone—such uses are found if there is sufficient support from the park's tenants. Where industrial

zoning and in some communities business park zoning are exclusive, however—that is, where only those uses specifically listed as permitted by right or use permit are allowed—these support uses are not allowed and would have to be located where they are permitted by zoning. And where they are permitted, employment in the park typically must be sufficient to support the planned retail activity, because in many jurisdictions, retail uses in a business park are required to cater primarily to on-site tenants. If they are not allowed in the park, they will probably be located at some distance or in adjacent commercial zones with designations such as "interchange commercial" or "heavy commercial."

When permitted in a business park, either by right or through a planned unit development or other special approval process, the most common of such service uses is a hotel or motel with meeting facilities. A hotel or motel can be an early addition to an interchange and serve not only the tenants of a business park but also the general public. Other uses in this service category include restaurants and fast-food outlets, convenience stores, banks, travel agencies, dry cleaners, health clubs, barber shops and beauty salons, automobile service stations, truck stops, daycare centers, copy centers, mailing and delivery services, office supply stores, and other support retail businesses.

It is unfortunate that current zoning practices in many communities exclude these uses from the new models for business parks, as these support services supply the growing density and diversity of employees found working in these facilities. It is hoped communities eventually will recognize that integration of these services into the fabric of business parks makes good sense, using land more efficiently and reducing traffic congestion by placing such services within walking distance of their users.

Nevertheless, developer-sponsored business services increasingly support the operations of business park tenants. Many business parks now offer a range of tenant and building services. Shared services, such as centralized

The Village at Beacon Centre is a convenience-oriented retail center that includes a travel agency, quick printer, dentist, dry cleaner, gas station, medical clinic/diagnostic center, and a variety of restaurants and business services. Offices are located on the second level of the center.

©John Gillan

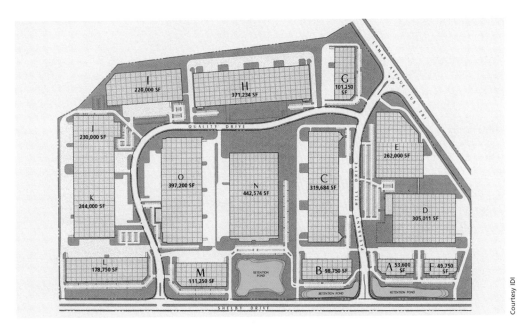

Southpark, a 200-acre (80-ha) multiuse business park in Memphis, Tennessee, was designed for small service companies and medium-size distribution and manufacturing, bulk distribution, and build-to-suit clients. Buildings are designed with high ceilings for greater stacking height and are deeper to minimize time to move goods.

Courtesy IDI

telephone systems, central receptionists, common meeting rooms, and office equipment and furniture rentals are popular with startup firms. Centers catering to incubator firms frequently offer secretarial, bookkeeping, and accounting services. Such business services provide a competitive advantage.

Services can be provided in several configurations, depending on the development strategy chosen. In smaller parks, service kiosks can be installed. In larger parks, a retail service center can be provided in an accessible location, preferably with pedestrian access for the park's tenants. Centers of this type are usually sited on an arterial street or parkway, often at the park's edge. A secondary entrance to the park may offer a convenient site where services can be seen and used by neighbors as well as the park's tenants. Specific uses in these centers vary widely. In parks with an industrial orientation, auto and wholesale services may predominate. In R&D and office parks, tenants prefer more upscale uses such as restaurants, personal services, and convenience shops. At LakeView Corporate Park (see the case study in Chapter 7), the developer was able to attract businesses that provide necessary services as the park matured. Now the park has a daycare facility that accommodates 240 children, a 120-room Radisson Hotel and Conference Center, a technical college for high school students, 100 outlet stores, restaurants, and a gas station.

A third configuration for service facilities is found where office uses predominate: individual buildings are designed to include one or more services on their first floors or basement levels. Fitness facilities and deli, cafeteria-style, or full-service restaurants are popular amenities in office buildings. Food service facilities require careful planning and consideration of venting to eliminate cooking odors, siting to maintain the image of the building and provide outdoor seating, and conforming to fire and safety regulations. Health clubs and daycare facilities are the most recent types of services to be provided in high-quality business parks.

A fourth configuration increasingly found in some of the most advanced business parks is a "town center," a pedestrian-oriented shopping district built to resemble a downtown main street. The Village at Beacon Centre (see the case study in Chapter 7) is a convenience-oriented retail center that includes a travel agency, quick printer, dentist, dry cleaner, gas station, medical clinic/diagnostic center, and a variety of restaurants and business services. Offices are located on the second level of the center.

Auto repair shops and gas stations can be useful additions to parks if they are carefully sited. Prominent sites at the development's main entrance should be avoided because they detract from the image tenants look for. Oil companies, however, would likely select this type of site. If the gas station closes, an additional problem arises as the site may be too small to be readily converted to a more dignified use suitable for a park entrance.

Notes

1. Institute of Traffic Engineers, *Trip Generation,* 6th ed. (Washington, D.C.: Author, 1997).
2. Transportation Research Board, *Highway Capacity Manual* (Washington, D.C.: Author, 1997).
3. One thousand square feet and 100 square meters are approximately the same size and therefore require about the same number of parking spaces.
4. Joseph DeChiara and Lee E. Koppelman, *Time-Saver Standards for Site Planning* (New York: McGraw-Hill, 1984).
5. Robert A. Simons, *Turning Brownfields into Greenbacks: Developing and Financing Environmentally Contaminated Urban Real Estate* (Washington, D.C.: ULI–the Urban Land Institute, 1998).
6. Jo Allen Gause, *New Uses for Obsolete Buildings* (Washington, D.C.: ULI–the Urban Land Institute, 1996).

5. Marketing and Leasing

Once the industrial building or business park is constructed, the developer or owner must lease or sell it at a price that will produce an attractive return on the investment made. If the developer's vision for the property reflects the realities of the marketplace, the property can be leased successfully by means of a good marketing program.

Marketing

Marketing an industrial project is a multistep process that revolves around creating an identity or niche for the development, identifying target users, convincing them that the space meets their needs, and negotiating the terms of the lease or sale.

Formal marketing goes into full swing at the start of construction, but the job of finding tenants should be started informally much earlier, as soon as the idea of developing the project at a specific location begins to take shape.

The major steps in marketing a project generally include making contacts with prospective users or tenants, developing a marketing plan, establishing a marketing

Located near London's Heathrow Airport on the site of a former landfill, Stockley Park has extensive landscaping, water features, and a regional park with a golf course and other recreational amenities.

budget, preparing and distributing marketing documents (brochures, technical service packages), and establishing a leasing program through in-house resources or with real estate brokers.

Without the right kind of promotion, even the best project can founder. This reality argues for the inclusion of marketing and public relations experts on the development team early in the development process to devise a marketing strategy. Marketing and public relations begin long before ground is broken and continue after the project is complete. An appropriate marketing strategy helps a broker meet the developer's financing requirements for preleasing or preselling. Good public relations can generate positive attitudes toward a project before it is even started or help defuse opposition.

Making sure the project serves its target market well is the first basic element of marketing. Thus, the marketing and sales process begins with market research, the goal of which is to project the absorption rate of the project based on analysis of demand and competitive supply. Several questions need to be asked: Who are the target markets? What project features and amenities do these groups want? Based on market conditions and the products in the market, what are target tenants willing to pay? What are competitive projects offering?

The second basic element is to effectively promote the project's attributes to prospective clients at a time when they are in a position to lease or buy. The direct marketing of an industrial project may begin with low-key, infor-

Timing is everything. The developer of this 721,000-square-foot (67,000-m²) industrial facility in Naperville, Illinois, pulled together a full proposal—including preliminary specifications and drawings—from scratch over one weekend to land its largest single facility ever developed.

©1999 Gary Knight and Associates/Courtesy IDI

mal contacts by the developer or owner with the types of firms that are targeted for the project, but as the development progresses, a more systematic approach to marketing produces the best results. The developer or owner must prepare and execute a strategic marketing plan, which should include goals for leasing and sales, budgets, and specific marketing programs.

In marketing, it is important to be guided by the market research–based vision for the project, especially in terms of planning and design, product (and tenant) mix, and quality of tenants. At the same time, if demand proves to be different from that anticipated, a flexible development plan becomes an important marketing tool. Business parks especially should feature a wide inventory of buildings open or under construction and remain responsive to changes in the demand for different products—speculative buildings, land sales, and build-to-suits.

Activity tends to breed activity. So having product available at all times is important to marketing. In multiuse projects, it is worth devoting considerable time and resources to preleasing to a high-quality "seed" tenant. An initial tenant with a good business reputation can set the tone for the entire development and create an image that will give the park or the building a competitive advantage in luring other tenants.

The challenge of selling a business park or industrial project is the focus of this chapter. For the most part, the word "sales" is used broadly to include both leasing and selling. Ideally, if members of the development team do a good job at research and product design, sales and leasing can be a relatively straightforward exercise. But even in the most ideal circumstances, prospective clients must still be convinced of the project's merits relative to the competition.

The Marketing Plan

The marketing plan identifies firms and other organizations in the target market and methods for convincing them to lease the space. It outlines goals for leasing and

sales, establishes programs for accomplishing those goals, assigns responsibilities and resources, and sets schedules. It is a working document that should be continually evaluated and updated to reflect changes.

A comprehensive marketing plan includes the following specific elements:

- A description of the project, the target populations, and an assessment of the project's relative position in the marketplace—in sum, an analysis of the project's situation. This situation analysis should seek to answer a number of key questions. Who are the prospective tenants? What are their needs? How can the project be differentiated from competitive projects? What marketing opportunities seem particularly promising? What particular marketing problems need to be dealt with? As background, the analysis should also include a summary of market conditions—asking rents, concessions, vacancies, lease rates and terms, typical tenant improvement packages, services and amenities at competitive projects, and absorption rates.
- A statement of the project's financial goals. The marketing plan should take into account the investor's goals for the project, including exit strategies. These financial goals should form the underlying basis for leasing decisions. Thus, the marketing plan should include short-term and long-term forecasts of expected financial results. The marketing team must keep in mind that the project's financial feasibility analysis will be constantly revised and updated throughout the development process and that changes in the pro forma leasing projections will necessitate corresponding revisions in the marketing strategy.
- A general marketing and leasing plan for the project, based on the analysis of market conditions and on the basic leasing assumptions from the pro forma leasing projections. How will the project—its location, features, amenities, services, and delivery schedule—be presented? What kinds of pricing structures will be estab-

lished? What kinds of promotional activities, including broker programs, will be undertaken? By what means will the marketing and sales staff get information to the target market?

• Specific marketing programs. As the marketing plan evolves, a list of specific marketing activities should be compiled. Roles and responsibilities must be assigned, schedules worked out, and budget allocations made.

The marketing plan is a multifaceted scheme for identifying and gaining the attention of potential tenants. A good marketing plan can be the major factor distinguishing a successful development from one that languishes. It provides answers to the following basic questions: What sectors or types of businesses will be pursued? How broad or narrow a net will be cast? How will leads be generated? How will the attention of prospects be gained? What image of the project will be projected? What kinds of marketing materials will be produced? How will on-site elements —architecture, landscaping, presentation space, and materials—be used to promote the project?

In organizing their marketing programs, some developers rely mainly on their in-house leasing/sales staff. Many developers market their projects mainly through the brokerage community, while many others combine in-house staff and brokers. Developers may be their own best salespeople, but even many of those who do their own leasing and selling often rely on outside brokers to bring a market perspective and additional prospects to the table. Some developers, particularly those lacking an in-house sales staff, use exclusive brokerage arrangements; others go with open listings. The marketing strategy for most industrial/business parks involves both local brokers and direct marketing efforts undertaken by the developer's own sales and leasing staff. The larger the project, the more likely it is that the developer will need an in-house marketing and sales staff to assist in marketing and other tasks such as designing space for specific users and negotiating deals.

Setting Marketing Goals

A successful marketing program requires a clear statement of what the developer/owner is seeking in terms of types and size of tenants, rental rates, lease terms and conditions, and length of the lease-up period. These marketing goals must be grounded in the realities of the marketplace as determined by the market analysis and any subsequent changes in supply, demand, and competitive conditions. They must also reflect the business objectives of the project's owners and investors. For example, depending on their exit strategy, some investors might prefer to emphasize short-term value and thus rapid lease-up, while others might prefer to hold out for opportunities for longer leases or institutional-quality tenants that can add prestige and value when the project is sold.

The Marketing Budget

The resources devoted to implementing the marketing plan must be commensurate with marketing goals. If, for example, the goal for a new speculative industrial building is to reach 80 percent occupancy within a year and it is only 15 percent leased at the end of the development period, achieving this goal is likely to require a fully staffed team of aggressive leasing agents armed with a full complement of marketing tools.

A first-year marketing budget generally ranges from 4 to 5 percent of the anticipated gross revenues of a proposed project. The developer should keep in mind that the marketing budget must be adequate to cover the entire marketing period, not just the flurry of marketing activity that usually accompanies a project's opening. Individual speculative buildings require ongoing supplementary marketing budgets throughout the life of the project.

While the major elements of a marketing program for an industrial project are fairly straightforward, as a practical matter it can be difficult to come up with a hard and fast estimate of marketing and leasing expenses early

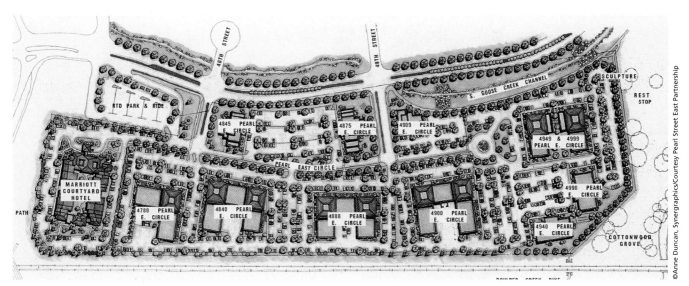

The plaza buildings at Pearl Street East Business Park combine office towers with first-floor flex space, which serves the high-tech Boulder market well. The concept has proved very leasable to a wide range of users, resulting in low turnover and minimum re-leasing costs.

in the development process. The size of the marketing budget depends on a number of variables, including market conditions, the number of competing properties, the developer's local reputation, and the quality of the project itself. Because of the need to establish a reputation, a developer's first project in a market area will probably need a larger marketing budget than subsequent projects in that market.

A rough estimate of how much should be budgeted for marketing can be achieved by compiling a comprehensive list of possible marketing activities. Members of the development team can prepare a reasonable but generous cost estimate for each marketing activity on the list, then scrutinize every item and delete any activities that do not justify their costs. The compensation scheme for marketing agents and the degree of reliance on outside brokers are also important variables in marketing costs, although they typically are separate line items from the marketing budget. In some cases, brokers assume marketing costs in their commission structure.

Another way of budgeting for marketing looks at what it will cost to achieve the desired absorption rate. Industrial marketing often relies heavily on active prospecting by members of the leasing and sales team, who make direct contacts with parties likely to be interested in the new project. Marketing costs depend on the rate of converting contacts to completed transactions, which in turn depends on numerous variables, including how well the target market is defined, how carefully the prospecting

is targeted, how competitive the project is, and how effective the marketing agents are. To estimate the grand total, it is necessary to predict how long it will take to lease the project. The market research conducted as part of the feasibility analysis should indicate absorption rates, but the amount to be spent monthly over the course of the marketing period is a judgment call.

It is critical to monitor the productivity of marketing and sales activity, measuring expenditures against leases produced or sales closed. To track the return on marketing dollars expended, developers should incorporate the line items in the marketing budget directly into the accounting system. It is also important to use continuing market research to measure effectiveness and to monitor changes in the project's trade area that may affect marketing.

Establishing the Project's Identity

An industrial project's visibility and image—the character it projects to potential tenants—are its initial selling points. The developer must establish an identity for the project that accurately reflects the quality of the project and create an image that tells prospects at a glance that this building or site is a location worth considering. Everything that is used to sell the project—from the sales center to the entrance signage to sales brochures to letters and phone calls—should support a consistent message. The development team should articulate a few of the key features of the development that make it stand out—

Tuttle Crossing's master plan has a carefully designed marketing program and marketing strategy that caters to many markets simultaneously: small office users, multitenant renters, larger corporate owner-occupants, and flex-type office/warehouse users.

Courtesy Edwards Land Company

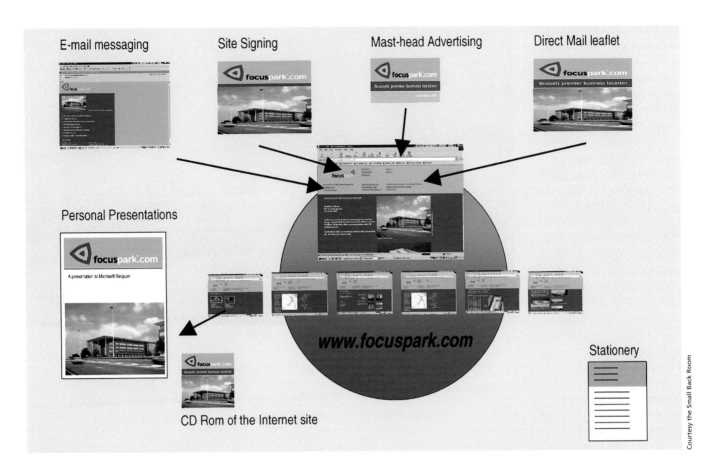

E-mail messaging Site Signing Mast-head Advertising Direct Mail leaflet

Personal Presentations

www.focuspark.com

CD Rom of the Internet site

Stationery

Courtesy the Small Back Room

The marketing plan prepared by the Small Back Room for Focus Park near Brussels, Belgium, provides a consistent image on all documents, from E-mail messages to brochures. International tenants are targeted through a multilanguage Web site, www.focuspark.com.

location, design, special features, high quality, affordable price, prestigious tenants, protective CC&Rs, the developer's solid reputation, a proactive management philosophy, for example. Tailoring the message to the target market can heighten the impact of printed sales materials and provide a focus for salespeople. Once the project's main selling points have been articulated, they should be publicized consistently in everything the marketing program produces.

As much as possible, all marketing and supporting materials for a project should be unified by theme, graphics, and style. A logo should be created to serve as graphic representation of the project. Putting the project's name and logo on stationery, presentations, and other early documents gives it visibility and establishes its identity. Naming requires some care. The project's name should be one that potential occupants and the community in general would find appropriate to the location and the project.

A design professional with experience in real estate projects can create the project's logo and a graphics style that serves to identify the project. The logo and identity theme should be used on all communications materials, from brochures to press releases to Web sites to space ads to the covers of lease proposal forms. The identity theme probably specifies a color scheme, and if it does, it is important to use that color scheme in all promotional pieces. Signage should also use the logo and be graphically related to the identity theme.

Lead Tenant

To obtain financing, some industrial/business park developers, especially those without a strong track record, are obliged to prelease a certain percentage of their space. Even before the overbuilding spree in the 1980s that largely brought an end to the financing of purely speculative projects, industrial developers tended to pay considerable attention to attracting a high-quality tenant at the outset of the development process. In the early stages of a project, industrial developers often directly seek out prospects among local and national corporations with operations that fit the targeted tenant profile. Securing a well-regarded lead tenant or tenants significantly contributes to the project's success, because it can set the tone for the entire development and help create an image for the park that will give it a competitive advantage.

Principles of clustering—the tendency of similar or linked industries to locate together—apply to industrial real estate. Often the lead tenant is the most relevant determinant of the overall tenant mix. Not only does the lead tenant attract similar or linked enterprises; it also seems to draw similarly sized operations. In recognition, large lead tenants often require incentives to make an early commitment.

Equally important, after a lead tenant has been secured, every effort needs to be made to avoid construction-related delays in occupancy. The developer's reputation and ability to deliver the project on time is critical, not

The master plan for Weston Business Center in Broward County, Florida, calls for six buildings containing more than 1 million square feet (93,000 m²). American Express, shown here, was the first tenant, with a 224,650-square-foot (20,900-m²) lease; less than one month later Anda Generics, a subsidiary of Andrx Corporation, leased the second building (152,000 square feet [14,130 m²]) at Weston. The third building, containing 182,000 square feet (17,000 m²), was leased to Office Depot.

only to the lead tenant but to other prospective tenants as well.

Marketing Materials

A variety of materials can be used to market a business park or industrial development. These materials should be designed and produced professionally and coordinated carefully with the other elements of the marketing program. They should express clearly the marketing message that the development team has articulated. They must be distinctive and descriptive, without unnecessary hype.

Brochures and Technical Service Packages. The quality and thus cost of the sales brochure required for successful marketing vary from project to project. In intensely competitive markets and for projects that the developer wishes to position as first class, more expensive four-color glossy presentations are warranted. In less competitive markets, less expensive, all or mostly black and white brochures may suffice.

Developers usually engage a public relations or advertising consultant to help design the sales brochure. A nine- by 12-inch (23- by 30.5-cm) jacket that accommodates a variety of inserted materials—single pages, stapled pages, and folded maps and flyers—is a traditional format. The inserted materials can be individually updated without having to redo the entire brochure.

A new format that has grown in popularity is the use of PowerPoint presentations to selected companies that have already shown interest in the project. These electronic presentations have the advantages of flexibility, timeliness, and easy transmission via E-mail to their audiences.

The sales brochure should present a thorough and clear description of the project that highlights its selling points. Complete factual accuracy is essential. It should be amply illustrated with renderings, photos, site plans, floor plans, and any other relevant graphics. The project logo should appear on all the individual pieces. Several elements should be considered for inclusion in the sales brochure:

- project description, including concept, tenant theme (with the identification of any leased tenants), features, and timing;
- the developer/owner's and manager's track record, including photos and renderings of other relevant projects;
- development plan identifying existing and planned roads, parcel configuration, parcel sizes, and the location and uses of existing and planned buildings;
- sample floor plans for various types and sizes of tenants;
- specific descriptions of any available space or available lots;
- relevant technical information about the site, which might include data on availability of and rates for electricity, natural gas, water, and sewerage, telecommunications infrastructure, fire protection, and security services;
- technical information on existing and proposed buildings, including heating and cooling capacities, truck loading features, clear heights, and column spacing;
- a summary of regulations applicable to the project, including details of protective covenants, zoning and land use regulations, setback requirements, floor/area ratios, building height limits, allowable building materials, design approval procedures, parking and service area locations and requirements, storage locations, and screening requirements;
- community context, including a location map, access routes, the location of nearby amenities such as hotels and restaurants;
- local and regional background information on population, the labor market, housing, transportation systems, taxes and business fees, and any industrial incentives or tax abatement programs.

Many industrial developers produce two sets of selling documents: a promotional brochure and a technical service package. The brochure, which serves as a narrative to introduce the project, is distributed widely to prospects, and the technical service package, which gives details that serious prospects want, is provided more narrowly to brokers. The technical service package contains detailed information on the topics listed earlier.

Web Pages. Increasingly, industrial developers and owners are using the Web to market their properties. It may in the form of an individual Web site for the property or a property listing that is accessed through the developer's or broker's Web site.

An advantage of Web pages is that they can easily be kept up to date. At a minimum, a Web page should include an overview of the project, with building and site data, floor plans, a summary of technical specifications, lease terms, and a location map. In addition, photos illustrating construction progress and updates on leasing activity are two powerful selling tools.

Another advantage of Web pages is that they can accommodate considerable ancillary information as well as provide links to other information on the Internet that a prospective tenant could find useful and convincing. For example, a developer might want to include newspaper and magazine articles that specifically mention the project in a favorable light or more general discussions of current trends in industrial space that illustrate the benefits of the project. Links to the homepages of the project's lead tenants or the sites of local development agencies or chambers of commerce that contain information on the area where the development is located can also help sell the project.

Newsletters. For a large and phased project, periodic newsletters or bulletins can be a cost-effective sales tool. A newsletter can also be an important tool to promote tenants' loyalty, serving to keep current tenants informed of changes, services, amenities, and issues. Expanding the distribution list of a tenant-oriented newsletter to encompass tenants in competitive local projects (and perhaps selected companies on the target list) provides the marketing team with a simple means for keeping the project in prospects' minds. It can also be used to ensure that brokers and other important contacts are informed about the project.

If a newsletter is to be used for marketing as well as an information tool for tenants, it should be (like all marketing materials) well designed and well edited. It need not be an expensive, four-color production—which may in fact give the wrong impression to occupants who recognize that they are indirectly paying for it.

A recognizable and appealing design using the logo should be adopted and consistently used. Stories should indicate to brokers and potential tenants what kinds of tenants occupy the project, what kinds of space are or will be available, and what kinds of services are provided. For example, the newsletter should cover new leases and sales, ground breakings, new tenants' arrivals, and the addition of new services or amenities. Some features included mainly to provide information to tenants—for example, a calendar of upcoming events associated with the project or a guide to restaurant, shopping, and cultural amenities in the neighborhood—can also be useful in marketing the project.

Merchandising

Merchandising the product encompasses all the visual impressions associated with the project. Brochures, Web sites, and other marketing materials are put together to tell prospective tenants about the advantages of a particular project. But project marketing needs to show as well as tell. On-site impressions are very important. Starting with curb appeal, merchandising is the use of on-site displays and practices to show the advantages of the project and create an environment conducive to sales.

Making a favorable impression begins at the project's entrance. A well-designed entrance to an industrial/business park or a speculative industrial building is a merchandising essential. As soon as practical in the construction process, the project entrance should be finished

A property can be leased successfully through a good marketing program if a developer's vision for the property reflects the realities of the marketplace. Shown is the Nestlé Building at Alliance in Fort Worth, Texas.

and landscaped. Extensive and environmentally sensitive landscaping sells space, can also facilitate the approval process, and makes for happier neighbors. A good landscaping scheme should be adopted, and, to the extent that it does not interfere with infrastructure and building construction, the developer should landscape strategically visible areas as soon as possible.

Even during construction, the overall condition of the site is important to successful merchandising. Prospective

A well-designed entrance to an industrial or business park is a merchandising essential. Shown here is Miami International Corporate Park.

clients will visit the site, so construction traffic should be regulated, trash should be collected, and all areas, especially those to be inspected, should be kept neat and well organized.

Signage makes impressions and is therefore an important element in merchandising that should be established early in the development process. A uniform set of sign guidelines is preferable to making decisions as the need arises. Some developers limit the number of signs that a parcel owner can put up during construction. Signs should be considered a key detail of the overall sales environment, and they should be designed, regulated, and placed accordingly.

Architectural quality can be another important factor in merchandising. In the period before construction is completed, serious prospects may require visual depictions of the entire business park as well as individual buildings. At this stage, renderings based on preliminary designs or based on designs permitted by the CC&Rs are appropriate rather than detailed architectural plans. Other tools that can help prospective clients visualize the finished product include three-dimensional models, aerial photographs, and site maps. These types of visual aids can be costly to produce, but they are often called for during approval and financing so the developer should make sure they are produced and maintained in a way that will make them useful to the marketing office later. Other visual tools for high-profile projects include slide shows, videos, and three-dimensional computer-aided design presentations. Although virtual tours are used largely for residential real estate, techniques such as 360-degree imaging or tours through buildings and sites are likely to increase for industrial properties.

An on-site marketing office can be an investment that pays off. To enhance the sales environment, such a facility should be well appointed, although some developers recommend that even a simple, unstaffed, small structure is better than nothing, serving at least as a place to meet and discuss lease terms during preliminary conferences with prospects. At a minimum, the sales and leasing office should have adequate space for displays and presentations and a comfortable setting for conferences with prospects.

The marketing office should provide take-home copies of all printed materials available on the project, the location, and the project team: the project brochure, the technical service package, the developer's and other team members' résumés, including the land planner, architect, project manager, and, if applicable, the broker. Published information on the city's or region's economy and attractions is also useful and may be obtained from local chamber of commerce offices or economic development and planning agencies.

Finally, satisfied tenants may serve as a project's best merchandising tools. In a mature project, marketing agents may take serious prospects through occupied space and have them ask the tenant questions. Few things are as encouraging or reassuring as testimonials from other companies that a location is good for business.

Developers work in partnership with logistics and corporate real estate professionals to help meet site selection requirements for companies such as Circuit City. Shown here is the company's 514,560-square-foot (47,820-m²) distribution center in Groveland, Florida.

©1999 Gary Knight and Associates/Courtesy IDI

Generating Leads

An essential task in marketing is generating leads. While it is tempting to start the process with a wide audience, it is important to keep in mind that a shotgun approach can be costly and inefficient. The target markets identified in the marketing plan should serve as the basis for focused marketing plans and programs. Depending on the nature of the target market, the program for generating leads might emphasize one or more of the following techniques: direct initial contacts, third party contacts, direct mail, cold calling, media advertising, and public relations. Even when the leasing and sales program relies largely on initiatives from brokers, a successful developer also seeks to generate leads independently.

Direct Initial Contacts. The initial marketing, which may be undertaken informally by the developer, generally focuses on already established relationships between the developer and prospective tenants. The headquarters office of national or regional developers is likely to have a network of contacts that can be explored for leads. When seeking tenants at the early stages of a project, developers often directly contact local and national corporations with operations that fit the target tenant profile.

Third Party Contacts. A variety of interested parties in every market can be helpful as a source of leads on prospective tenants: city and county development and redevelopment agencies and officials, planning commissions, state development agencies and officials, councils of governments, local bankers, local utility company executives, chambers of commerce and other business associations, local educational and training institutions, and public/private economic development coalitions, for example. Many of these organizations and people will have been contacted during the early phases of the project's development for data, advice, and permissions, so they will already be familiar with the project; however, it is essential to ensure that the relationship is maintained and that they are kept up to date on the development's progress.

Professionals who are active in industrial recruitment in the area or who are in a position to hear of firms and organizations that might be considering a move or expansion should also be cultivated. Establish procedures that will keep the communications lines open. Call them occasionally to find out what they know and let them know what is happening at the project. Put them on the mailing list for brochures, newsletters, and announcements. Include them in events like ground breakings and grand openings. Target firms are likely to belong to national trade associations; membership rosters can be useful in identifying key executives of those companies.

Current tenants can be another good source of leads. Visit your own tenants regularly, keep them happy, and encourage them to give you the names of associated operations, suppliers, and other companies that might be looking for space. Providing brochures to state and local development and redevelopment agencies for their use in responding to site location inquiries can also produce leads.

Direct Mail. Direct mail should be targeted to be most effective. If the target market contains many thousand firms, bulk mailings may generate enough leads to be cost effective. But scattershot untargeted mailings are not likely to justify their costs. If bulk mailings are to be part of the marketing plan, a low-cost flyer should be designed, saving the more detailed sales brochure for more serious prospects.

A direct-mail campaign must be followed up to be successful. In a campaign directed at brokers, for example, two or three mailings over a four-month period may be needed to gain their attention. Because the cost of multiple mailings can add up quickly, the careful selection of recipients is a critical task. Many developers focus their direct-mail campaigns on the brokerage community. Some make a point of including on the list of recipients nonbroker third party contacts—officials of economic development agencies, utility company executives, chamber of commerce staff, and so forth.

Site maps and renderings such as these for Cantera Business Park in Warrenville, Illinois, help prospective clients visualize the finished product.

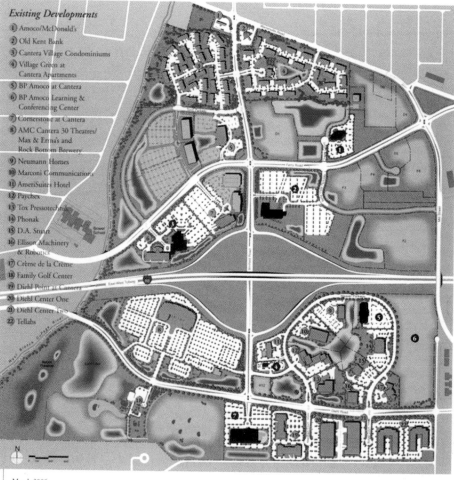

Existing Developments

1. Amoco/McDonald's
2. Old Kent Bank
3. Cantera Village Condominiums
4. Village Green at Cantera Apartments
5. BP Amoco at Cantera
6. BP Amoco Learning & Conferencing Center
7. Cornerstone at Cantera
8. AMC Cantera 30 Theatres/ Max & Erna's and Rock Bottom Brewery
9. Neumann Homes
10. Marconi Communications
11. AmeriSuites Hotel
12. Paychex
13. Tox Pressotechnik
14. Phonak
15. D.A. Stuart
16. Ellison Machinery & Robotics
17. Crème de la Crème
18. Family Golf Center
19. Diehl Point at Cantera
20. Diehl Center One
21. Diehl Center Two
22. Tellabs

March 2000

Under Development

1. Orthopedic Associates of DuPage
2. Navistar International
3. Full-Service Hotel
4. Lion's Choice
5. TerraView at Cantera
6. Jones Lang LaSalle Development, Inc.
7. LifeTime Fitness

Sending brochures directly to prospects can be an effective strategy for generating leads, especially when the prospects are carefully identified from the market analysis. Many developers include on their mailing lists all the tenants in competitive projects. A proactive marketing program may identify the executives and corporate real estate managers of firms and organizations in the target market for inclusion on the direct-mail list. Some developers advocate conducting spot checks of the impact of direct mailings, calling perhaps ten recipients a week, asking whether they received (or remember) the mailing, and inquiring about their reaction to it.

Cold Calling. Projects with their own leasing/sales staff often generate leads through "cold calls," that is, calls to potential prospects initiated by a salesperson. Cold calling is time-intensive, but it can generate leads and, at the same time, help keep salespeople in touch with market trends.

Paid Advertising and Public Relations. Advertising and public relations are integral parts of the marketing strategy that can be used to promote the image of the project and attract the interest of prospects. High-impact marketing in the form of extensive advertising and public relations work is not required in all markets, however. In markets with little available space, for example, brokers will be familiar with the few projects that contain space that could meet their clients' needs. Some developers coordinate the advertising of their projects in house, while others work with their brokerage firm or hire a marketing or public relations consultant. Whichever route is taken, the design and content of advertising and public relations materials should be supervised by marketing professionals.

Help in leasing and selling may not be the only use that an industrial development has for a public relations consultant, so the developer should determine whether the project has other needs—such as help in obtaining approvals or help in dealing with neighbors—that should be considered in choosing such a consultant and in deciding when in the project cycle it should be brought on board. The consultant should specialize in the type of project that is being developed and be strong in whatever marketing services the development team determines the project needs—approvals, community relations, press relations, materials design, advertising placement, and so forth.

If the developer decides to use an advertising/public relations consultant, one may be identified through referrals from other developers and from the pages of local business journals. Membership of a consultancy's principals or employees in the Public Relations Society of America (which administers a voluntary APR or "accredited in public relations" program for public relations professionals) or the American Marketing Association provides some indication of professionalism. Advertising/public relations consultants may be hired for one-time projects at an hourly rate or for a fixed fee. For large projects, many developers prefer to keep an advertising/public relations consultant on a fixed retainer with monthly billings for time spent to secure marketing and public relations services through all phases of the project.

Like all marketing initiatives, paid advertising should express clearly the marketing message that has been established for the project, and it should carry the project's logo and be consistent in style. To generate leads and impress prospects, industrial projects in general rely much more on brochures, direct-mail pieces, Web pages, and audiovisual and other types of merchandising displays than on paid media advertisements. But a judicious program of paid ads and a public relations program aimed at obtaining favorable media exposure can help the marketing effort by drawing attention to the project. Because such advertising and public relations tend to not be directly productive, their place in the marketing strategy needs to be considered carefully and their benefits assessed against their costs.

Industrial developers advertise mostly in local general audience and targeted business and real estate newspapers and in trade and professional publications targeted to specific businesses and industries. They rarely advertise in national general audience or business papers like the *New York Times* or the *Wall Street Journal*, because the cost is too high and the readership too general, and they seldom use local radio or TV programs for advertising property for lease or sale.

Many industrial developers find little value in extensive media advertising. They may advertise a project relatively heavily in selected publications as the leasing/selling phase begins in earnest but then taper off to nothing or nearly nothing. When they have small spaces to lease, some industrial developers take out classified ads in general interest or real estate newspapers. A number of industrial developers announce their projects in print ads designed to trumpet the company's name or in "tombstone" ads touting project completions or leases negotiated with major tenants.

The target markets should suggest the appropriate print vehicles for an ad campaign. Which newspapers and periodicals, including the publications of trade and professional associations, are the decision makers in target firms likely to read? The cost of advertising in specific publications is usually a deciding consideration. Four or more small ads may cost the same as one full-page ad, and, generally speaking, smaller ads repeated at intervals of time capture the attention of more readers than a single larger one. Spot advertising in trade journals or professional publications is usually more effective in promoting an image—of the project or the developer—than it is in directly generating leads.

The Internet provides another method of advertising. Some Web-based property listing services charge a fee, and some are free. Some provide space for photos, maps, and plans. For an industrial developer considering listing a property, a key consideration is whether the site is visited by serious shoppers. Examples of Web sites used for this purpose include propertyGo.com (www.propertygo.com), CoStar Property (http://www.costargroup.com), LoopNet (http://www.loopnet.com), and Commercial Realty Online (http://www.comro.com).

Billboards and other advertising signs should not be overlooked as advertising tools. Large signs visible from highly traveled transportation routes can serve to remind passersby, some of whom may be representatives of companies that are looking for new space, of the existence of the project. To be effective, billboards need to be comprehensible at a glance; industry standards recommend no more than seven to 11 words on any billboard. Show the project's location, say that space is available, and provide a telephone number. Billboard advertising is not cheap, but a good ad that is seen daily by thousands of business commuters can be effective in promoting the project to a wide audience.

Projects with highway visibility may offer an opportunity for on-site "space available" signs—unless the presence of such signs will detract from the image that the project is seeking to promote. If on-site advertising signs are used, they should be designed to mesh with the overall character and architecture of the project and placed where they will be mostly inconspicuous to tenants. In master-planned industrial parks, such signs should be set, if possible, in landscaped areas to help convey the project's parklike character.

The efficacy of other banner advertising—on buses and commuter trains, in bus shelters and train stations, in stores—depends on how many of the right people it grabs and how often. Such advertising is usually too costly for the number of leads it produces.

Being favorably noticed in the media (and by brokers) is the chief aim of public relations. Most public relations campaigns for industrial projects focus on three techniques: media relations, promotional materials, and promotional events.

The establishment of good press relations can be useful in marketing an industrial project. Coverage of the project or the developer in local newspapers and business journals and on local news broadcasts is generally most productive, which requires establishing relationships with the real estate, business, and city reporters and editors. For projects with unusual development processes,

On-Site Amenities Blur the Line between Business and Pleasure

Company executives worldwide are acting on the understanding that the work site is no longer a spot for the 9-to-5 drudge. With competition for high-quality employees at an all-time high, a facility must be as attractive as the job description.

In addition to a barber shop/beauty salon, sundries store, and dry cleaning service, for example, Sprint Corporation's new world headquarters includes a Sprint store that features company merchandise, according to Hugh Zimmer, chair of the Zimmer Companies, developer of the project. The first of an expected 14,000-member employee base began working at the Overland Park, Kansas, site in July 1999. When completed in late 2002, the 4 million-square-foot (372,000-m²) Sprint facility will include a 450-child capacity daycare center and health care facility. "Sprint is taking the needs of its workers seriously and designing the facility so that families will want to visit after work and on weekends," Zimmer says.

For the last 11 years, Zimmer has been sprucing up the 300-acre (121-ha) Southlake Technology Park in Lenexa, Kansas. Southlake, 12 percent of which is dedicated to park and recreational space, is shared by 3,500 employees working primarily at data, communications, and software development companies. On any given day, one can find employees catching their breath along the exercise stations throughout the park's four-mile (6.5-km) jogging path, baiting a hook at one of nine fish-stocked lakes, or dropping their children off at the daycare center. The reason for the extras is simple: "We're adding amenities to our business parks because that's good business," Zimmer says. Good business is also why the Zimmer Companies allows a major area hospital to run an outpatient medical clinic on the park property.

Companies at Southlake are not the only ones to take advantage of the perks related to an ample supply of space and a developer willing to fill it with extras. In warmer climates in particular, there has been a shift to campus-style office parks—low-rise buildings (four stories and under) surrounded by open space. Santa Monica's MGM Plaza, for example, comprises seven low-rise buildings on more than 15 acres (6 ha) of path- and patio-laden land, says Peggy Moretti, vice president of public relations at Maguire Partners, a southern California commercial real estate developer. A campuslike setting may be crucial in some instances. In California, for example, an on-site child care facility is required to have a specific amount of outdoor space available, according to Moretti.

When company executives sit down to map out their dream site or consider taking on a 2 percent increase in lease payments for that fully loaded exercise facility, some important bases must be covered first. A location that makes good business sense, a reliable on-site maintenance staff, and good lighting never go out of style. "Is a company going to relocate because of a convenience store? Probably not," says Moretti. "But if the decision comes down to two spaces with all of the basics, the company will probably go with the one with more amenities."

The same goes with employees. If two companies are running neck and neck when it comes to luring a potential employee, amenities may be the tiebreaker. A facility with a lot of amenities is likely to give a potential employee the sense that the culture of the company is friendly, which may be the key when deciding whether or not to take a job. ■

Source: Adapted from Tracy Bertman, "Pay for Play? On-Site Amenities Blur Line between Business and Pleasure," *Plants Sites & Parks,* August/September 1999, pp. 30–32.

construction or architectural features, or tenant amenities and services, efforts may be made through media relations to secure coverage in the national real estate press. A reprint of an *Urban Land* article that focuses on some noteworthy aspect of the project, for example, can make an impressive insert in the marketing brochure.

Many events that are appropriate subjects for news releases occur throughout the course of development, including completion of site acquisition, milestones in the construction process, innovative program or design elements, and tenant signings. A project can improve its chances of getting noticed in several ways: by assembling a good press list, issuing substantive and newsworthy press releases, and cultivating reporters and editors by, for example, inviting them to events, distributing promotional items, and practicing an open-door policy that facilitates access for the press to the key members of the development team.

If the project is outstanding or innovative in one or more aspects such as site planning, design, or mitigation of environmental issues, the developer or project architect may wish to submit its name to appropriate local and national award programs. There are many such programs, and a marketing/public relations consultant specializing in industrial real estate should be aware of them. Submissions require some time to prepare and usually a fee, but an award from a reputable source can be a strong selling point.

Some developers or their brokers send promotional items with the project's logo such as pens, paperweights, coffee mugs, mousepads, and coasters to reporters, other brokers, and prospective clients to help keep the project in the forefront. In marketing the Meadowridge Business Park in the Baltimore/Washington, D.C., area, leasing agent Colliers Pinkard distributed "view finders" with photos and graphics of the project to key businesspeople around the country. These toys provided a whimsical way of getting the marketing message across for a major business park.

Promotional events such as ground-breaking ceremonies, opening parties, and project tours can be used to present the project to reporters and community dignitaries and to garner media coverage. Developers need to carefully calculate the cost-effectiveness of special events, however, because they can be expensive to mount and the results are not easily quantified. Support for community or charitable concerns—the lending of space for a PTA's Saturday plant sale, the dedication of land for a public recreational use—is also a good way of attracting media attention and gaining support in the community for the project.

Leasing

The lease is the foundation for the successful financial operation of an industrial development. This negotiated contract between a tenant that will occupy space and the owner of the project establishes the level of income that

Building 01 at Beacon Tradeport in Miami was 100 percent pre-leased within weeks of beginning project infrastructure.

Courtesy Ernst & Young

can be expected from the project. It also clarifies both parties' responsibilities.

Leasing involves considerably more than quoting a price per unit of measure. The term of the lease, escalation provisions and renewal options, the allocation of various operating costs, the identification and satisfaction of different users' needs for above-standard electrical or HVAC capacity and other special needs, and the allocation of responsibility for tenant improvements, repairs, and maintenance are among the many negotiated elements of a lease that have important consequences for the bottom line. This complex process has a significant impact on the financial success of a development, so it must be undertaken by experienced professionals who are adept at meeting the objectives of all parties involved.

Organizing the process that brings prospects to the negotiating table is the first essential task of sales and leasing. The second is the negotiation process. The time to start thinking about specifics of the lease—its structure, rates, renewal options, expansion options, and other key terms—is during the development's planning phase, when the project is being positioned in the market. Establishing realistic lease terms is essential for determining the project's financial feasibility. The method of allocating costs between the owner and tenant is also important; it depends on a variety of issues, such as current market practices and the competitiveness of the project.

Organizing the Leasing Effort

A fundamental issue in the marketing process is how to conduct the leasing/sales operation: with an in-house staff? under contract to an outside agency? by means of an open listing in the brokerage community? or through some combination of staff and brokers?

Each choice has its pros and cons. Through an in-house leasing and sales team, the developer can establish its own marketing priorities and ensure that specific procedures are followed. But this advantage in control generally en-

GTE Communications Network (shown) and GTE Supply occupy more than 400,000 combined square feet (37,200 m²) of space at DFW Trade Center and Valwood West in Dallas.

tails added financial obligations and management responsibilities. Alternatively, the developer may enter into an exclusive arrangement with a brokerage agency. Such an agency can provide market experience and a professional sales force, thus reducing the developer's administrative burden. It does increase the developer's reliance on an outside consultant to perform effectively, and depending on the agreement, it can be more expensive as a result of commissions paid. A third choice, an open listing, is the system many industrial developers select, especially for large projects in competitive markets. Developers who work through open listings often retain their own leasing staff, even if small, to coordinate marketing activities, maintain contacts with brokers, and negotiate lease terms.

Open Listings. In markets where competitive brokerage activity is strong, the most efficient method of marketing an industrial project may be to collaborate with the area's brokerage community through an open listing system. Because this informal system involves no formal agreements between developer and broker, it is important to keep brokers informed about the project and to play the broker-relations game openly, fairly, and supportively. Brokers must be assured that they will receive fair and timely financial remuneration in bringing clients to projects for which they are not directly responsible and that might actually compete with projects they represent more formally.

In an open listing, the main audience for the project's marketing documents—brochures, technical service packages, news releases, and promotional items—is brokers. Keep local brokers up to date on the project—and interested. Keep information—pricing modifications, new leases and sales, changes in plans and policies, new products—flowing so the project is fresh in their minds. When the project is ready for leasing, arrange to make regular presentations at leading brokerage firms and to real estate boards and other brokers groups.

Developers and owners should make an effort to be accessible and responsive to inquiries from brokers.

Highly personal approaches to high achievers can sometimes produce extraordinary results. Some developers and leasing agents find that it pays to identify the area's or project's top producers and to schedule regular individual get-togethers such as a breakfast or lunch.

Most important is to clarify the rules regarding registration of prospects and commissions. To attract brokers' interest and efforts on behalf of the project, it is important to protect the broker's stake and to remain competitive in their compensation. The commission schedule and registration policy should be included along with a typical registered broker agreement in the information packets provided to brokers.

A prospect registration system gives credit to the appropriate broker for bringing a prospect to the project and ensures that if the prospect signs within a certain period of time, say six months, the broker will get the leasing commission. Some owners require receipt of a letter from the prospect authorizing the broker to be its representative on the project before registering the broker, and they may also require a meeting with the broker and client within a certain length of time, perhaps two weeks. The owner must have a clear-cut (and publicized) policy for who gets the commission if more than one broker shows the project to the same prospect. Generally, the registered broker is required to keep the lead active and to be directly involved in negotiations to consummate the deal.

Owners should execute broker agreements that make their registration and compensation policies transparent. A typical broker agreement guarantees a commission if the prospect signs a lease within a certain period. It may stipulate that if the broker's client is willing to accept specified lease terms—term, rates, escalations—or, more generally, terms "acceptable to the owner," the commission will be paid. The broker agreement should state the amount and timing of the commission payments and conditions pertaining to the broker's claim to any renewal commission. Owners typically decline to pay renewal commissions if the broker has no direct role in convincing the tenant to renew its lease.

Broker commissions are typically expressed as a percentage of rental income (usually 5 to 6 percent). Rental income is specified in the lease and can be defined in a variety of ways, including net rent, rent plus expenses (gross rent), and rent plus a portion or all of the fully amortized tenant improvements. In almost all cases, the commission structure calls for a declining percentage of income for the later years of a lease term, generally after the fifth year. The typical payment schedule for commissions is half upon signing and half upon occupancy or at the time rental payments begin.

The developer/owner's ability to establish a smooth relationship with the brokerage community can pay many dividends. Brokers are naturally more likely to direct their clients toward projects with cooperative owners. Strive to be honest and dependable in your dealings with brokers. Conversely, deal only with trustworthy brokers. Pay brokers on time. Maintain the standard commission. Do not get involved in cutting commissions.

To underscore the team approach, some owners make it a point to invite the broker to the closing of any lease or sale and to recognize the broker's contribution. In press releases or newsletters to publicize successful deals, the participating brokerage company and appropriate individuals should be mentioned.

Exclusive Listings. An exclusive listing with a full-service brokerage firm can offer a variety of services. Developers who choose this option may lack in-house leasing or sales skills, or they may be seeking multiple marketing services, including a strong knowledge of trends in the type of industrial product being developed, extensive contacts in the target market, and lease negotiation skills. Other development services provided by the broker may also be an incentive for establishing an exclusive relationship—market research and feasibility analysis, development advice, or assistance in structuring the financing, for example. In some communities, exclusive arrangements are essential for gaining the necessary attention of a prominent brokerage firm, especially for smaller projects. In some cases, lenders favor an established brokerage firm over an in-house marketing team.

Often an exclusive broker works with a network of cooperating local brokers in an arrangement that operates like an open listing program. (And the agent's cooperative brokers should be treated with the same courtesy and timely remuneration as open listing brokers.) Commission costs can become even higher for deals involving cooperating brokers if the local practice is for the "procuring" broker to receive the full normal commission and the exclusive broker to get a half commission. But it is presumed that the superior leasing skills brought to the table by the right broker will compensate for these expenses by bringing in more deals faster and, more important, the expertise to negotiate better terms and higher rents, resulting in a better return for the developer. An agency that is well known and respected in the area adds credibility to the project. More than one successful mar-

keting program has been built around the credibility of the brokerage agency handling the leasing and sales.

Selecting the right broker can make or break a project. The agency should have a proven record of success in leasing industrial projects of the same type in the market area. It should have the reputation of being able to aggressively prospect and engage tenants so that the goals of the leasing program are met. As lease negotiators, contracted consultants must be knowledgeable in the legal and commercial aspects of leases and able to represent the developer's wishes and objectives. An exclusive arrangement may hold the broker accountable for a portion or all of the marketing and promotional activities. When entrusting the leasing enterprise to an outside agency, the developer/owner needs to exercise careful oversight through periodic monitoring of the number of client inquiries, direct contacts, and presentations to prospects.

If the agency under consideration is marketing similar projects, it should be assessed carefully. It is a potential issue, but it does not necessarily obviate the company's effectiveness in marketing the project. The question of whether projects are targeted to the same users is one consideration, because in many cases, seemingly competitive projects may actually have a different focus and different target markets. Other issues are the size of the firm, available resources, and the actual personnel designated for marketing the project. An agency that is not as well known and has no client conflicts may have more staff to devote to the job but may also have fewer contacts among firms in the project's target market.

Contracts with exclusive brokers need to be carefully drawn. Among the provisions requiring particular care are the term of the contract, the scope of work that the broker is expected to perform, commissions, responsibilities for marketing expenses, flexibility in negotiating lease terms, submission of activity and progress reports by the broker, and remedies the developer can follow in the event of the broker's poor performance. The term of an exclusive listing should depend on the size and phasing of the project and on the product type—a term of at least several years plus renewal options for a large phased park development, six months to a year for a single multitenant building, up to six months for a 10,000-square-foot (930-m²) block of space, a year or two for a build-to-suit. Check the relevant state regulations, because they may limit terms to one year, subject to renewal thereafter.

The scope of work is generally premised on the developer's approved marketing plan, which should be an exhibit in the contract. Compensation depends on the scope of the work and the agency's normal charges. Commissions are generally higher for net leases than for gross leases. If the broker is to work with cooperating brokers, the basis for their commissions must be spelled out. The exclusive broker is aware of the owner's requirements concerning the rates, term, and special provisions in executed leases. To ensure that these requirements are met, it is advisable to include a clause in the broker contract stating that the terms of any negotiated lease must be acceptable to the owner.

In-House Leasing Agents. Large developers often employ in-house leasing agents who can get to know the property and its attributes more intimately than outside brokers and provide continuity for the marketing program. A possible downside to an in-house leasing staff is that the developer's leasing personnel are removed slightly from the larger market and might not have the contacts or market knowledge of an agent associated with a large firm.

The decision to rely on in-house leasing personnel depends largely on conditions in the market, the size and personnel of the development/management company, the size of the project, and the particular marketing issues. The ongoing leasing needs of a large project or of a landlord who operates a number of buildings in the same geographic area may justify the establishment of an in-house sales staff.

Depending mostly on its size, a project being leased by an exclusive broker may not require in-house leasing agents on site. But fitting out an on-site sales office where brokers can meet with prospects may still be productive. Most projects being marketed under open listings use on-site agents to handle walk-ins, telephone inquiries, new lease negotiations, and lease renewals. Often the in-house leasing agent is part of the property management team.

Selling Prospects and Negotiating

Making a sale hinges on convincing the prospect that available space in the project meets its needs functionally and economically. A good salesperson knows the project inside and out and is skilled in determining which factors weigh most heavily in the prospect's decision about where to locate. Questions about occupancy for most prospective industrial tenants are not restricted to price. They also relate to location, functionality, and the landlord and management company.

Knowing the project and the prospect's objectives for occupancy, a successful leasing agent will be able to articulate clearly and persuasively the reasons that this location, this space, this developer, and this management style can be a perfect fit for the prospect. The importance of familiarity with the project is the reason that many developers who work through the brokerage community still prefer to retain their own leasing team. The importance of understanding the prospect's concerns about occupancy is the reason developers seek marketing and brokerage consultants with industry expertise for their development teams.

The ability to communicate clearly and compellingly is the foundation of professional salesmanship. Different styles of selling make people comfortable or uncomfortable. A successful agent recognizes personality types and varies his or her selling style—friendly, relaxed, down to business, high powered—to fit the prospect. A good salesperson seizes the moment and is very attentive to the prospect. He or she rounds up whatever information the prospect requests as soon as possible and quickly follows up on meetings with a phone call, a letter

Pinnacle Micro, designer and manufacturer of optical disk drives for computers, was provided with two identical two-story structures with the flexibility for uses from corporate offices to R&D with limited light truck service and capability for product stacking.

When CIGNA invested in 1,025,545 square feet (95,300 m²) of space at Shawnee Ridge in Atlanta, developer IDI entered into a partnership so that it could retain 10 percent ownership of the six buildings purchased by the insurance company.

©1999 Gary Knight and Associates/Courtesy IDI

summarizing the issues discussed, or, if appropriate, a proposal.

Once a prospect has committed to negotiating a lease, a prudent developer/investor undertakes due diligence on the prospective tenant's financial viability. A Dun & Bradstreet or TRW credit report is a good start, but additional research may be necessary if the dollar amount of the lease warrants it. Institutional-quality tenants improve a property's investment value, while at-risk tenants can substantially reduce it.

By their nature, lease negotiations involve the resolution of conflicting financial goals. The prospective tenant wants to minimize occupancy costs, customize the space to fit particular needs, and retain a flexible option to vacate space or expand into adjacent space should circumstances change. The owner wants to maximize and stabilize cash flow and enhance the investment value of the property. Taking all parties—the owner, the prospect, and the lenders—through the lease negotiation process to closing requires professional negotiating finesse, which is what a competent broker or leasing agent is trained to provide.

In lease negotiations, the art must yield at times to the reality of the marketplace. When overbuilding and high vacancy rates are common, the fact that tenants can shop around for deals pushes developer/owners to agree to lower prices or smaller escalation rates, higher tenant improvement allowances, and other concessions they would not dream of in a strong market. Prestigious tenants the developer would like to land to enhance the development's image can have this same effect on the developer's negotiating strength.

The most basic rules for successful lease negotiations are to plan ahead, to approach the process as a cooperative endeavor in which the goal is a transaction that is agreeable to all parties, to be open to creative alternatives, to keep emotions out of the process, and to be capable of saying "no." The following seven steps can be useful in dealing with "a hardheaded potential tenant."

- Set up a plan. You need to base the plan on a bottom line, which is the combination of lease terms that produces the minimum acceptable economic return.
- Be aware of available alternatives. While a bottom line may keep you from accepting a bad deal, make sure that it does not keep you from being creative and open in the search for alternatives.
- Remain flexible.
- Track the issues. Concentrate on exploring and emphasizing areas that the landlord and tenant have in common.
- Sidestep attacks. Negotiate by asking, learning, exploring, discussing—which is managing rather than dominating the negotiations. One of the most important skills in negotiating is to be able to see the situation as the other side sees it. When an unacceptable proposal is put forth, neither accept nor reject it but look for how it may contribute to a resolution of the issues.
- Resist commitments on subsidiary points. It is unwise to agree on individual points until there is agreement on all issues. Get something in return for each concession, and keep each concession conditional.
- Resist the emotional commitment to make a deal. Not every negotiation should end in a deal. Consider your alternatives.[1]

The Lease

Lease agreements come in a variety of forms and can contain all manner of terms and conditions. A single-tenant building typically is leased on a net basis, with the tenant responsible for maintaining the building and the site. Space in multitenant industrial buildings, on the other hand, is often leased on a gross basis, with tenants responsible for a prorated share of expenses. Net leases are becoming more common.

Under a gross lease, the tenant pays a fixed amount of rent and the landlord pays all operating expenses. In gross rent deals, individual tenant spaces are generally separately metered so that tenants pay their own utilities.

Technology firms are forcing many real estate owners and investors to rethink their approach to the landlord and the function of real estate services. What are the special real estate needs of dot.coms and technology firms? What kinds of real estate solutions work for them—and the property owner?

A real estate owner may have to model a property after the very tenants it hopes to attract. By taking the partnering approach to new economy tenants, Divco West, a Silicon Valley real estate owner/operator, has gained some insights into their needs and has adopted many of the techniques of such tenants and clients as Cisco Systems, Oracle, Polycom, New Access Communications, and bartertrust.com. For example, it has a cross-industry advisory group that ranges from real estate finance guru Ethan Penner to venture capital principals from Sand Hill Capital and Mayfield Fund, and Divco invests its principals' time in advising venture capital firms on real estate issues. "New economy firms need new types of real estate and new financial structures," says Divco CEO Stuart Shiff. "Our job is to try to match those needs with flexible solutions that work for them and provide good returns."

Some of technology firms' special needs include:

- Collaborative Space—The first thing that strikes many real estate firms about technology companies is their open, collaborative culture, notes Shiff. "New economy firms want a physical environment that reflects the openness and idea sharing that have helped fuel their growth—with plenty of plazas for Friday afternoon social hours, walking-oriented amenities, sport courts, and the like. Technology executives often run into venture capital people or other CEOs at restaurants or during impromptu volleyball games in a parking lot and share their ideas without a second thought," he adds.
- Employee-Recruiting Space—Technology firms in high-tech markets such as Silicon Valley, Austin, and New York are finding that space itself is an advantage in recruiting employees. The young, high-energy talent they are competing for is drawn to unusual converted warehouses, unfinished interiors, lawns and green spaces, operable windows, and nontraditional amenities. Divco has taken to staging some of its office space by finishing out a tenant lobby on spec or installing table tennis and other games that the tenant can keep if it signs a lease.
- Speed-to-Market Space—"Every early-stage company is motivated to get its business up and operating before its competitors do, and many people think incubation space is the answer," says Shiff. "We're finding that promising new companies prefer to incubate in office buildings where they mix with all types of busi-

nesses and don't face as much of a recruiting war. A solid startup may want to get a small space at first, with staged expansions that quickly mushroom to 40,000 or 50,000 square feet (3,720 or 4,650 m²)."
- Flexible Leases and Financial Structures—"We start with a clean slate and ask tenants what they want. Their varied answers often uncover a key issue that is crucial to them," observes Mike Dumke, a director for Divco. Short leases and very low credit, for example, do not have to be deal breakers, he says. "You develop a sense of the risk factors and the reward potential and draw a conclusion." Blends of credit, weighted lease obligations, and other strategies can help a company with a good business plan get off the ground—and build a relationship with the landlord that keeps it in the fold.
- Warrants and Other Partnering Strategies—Technology firms seeking space in highly competitive markets may offer stock or warrants as a tradeoff against cash payments. In early 2000, it became a virtually standard part of deals in San Francisco's South of Market technology corridor and in many of Silicon Valley's most sought-after submarkets. Further, real estate firms have shown interest in getting a small piece of the tenant as a demonstration of their partnering approach and of their desire to share in the tenant's stock and venture capital plays—although recent volatility has changed things. It can be lucrative, but there is no simple formula that can be applied.
- Venture Capital Strategic Real Estate Alliances—Venture capital firms are starting to pay attention to real estate—and the lack of it. "Venture capital firms shepherd their startups into second- and third-round growth strategies, then hit a major obstacle when these firms can't find space close to their employee base," says Shiff. "Now, venture firms are seeing the advantages of synergistic real estate relationships to help assure their companies a home." ∎

Source: Ron Heckmann, "The Partnering Approach," *Urban Land*, May 2000, p. 99.

A single-tenant building is usually leased on a net basis, with the tenant responsible for maintaining the building and the site. Nike was among the first tenants at Southpoint Industrial Park, Forest Park, Georgia.

For short-term leases, increases in operating expenses can be predicted and accounted for in the calculation of rent. But for terms longer than a year, gross leases are risky for a developer/owner, whose net rental income stream can be eroded by inflationary operating expenses. Some of this risk can be mitigated by the inclusion of periodic rent escalations in the lease, either predetermined or contingent on some indicator such as the consumer price index. Or, more commonly, the lease may contain provisions for the tenant to pay its prorated share of increases in expenses over the base year amount.

Under a net lease, the tenant pays a base rent plus its share (based on use or occupancy share) of certain operating expenses of the building. Thus, the developer/owner passes through to the tenants some or many of the variable expenses that are associated with operating an industrial building—utility and other operating costs, maintenance and repair costs, insurance, and property taxes. Which specific expenses are passed through is sometimes designated by a differentiation in interpretation of net lease, net-net (double net) lease, or net-net-net (triple net) lease. But one term may mean different things in different markets, so it is best to clarify terms at the start of leasing discussions. What is included in base rent, whose responsibility it is to perform repairs and maintenance, and whether or not increases in expenses are passed through are all subject to interpretation and negotiation.

The time to start thinking about specifics of the lease —gross or net, rates, and other key terms—is during the project's planning phase, when the project is being positioned in the market. Establishing lease terms is essential for determining the project's financial feasibility. Knowing what will be the owner's share of the operational expenses is an important factor in the design and construction of building systems and in other design decisions.

The lease terms that can be achieved depend on general market conditions. Developers are wise to bring in brokers as consultants during the feasibility stage when the marketing strategy is being developed. The leasing strategy must be firmly grounded in the reality of the local market and must also try to anticipate how market conditions might change over the planning and lease-up periods.

Any lease for industrial space should include the following information:

- size and location of the space;
- the method of measuring leased space;
- options for expansion, if any;
- duration of the lease, renewal options, and cancellation privileges;
- rent per unit and escalation provisions during the term of the lease;
- utilities and services to be provided by the owner;
- method of determining the tenant's share of the costs of utilities and services;
- responsibility for repairs to tenant spaces and common areas;
- due date for rent payments, to whom rent is payable, and penalties for late payments;
- interior work to be performed by the developer that is covered by the basic rent;
- responsibilities for repair and maintenance to the roof and structure of the building;
- operating hours of the building;
- number and location of parking spaces and terms of their use;
- allowable uses of the leased space;
- date of the tenant's possession; and
- provisions for subleasing and assignment of space, if any.

The developer is likely to require a security deposit to guarantee compliance with lease conditions as well as to compensate for any damage to the premises beyond normal wear and tear. In cases where the lessee does not have strong financial capabilities, a letter of credit or guarantee from the parent company may also be necessary.

A lease in today's complex world of real property is a sophisticated legal document. In addition to the advice provided by brokers on the commercial terms, an experienced real estate attorney needs to be consulted on the legal aspects of the lease. A standard lease form is only the starting point; all industrial leases need to be tailored to the individual transaction. Technological change is driving much of the industrial market today, and the changes are showing up in the length of lease documents.

From the landlord's perspective, some common clauses should be avoided or limited:

- Right to Expand into Adjacent Space—Many tenants would like to hold their options open at the expense of the landlord's flexibility. A tenant's unqualified right

to expand into new space after a certain number of years can result in the landlord's having to hold space vacant. While developers may be able to say "no" to small tenants, they may have to make some arrangement to satisfy the needs of large tenants. They may be able to get by with offering the tenant a right of first refusal on expansion space as it becomes available. But a right of first refusal can come back to haunt the owner if the space is unknowingly re-leased without notification to the tenant holding the right—an easy mistake to make. Confronted by a prospective tenant who wants expansion space, developers may agree to preserve expansion space by leasing it for short terms only, but finding interim tenants for space so constrained may be difficult.
- Tenant's Right to Terminate the Lease—Major tenants often want a right to terminate the lease if a condem-

Public/Private Partnership Attracts Build-to-Suit Headquarters

In its heyday, the sprawling 86-acre (35-ha) Hughes Aircraft Co. R&D facility in the San Fernando Valley area of southern California was home to more than 6,000 aerospace engineers, who designed and analyzed top secret guided missile systems. In 1994, however, less than five years after the Berlin Wall came tumbling down, Hughes, already forced to reduce its workforce to 1,900 workers, shuttered its home of 35 years and relocated to Tucson, Arizona.

Today, the site is once again abuzz with activity, thanks in large part to the efforts of the private sector and city officials like Los Angeles Mayor Richard Riordan. Riordan, his LA Business Team, Hughes Aircraft, and the Valley Job Recovery Corp.—an agency formed to help the community rebound from the aerospace slowdown—deliberated over how to keep the crippled R&D facility from becoming a ghost town. At the urging of officials from the mayor's office, Cost Federal Savings, a local

lender, became involved. The institution, later purchased by Washington Mutual, wanted to relocate 750 employees scattered throughout the San Fernando Valley.

In late 1995, Hughes sold the entire facility to the Valley Job Recovery Corp. for the below-market figure of $14 million. The nonprofit corporation in turn sold the entire site to Coast Federal for the same amount. As part of the agreement, Valley Job Recovery would retain an option to purchase 30 acres in the northernmost part of the site at a discount.

Plans to put the former Hughes site back on the business map surfaced quickly. In June 1996, the Los Angeles City Council voted to buy 5.5 acres (2.2 ha) of land from Coast Federal for a $25 million, 50,000-square foot (4,650-m²) 911 dispatch center. Not long after, DeVry Institute, a Chicago-based trade/technical school opera-

West Hills Corporate Village in Los Angeles, California.

Courtesy Regent Properties

nation takes place or if access to the property is impaired. Options to terminate leases for any reason may make long-term financing impossible to secure.

- Requirement for Reconstruction—An option to terminate the lease in the event of an uninsured loss is preferable to the tenant to a requirement that the developer reconstruct the space.
- Landlord's Responsibility for Repairs—Such responsibility for repairs necessitated by tenants' use of areas such as parking lots or truck courts is to be avoided.
- Proposition 13 Tax Increase Exclusion—When property in California is sold, the property tax is reset at 1 percent of the sale price. Smart tenants try to keep tax increases triggered by sale of the property from being considered as a pass-through expense. Owners, however, resist, because such an exclusion makes the property less salable. Developers may be able to compromise on this issue by negotiating a limit to the number of sales in a ten-year period on which the tenant will have to pay the increase in property taxes.

Many developers start lease negotiations with a standard lease form they have developed that contains the terms and conditions under which they prefer to make a deal. But it is usually only a starting point and a method for ensuring that the negotiations cover all the key points. Many large tenants also have their own lease forms, and the first issue to be negotiated is which form to use as the base.

While the lease terms and conditions are ultimately a function of what the market will bear, executed leases must also satisfy lenders' requirements. Different lenders have different concerns. If the developer fails to ascertain the lender's requirements, it runs the risk of having

---

tor, agreed to purchase 15 acres (6 ha) from Coast to operate a 100,000-square-foot (9,300-m²) campus in the southeast corner of the property.

Three weeks later, Valley Job Recovery exercised its option to purchase 30 acres (12 ha) and negotiated an agreement with Beverly Hills–based Regent Properties and Shamrock Holdings of California (a Roy Disney family–owned company) to undertake the newest phase of improvements at the site: a 590,000-square-foot (55,000-m²) business park called West Hills Corporate Village. The goal was to preserve and enhance the site's campuslike environment by renovating existing office buildings to include generous amenities, ample parking, extensive landscaping, and open space. The city of Los Angeles took over the entitlement process and rezoned the project in seven months, paving the way for complete rehabilitation of the 30-acre (12-ha) site. The original entitlement process covered the existing 470,000 square feet (43,700 m²) on the site; however, as part of the public/private partnership, the Regent/Shamrock group was able to receive entitlements for the expansion of the office park to a total of 590,000 square feet (55,000 m²), in the form of two build-to-suit projects.

The building core and shell of the four existing buildings left by Hughes have been upgraded into contemporary office space. New exteriors feature attractive entrances and energy-efficient glass with granite accents. Interiors are finished to Class A standards, with spacious and well-appointed lobbies. The project has two fiber-optic cable feeds and features state-of-the-art systems for optimum service, energy efficiency, and cost control. Both the HVAC and electrical systems have excess capacity and redundant equipment. In addition, seismic upgrades already have been completed in each existing building so they comply with new city seismic codes.

Marketing of the West Hills Corporate Village began in mid-1998, and in October 1998, the Boeing Company announced it would occupy one of the four existing buildings, relocating 275 employees throughout Ventura County and 220 employees from its Canoga Park facility. Boeing's new West Hills Campus encompasses 170,000 square feet (15,800 m²) of building space for research and development of defense and aerospace laser and electro-optics. The ten-year, $35 million lease, facilitated by the LA Business Team, represented the second largest real estate transaction in the west San Fernando Valley in the last five years.

In April 1999, Sterling Software's information management group agreed to relocate to West Hills, signing a ten-year lease for a new 135,000-square-foot (12,550-m²) build-to-suit headquarters building. Located in nearby Warner Center, the company had been considering relocating to Calabasas as an alternative to Los Angeles, and the public/private partnership proved a deciding factor in its decision to stay in Los Angeles.

A week later, Software Dynamics, a leading developer of software for the financial services industry, agreed to move its headquarters unit from Chatsworth to West Hills, signing a ten-year lease to occupy approximately half (30,000 square feet) (2,800 m²) of the second floor of a completely renovated three-story, 160,000-square-foot (15,000-m²) building.

Recently, leases have been executed with Pitney Bowes, Page Net, Xerox, and IBM, bringing the project's occupancy level to 75 percent. Discussions are being held with other *Fortune* 500 high-tech firms, which should bring the campus to full occupancy. ■

Source: Jeffrey Dinkin, "Public/Private Partnership Attracts Build-to-Suit Headquarters," *Urban Land*, May 2000, pp. 50–51.

Since the late 1990s, the popularity of build-to-suit transactions has grown for a number of reasons. Rapid corporate growth in many industries coupled with healthy corporate egos—in the software and entertainment industries, for example—have inspired corporate owners to seek a distinctive image and visibility. Moreover, even with the resurgence of available capital, developers and capital sources still strongly prefer the preleasing of a build-to-suit facility to riskier speculative development.

Of central importance in structuring build-to-suit leases are the improvements that are the objective of the transaction and the problems inherent in providing for future built space. Further, certain conditions must be satisfied before the project can be completed—issues concerning the closing of the purchase of the site, finalization of government entitlements for the site, finalization and receipt of a commitment to finance the construction of the project, and actual commencement of project construction.

Because a prospective tenant wants to avoid locking itself into a deal that may not materialize, safeguards to reassure the tenant are necessary. Thus, a transaction must be structured to allow the developer the time and flexibility to satisfy the conditions while giving the tenant enough flexibility and leverage to ensure that the developer exercises due diligence in completing the transaction—or faces possible termination of the lease.

To ensure that each party is content at each step of the leasing process, several tenant termination rights based on certain milestone ("blowout") dates must be established and carefully spelled out. They may include, for example, the dates that fee ownership must be obtained, entitlements finalized, financing secured, and construction started. When structuring such conditions, a number of issues need to be addressed.

Land acquisitions increasingly are predicated on finding a lead or preleased tenant before closing purchase of the site. In such cases, a fee purchase condition is appropriate, but this condition also can be easily defined as when the developer records the deed and receives title insurance. If the project entitlements have not been solidified, an entitlement precondition also may be appropriate. Satisfaction of an entitlement blowout date must be specified and include some flexibility, because, in most cases, entitlements are subject to administrative and/or state court appeals and motions.

Even in the face of competitive capital markets, land acquisition and construction financing are still major concerns for tenants and may become a precondition. The recordation of a mortgage securing a certain loan amount—or the lender's delivery to the tenant of a pre-approved loan commitment—should be a sufficient guarantee of financing. The developer can then avoid giving the tenant access to all the loan and financing terms.

When the timing of the tenant's move into the building is critical or when there is no financing—for example, when the developer is a REIT—the project construction date becomes vital. The date construction of the base building begins can be designated as the start of post-excavation foundation work. If hazardous waste is a problem, soil remediation may be required before foundation work can begin, the time for which would have to be factored into the development schedule.

Certain events should satisfy blowout conditions, even if specific terms are not met. For instance, the issuance of all building permits and the start of significant on-site construction should obviate the need to meet other stated entitlement conditions. The issuance of a temporary or permanent certificate of occupancy should obviate the need to meet other conditions for any blowout dates. This commonsense approach should allow the developer to proceed quickly through the development timetable without having to make submittals to and hold discussions with the tenant at every step.

The developer should negotiate for the right to extend the various blowout dates for short terms such as 30 to 90 days, based on proof that the particular contingency can be satisfied during the extension period. With this time cushion, the developer can then take aggressive action to satisfy the contingencies without fear that a near miss will allow the tenant the right to terminate the lease. For instance, it is reasonable to extend a financing contingency blowout date 30 days if the developer can deliver an unexpired loan commitment and/or a certification that the loan will be consummated within the 30-day period.

The developer also should negotiate for the right to renegotiate the blowout dates if unanticipated circumstances throw off the entire development timetable. For example, if a lawsuit will delay entitlements for at least two years, the developer should be able to present the tenant with a choice between committing to new blowout dates or terminating the lease immediately.

Whether or not a renegotiation right exists, the lease should address how events beyond the developer's control will affect blowout dates. The concept of force majeure traditionally has been applied to extend blowout dates for the start of base building construction.

The developer also should have the right to terminate the lease at a certain point, especially if it lacks the right to renegotiate blowout dates. Otherwise, the lease could go on indefinitely even though completing the project becomes infeasible from the standpoint of entitlements, financing, or construction scheduling.

If a blowout date is not met, the only remedy that the tenant typically can resort to is the right to terminate the transaction. Terminating the lease makes many tenants uneasy, especially if the time left to relocate is prohibitively short. To reassure the tenant, the developer usually needs to commit to covenants of performance, which assure the tenant that it intends—within reason—to satisfy the blowout conditions and complete the project.

The ultimate issue becomes what damages the tenant is entitled to collect if the developer breaches its covenants of performance. To protect the developer from rampant and unfair liability, it is imperative that damages be strictly limited. One approach is to limit damages to out-of-pocket expenses that the tenant reasonably incurs in connection with the lease, including legal and design fees. The sting of breaching such covenants for the landlord, however, could be obviated by the traditional "nonrecourse" or "recourse only to the value of the project" clause and the waiver of the consequential damages clause found in almost all leases. Such mitigating clauses are almost bulletproof for single-purpose development entities that breach a performance covenant even before fee title to the project site is obtained. ∎

Source: Adapted from Anton N. Natsis and Allison L. Malin, "Build-to-Suit Transactions," *Urban Land,* September 1997, pp. 71–85.

to renegotiate initial leases to finance the project. Among lenders' concerns are assignability, condemnation and insurance claim payments, and exclusions in pass-through expenses.

In the event of the borrower's default, lenders wish to have the means to obtain control of the project's cash flow before foreclosure so they can continue to maintain the project and provide tenant services. Thus, lenders require assignable leases, that is, leases that allow the lender to receive rent directly (take assignment of the rents) in the event of a default.

Many lenders want to be awarded any condemnation payment or insurance money from a covered calamity, which they then pay to the owner as they deem fit. Owners, on the other hand, usually want to get insurance payments directly for restoration expenses, especially if any leases require that damages to tenants' premises be repaired by the owner.

Lenders dislike whatever reduces owners' ability to cover increased costs. Sometimes the arrangements to pass operating expenses through to tenants exclude certain expenses, for example, increases in management fees. Lenders prefer pass-through arrangements with zero exclusions.

Everything is negotiable. The developer/owner should try to determine before negotiations begin what is most important to the prospective tenant and then focus on the relevant elements of the lease. Lease negotiations typically focus on the term, the rent, and tenant improvements.

Term. Opinions tend to vary among landlords and tenants as to what constitutes the ideal lease period, and for both parties the ideal period expands and contracts over time in response to changing economic and market conditions. Recent fundamental changes in the processes of product manufacture and distribution—not to mention a rapid rate of invention of new products/services and new types of companies—have made options for altering the term of the lease an important factor. Executing short leases is a key way to keep open a company's options to change.

From the landlord's perspective, the benefits of a short or long lease depend somewhat on what market conditions will be at the time of its expiration. Value is based on cash flow in place, however, so longer terms with set increases are generally valued more highly than short-term leases. For example, a developer with too many short-term leases may find it difficult to secure long-term financing. From a practical standpoint, though, it may be useful to allocate a certain percentage of space in a building or business park to short-term occupants to maintain flexibility in accommodating the expansion needs of large tenants.

Companies in highly fluid sectors of the economy put great store on flexibility in lease terms. A five- to ten-year lease model does not work for information technology companies, because many of them cannot predict where their business will stand in a year or two. These companies need shorter-term leases of one to three years without huge penalties for breaking the lease.

ConAgra, one of the world's largest food companies, describes itself as a "successful family of companies growing in partnership with the land." Its corporate campus in Omaha, Nebraska, captures its spirit through a pastoral setting with extensive landscaping, graceful architecture, and interior tenant improvements in an earth-tone color palette.

Companies that operate on contracts—third party warehouse operators, defense contractors—often insist on escape clauses in their leases to protect themselves from unrenewed or canceled contracts. Large tenants tend to commit to longer leases (ten or more years). The leases negotiated for a project's lead tenant and for a build-to-suit tenant are typically long (ten to 15 years) to compensate for lower rents or higher levels of tenant improvements.

Most tenants seek to have renewal options included in the lease because they ensure that the space will be available in the future. From the perspective of the landlord, renewal options reduce flexibility. And renewal options at a rate agreed on in advance are especially treacherous in that they may promise the space at a rate that may be below market at renewal time. Sometimes landlords offer renewal options at an arbitrated rate, but this choice too can end up costing rent. If a renewal option is necessary, the landlord should seek to allow it at a market rate determined by the landlord at its sole discretion or by third parties such as brokers or appraisers.

Another consideration for developers related to the term of leases is that it is best to try to stagger lease rollover times so that a large proportion of a project's leases do not expire all at once.

Rent. After location and the physical plant, the top concern of industrial/business park tenants is effective rent, which is their cost per unit after all concessions have been deducted. Tenants pay rent at the stated rental rate multiplied by rentable square feet or square meters. In most industrial facilities, unlike offices, it is unusual for common area charges to be included. Therefore, "usable" is the same as "rentable" in most cases.

Any pass-through operating costs also add to tenants' occupancy costs, so tenants are also sensitive to what cost items will be passed through, how operational costs will be accounted for, management's incentives for cost control, and other issues affecting operational expenses.

Rental rates vary with the amount of space a tenant takes, with large occupants typically getting a break. They also vary with the stage in the project's life at which the lease is negotiated, with lead tenants typically receiving lower rates and other favorable lease terms.

Determining achievable rents can be a complicated procedure. Quoted rates differ significantly from real rates once items such as rent concessions, tenant improvement allowances, allowances for moving, and lease buyouts are factored in. Generally, market rents for the project's product type and class set the limits; however, a superior product may be able to command higher rents.

Scheduled rent increases are an important element. In tight markets, the developer can usually negotiate annual increases in rent ranging from 2 to 4 percent based on increases in the consumer price index.

Tenant Improvements. The tenant improvement allowance is often a key negotiating point during the leasing process. As part of the lease, developers usually provide a set allowance for tenant improvements that covers finishing the interior space, including ceilings, walls, floors, and electrical and phone outlets. For most industrial projects, the tenant improvement allowance is fairly low, ranging from around $2 to $4 per square foot ($21.50 to $43/m²).

Developers generally offer a fixed dollar allowance per square foot of leased space or a certain level of specific improvements. The latter is expressed as a ratio, such as one linear foot of partition per 100 square feet (9.3 m²) of space or one electrical outlet per 150 square feet (13.9 m²). Generally, a tenant can upgrade any standard building item if it pays the difference in cost. The fixed allowance may be as cash or in the form of a rent credit.

For most industrial/business park uses, the key steps in determining tenant allowances include:

• Establishing the Budget—The tenant pays for improvements over and above the agreed tenant improvement allowance.
• Preparing the Space Plan and Designing Improvements—The space planner may be under contract to the developer or the tenant. Because the developer usually owns the improvements, it has a strong interest in controlling the design and quality of construction.
• Obtaining Approval—Depending on the extent of work, local agencies must approve tenant improvements through the issuance of building permits.
• Selecting a Contractor—The developer typically selects and oversees the contractor, but tenants may do this work with the approval of the developer. Improvements constructed by the tenant must usually be preceded by the landlord's provision of certain basic improvements.
• Overseeing Construction—The developer typically is required to oversee construction and to ensure that the tenant can move in on time. If the tenant does

the improvement work, the developer retains responsibility for making sure that it meets code standards.

In general, developers should seek to avoid costly tenant improvements that may not be usable by a future tenant and may be expensive to remove. The proliferation of certain high-tech tenancies presents a challenge to developers in this respect. Forethought and careful documentation can enhance the opportunity presented by specialized technology industries. Specialized scientific fixtures, equipment, and other improvements can mean higher rents throughout the term of the lease. To the extent the fixtures are reusable by future tenants, they may also have residual value if the landlord owns them. Determining what is the landlord's and what tenants may remove is essential and must be spelled out in the lease.

Note

1. Norman D. Morris, "Seven Steps to 'Principled' Negotiation," *Real Estate Review,* Summer 1990, pp. 51–54.

6. Management and Operations

As the "enterprise concept" of real estate has gained currency among institutional investors and investment advisers, real estate owners have devoted much more attention to operational concerns and issues. The institutionalization of real estate has prompted this process and, at the same time, has encouraged greater professionalism in reporting and the management of real estate assets.

As an operating enterprise, real property requires attentive, qualified management that considers not only physical plant operations and maintenance but also tenant services, marketing, and an exit strategy to respond to changing markets. When a project is viewed as an ongoing business rather than only bricks and mortar, the importance of proactive management to the project's success becomes clear.

Industrial development and investment has been the slowest real estate sector to incorporate the enterprise concept into development models, but today industrial developers and investors are much more management conscious and more proactive in the management of their buildings and business parks. This attention is in response to increasing complexities in the types and operations of industrial real estate as well as greater demands from tenants and investors.

Professional property development is key to enhancing the long-term value of corporate assets. Shown at left is the lobby of Compaq Computer's headquarters in Houston, Texas.

As is the case for all types of investment real estate, an industrial property can be managed on three levels—as an operating property, as an asset, and, if it is a piece of an investor's portfolio, as a portfolio performer. The concerns and responsibilities of the property manager, the asset manager, and the portfolio manager—who may be one, two, or three entities (or individuals)—are interrelated but distinct and often blurred in practice.

This chapter covers property management and asset management, which generally overlap and have a direct bearing on the performance of the property. Portfolio management, on the other hand, is not generally relevant for industrial property operations and management, except to the degree that investors with substantial industrial properties, like some REITs, subscribe to specific property or asset management theories. Many industrial REITs, for example, aggressively manage their properties as a way of adding value, thus upping the management ante for competitive projects in the marketplace. Conversely, some other investors in property portfolios pursue goals other than long-term value; they would therefore be reluctant to invest significant resources in upgrading or repositioning individual assets.

The chapter addresses the importance of determining management goals and strategy, provides guidance on establishing a management function, discusses practices relating to various ongoing management tasks, and addresses issues related to asset management.

Property Manager

- tenant retention
- rent collection
- operating budgets
- control of operating expenses
- record keeping and financial reporting
- preventative maintenance and repair
- tenant services (complaints and follow-up)
- tenant improvements
- crisis management
- legal issues
- security
- insurance and risk management
- enforcement of project rules and standards
- compliance with laws, regulations, and the lease agreement
- building safety and hazardous materials plans and controls
- public relations and community relations
- monitoring tax appraisals and bills
- tracking as-built drawings and design specifications
- communication with asset manager/owner
- leasing (if not provided by a broker)

Asset Manager

- strategic plan and budgets for the property
- performance monitoring
- ongoing market analysis
- oversight of property management
- capital investment and repositioning analyses
- hold/sell analyses
- tenant relations
- communication with portfolio manager

Portfolio Manager

- communicating with and reporting to investors
- setting portfolio goals
- investment criteria
- investment strategy
- acquisition and disposition decisions
- capital investment decisions for individual property assets
- oversight of asset management

Owner

- set goals and objectives for each property
- communicate with managers   ■

Management Goals and Strategy

To a far greater extent than even a few years ago, industrial developers and owners rely on principles of professional property management to enhance the long-term value of their buildings and business parks. Many factors have contributed to this trend: growing competitiveness in the industrial space market, the emergence of REITs and other portfolio investors as primary players in industrial property markets, the increasingly sophisticated and varied space needs of many technology-oriented industrial tenants, and computer- and Web-based technological advances that have enlarged the capacity of organizations to manage property.

Even developers who do not intend to hold a project as long-term owners are concerned about long-term profitability, especially if their financial return involves some participation in the value created through the process of development. The creation of value results when the expected future benefits that accrue to an investor exceed costs. And those long-term benefits accrue to the investor only when the property functions well over its expected economic life. Prospective future investors in the development are interested in how the constructed space and the management provided by the developer will perform over the long term; thus, they price the investment accordingly. Developers who fail to pay attention to management issues will be forced to sell or lease at lower prices and eventually lose out in a highly competitive environment.

In all income-producing real estate sectors, including industrial real estate, property management increasingly is considered a strategic factor. Property managers are forging new relationships with owners that allow them to operate more like partners than managers. Successful managers not only differentiate their services to tenants but also find ways to create greater portfolio value through techniques such as creative financing, more efficient operation of properties, or new revenue opportunities.

Property management has become in effect asset management, and development therefore is not complete until the day of a project's disposition. Managing real estate as an asset requires strategic planning and entrepreneurial responsiveness to changing market conditions. The manager's strategic goal should be to meet the owner's investment objectives as well as tenants' needs. For a large-scale planned business park, respecting the concerns of the project's neighbors is another key element of strategic management. Effectively meeting the often conflicting objectives of owners, investors, occupants, and neighbors requires that the manager be able to focus on a variety of issues: property maintenance, the retention of tenants, operational efficiency, ongoing market-sensitive and investor-sensitive modifications, and the space and services the project offers.

The developer should obtain the input of experienced property managers and establish the broad elements of the property management plan early in the development process. The market analysis should set forth management expectations and concerns of prospective tenants,

The three main goals of business park and building design are functionality, economy of construction, and easy long-term maintenance. Shown here is the Short Run facility, Philips Plastics Corporation, New Richmond, Wisconsin.

©Don Wong Photography/Courtesy Julie Snow Architects

©Don Wong Photography/Courtesy Julie Snow Architects

which can then be accommodated through design of the project and incorporated into the financial pro forma. For example, if targeted tenants consider a high level of security to be a priority, the developer may emphasize lighting and visibility of entrances, install perimeter fencing or an electronic security system, or budget for round-the-clock security guards.

Including the perspective of a property manager on the development team can be beneficial throughout the development process. Input from experienced property managers during the design process can help achieve the last of the three main goals of industrial park and building design: functionality, economy of construction, and easy long-term maintenance. There is no substitute for actual property management experience in identifying the probable effects of specific design decisions on daily and long-term operating expenses. Early input by a property manager also can help reduce later insurance costs and lessen liability. Input from a property manager is also useful in the feasibility analysis to estimate operating costs, which are a component of the property's value. When tenant specifications are negotiated and construction contracts signed, a determination must be made that the project will be able to provide the level of services that tenants expect at the costs specified in the operating pro forma based on the project's design.

During construction, property management should be a consideration when any changes to accommodate tenants' needs are contemplated. Both the initial cost and the ongoing operating expenses and capital costs for such changes need to be assessed to determine whether they mesh with the long-term goals of the project's investors. Including the property manager as a player in the construction process ensures that changes made during construction will not seriously affect the ability to operate the property or the costs of operation.

Establishing a Management Function

One of the biggest decisions regarding property management is whether to use in-house managers or to contract with a property management firm. A major factor affecting this decision is whether the property is one building or an entire business park, but other factors include the character and location of the project, the developer/owner's in-house staff capabilities, and the type of tenants. Many large industrial developers and portfolio holders have management divisions or subsidiary companies that handle property management for their own account and sometimes for other clients as well. These developers usually cite two principal reasons for including a management component in their businesses: property management services generate fees that can provide a steady source of income for a development company, and managing its own properties allows the developer to maintain close ties with the tenants, tenants who may maintain or expand their space at the current park or at the developer's future projects.

Industrial developers/owners who lack the in-house capability to manage their properties must secure the services of a well-staffed professional property management company. Firms specializing in property management can offer the advantages of advanced management techniques and systems that individual property owners generally do not possess. A management firm should be selected on the basis of its existing portfolio, its specialties, and its fee structure. Noting that more than 10,000 firms in the United States offer property management services, Athena Z. Harman, president of Harman Companies, a commercial realty and management company in La Jolla, California, offers several tips on what to look for in a management company:

- Relevant Experience—What other properties does the company manage? Is it experienced in handling the particular management needs—marketing, tenant

Property management firms often provide tenants with on-site services from company engineers rather than an outside contractor. Building Services Engineers for IDI Services Group stands ready to provide a host of on-site services to industrial tenants, such as Peterson Aluminum in Building A of Atlanta's Northpark Industrial Park, shown here. Among the services provided by the on-site engineers are repairs to plumbing, lighting, electrical fixtures, and HVAC systems.

Project Data: Avis Farms Research and Business Park

Land Use Information

Site Area   156 acres (63.1 ha)

	Completed	At Buildout
Gross Building Area (GBA)	382,176 square feet	800,000 square feet
	(35,504 m²)	(74,320 m²)
Number of Buildings	15	28
Parking (all surface)	1,250 spaces	3,200 spaces

Land Use Plan

	Acres (ha)	Percent of Site
Buildings	18.5 (7.4)	11.9%
Paved areas[1]	35.0[2] (14.1)	22.4
Landscaped areas	73.0 (29.5)	46.8
Wetlands and water features	29.5[3] (11.9)	18.9
Total	156.0 (63.1)	100.0%

Tenant Information

Occupied net rentable area (NRA)	98%
Average annual rent	$11–13 per square foot ($120–140/m²)
Average length of lease	5–10 years
Typical terms of lease	triple net
Typical tenant size	15,000 square feet (1,393 m²)

Development Cost Information[4]

Site Acquisition $321,000

Site Improvement Costs[5]

Excavation and grading	$61,000
Sewer/water/drainage	56,000
Paving	47,000
Curbs/sidewalks	38,000
Landscaping/irrigation	56,000
Fees/general conditions	71,000
Total	$329,000

Construction Costs

Superstructure[6]	$516,000
HVAC	156,000
Electrical	261,000
Plumbing/sprinklers	66,000
Finishes	261,000
Fees/general conditions	140,000
Total	$1,400,000

Project Management Costs

Architecture/engineering	$70,000
Leasing/marketing	15,200
Legal/accounting	2,000
Taxes/insurance	3,000
Title fees	1,800
Construction interest and fees	56,000
Other costs	102,000
Total	$250,000

Total Development Cost $2,300,000

Developer

Palm Beach Financial Ventures
900 Avis Drive
Ann Arbor, Michigan 48108
734-761-2800

Architect

The Heil Partnership
26400 Lahser Road, Suite 325
Southfield, Michigan 48034
248-799-9111

Engineer

Atwell-Hicks
540 Avis Drive
Ann Arbor, Michigan 48108
734-994-4000

General Contractor

J.S. Vig Construction
16650 Racho Road
Taylor, Michigan 48180
313-283-3002

Development Schedule

1965	Site purchased
1985	Planning started
1985	Construction started
1987	Leasing started
1991	Phase I completed
2001	Completion expected

Notes

[1] Surface parking and roads.

[2] At year-end 1998, 29 acres (11.7 ha) of paved areas had been completed.

[3] At year-end 1998, 9.5 acres (3.8 ha) of wetlands and water features had been completed.

[4] For a typical four-acre (1.6-ha) site and 30,000-square-foot (2,787-m²) building.

[5] Includes on-site and off-site costs.

[6] Includes steel, masonry, windows, roofing, and so forth.

Beacon Centre

Miami, Florida

Beacon Centre is a 205-acre (83-ha) business park primarily made up of speculative warehouse buildings, but also including office and retail uses. The project uses innovative architecture and extensive landscaping around buildings and parking lots and along major streets to create a parklike atmosphere that is more appealing than that of many warehouse-oriented business parks. The retail component of the project has been used to create amenities for on-site users and to allow the project to be largely self-sufficient. Facilities such as restaurants, banks, and office products stores serve the daily needs of Beacon Centre's workers and tenants and nearby businesses.

While acknowledging the inherent orientation of this kind of development toward industry and transport, the developer has succeeded in creating a pleasurable working environment that sets a high standard for the area and for warehouse-oriented business parks in general.

Site and Development Process

The south Florida area has become an important base from which international companies move goods and services to and from South America. Miami International Airport's cargo facility is a major center of international trade activity, and Beacon Centre, located just west of the airport, is well positioned to tap the region's international trade market. The project's proximity to the airport and the flexibility it offers for combining corporate offices with warehouse/distribution space are enticing features to tenants engaged in international trade.

The site is rectangular in shape and is bordered by arterial roads carrying local traffic. To the north is 25th Street (a major corridor for truck traffic); to the west is 87th Avenue (a major north/south artery); and to the east are bulk storage facilities. Directly to the south is the East West Expressway (State Road 836), which provides easy and quick access to the airport and to Route 826, a major north/south expressway.

The development partnership and plan have evolved considerably since the land was first acquired in the late 1960s by Benenson Realty Company and the Tisch Family Interest. In 1987, a new ownership partnership replaced Arvida Corporation as the developer partner. The new developer partner was the Codina Bush Group, which is now called the Codina Group, a full-service real estate firm made up of several operating companies, including Codina Development, Codina Construction, Codina Realty Services, and Codina Real Estate Management.

When it came on board, the Codina Group took a fresh look at the project, which had originally been planned primarily for office uses, and developed a new concept emphasizing warehouse and distribution space. It also reconceptualized the Village at Beacon Centre, shifting from a focus on specialty and boutique shops to a focus on service retail stores catering to the daily needs of employees and tenants in the park and surrounding area.

After reviewing the market and demand, the developer came up with several key objectives: 1) create an aesthetically pleasing architectural style, 2) pay special attention to landscaping, which would add value to the land, and 3) segregate truck and auto traffic.

Planning and Design

The plan is based on a simple framework of internal roads that connect with and blend into the surrounding grid of streets. By maintaining the fabric of the surrounding street grid, the plan makes locating internal building addresses easy. Moreover, by adhering to the property's rectilinear geometry, the plan maximizes land use efficiency and parcel size flexibility. The internal road framework—with 84th Avenue (also called Beacon Centre Boulevard) as the spine—channels project traffic efficiently.

Five major entry points—each with major entry and identity features—funnel truck traffic to its destinations with minimal impact on retail and office areas.

The plan segregates uses. Retail is located on the front of the site at the southern end. Warehouse uses occupy the center of the site. And office, showroom, and retail uses are located on the northern and western edges. The plan also pays special attention to the aesthetic treatment of the leading edge of the warehouse zone. By containing truck traffic, screening loading docks within the zone, and placing smaller-scale, build-to-suit buildings in front of the larger bulk storage structures, designers made this edge an effective transition zone that has sustained significantly higher square-foot land values for adjacent retail and office sites.

The flex/warehouse buildings themselves generally feature 10 to 15 percent office space in the front and warehouse facilities in the rear. Most are located along 84th Avenue and have truck loading facilities either at the rear of the buildings or in truck courts that run perpendicular to 84th Avenue. In many cases, warehouse buildings are arranged back to back, with shared loading dock areas served by cross-access easements. This results in a public street/service alley arrangement that minimizes visual and acoustical conflicts between adjoining front-of-house and back-of-house operations.

John Gillan

The warehouse buildings are of tilt-up concrete construction and include simple decorative features, corner towers, attractive signage, colorful awnings, and other interesting architectural elements. The first buildings had 22-foot (6.7-m) clear heights, but most of the later buildings have 24-foot (7.3-m) clear heights. Roofs are made of lightweight concrete for hurricane protection. All buildings are painted a salmon color and designed in keeping with the southeast Florida style pioneered by Addison Mizner. Most of the buildings were designed by Bruce Retzsch Architects of Boca Raton, Florida.

Rigorous landscape standards require that the seams between buildings and parking and between parking and the street be heavily landscaped, with a border of shade and street trees and hedges where appropriate. Streets and roads are all heavily landscaped, especially 84th Avenue and N.W. 17th Street, both of which include planted medians.

Situated on the southeast corner of the site, the Village at Beacon Centre is a convenience retail center that includes a travel agency, quick printer, dentist, gas station, medical clinic/diagnostic center, and a variety of restaurants and business services. Offices are located on the second level. The most recent portion of the project to be developed is another retail facility on the southern end—the Plaza Center—a power center featuring Wal-Mart, OfficeMax, Circuit City, and Sam's Club.

Marketing and Management

Most of the buildings in the project, which currently is 94 percent occupied, have been built on speculation. Beacon Centre has been successful in attracting both new entrants to the market and tenants from nearby projects. Prospects seeking out the project have been the source of much of the leasing, but some activity has been generated also by mailings to prospects by Standard Industrial

Beacon Centre combines attractive architecture and extensive landscaping to create an exemplary business environment.

The Panalpina Building is a build-to-suit distribution facility.

A multitenant, rear-loading warehouse facility features freestanding exterior panels to add architectural interest.

The front of Warehouse Building 5.

Classification code and by zip code. Codina Realty Services, one of the operating companies of the Codina Group, handles leasing.

Warehouse tenants in the project range from computer companies to freight forwarders to flower importers. Buildings are leased both to domestic and foreign companies, including Merisel, Sextant Avionique, DTK, TNT, Kuehne & Nagel, LEP Profit, Black & Decker, Acer Latin America, ADI (Ademco), Aerotek, Techdata, CHS Electronics, Circuit City, Eastman Kodak, IBC, Shell Oil, Virgin Atlantic, and DHL. Before it will lease space, the developer requires financial statements from each potential tenant.

Some of the best years for the project occurred during the recession of the early 1990s. Because of a sewer moratorium, supply was constrained in the market and the approval process was lengthy. Speculative building was not only possible but desirable, for it was the only way to ensure that product could be made available within a

reasonable time frame. Warehouse rents currently are $6.75 to $7.75 per square foot, the highest warehouse rates in the market.

Codina Real Estate Management manages the property. Security is provided 24 hours a day by Wackenhut Corporation in the form of a roving patrol.

Experience Gained
- Industrial buildings can be an attractive addition to the urban environment if developed sensitively. Innovative yet cost-effective architecture and artful landscaping can go a long way toward improving the image of warehouse/distribution developments.
- Service retail and restaurants are important amenities even for warehouse-oriented business parks, and can provide a distinct leasing advantage.

Site plan.

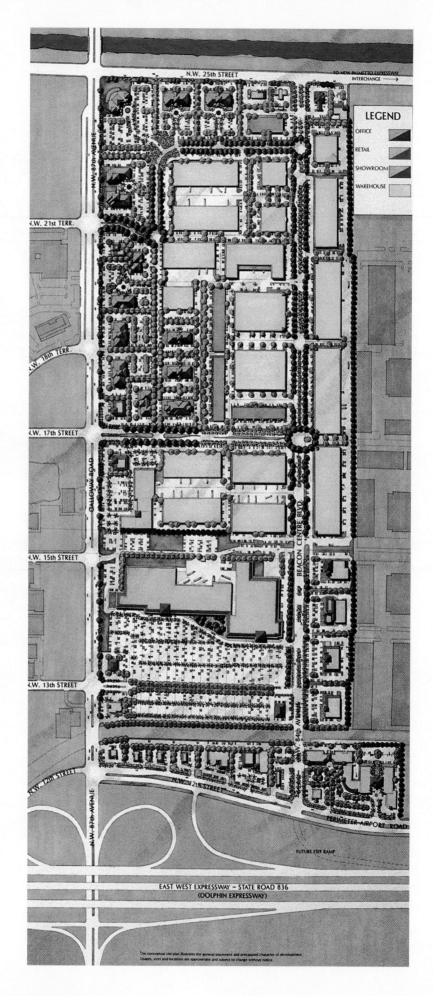

nates the need for individual projects to provide on-site stormwater detention facilities.

Marketing

The development philosophy that if you build it, they will come worked for LakeView. The development offers not only a beautiful setting, but also some of the lowest electric rates in the country and among the lowest business park land prices in metropolitan Chicago, as well as Wisconsin's attractive business taxes. Land values have more than quadrupled, from about $.50 per square foot in 1988 to about $2.25 per square foot in 2000, producing significant gains for initial owners.

Many of the park's tenants are large industrial operations. Before Pleasant Prairie was incorporated as a village, Rust-Oleum committed to the park and later moved its Evanston, Illinois–based production and research facility to a 28-acre (11.3-ha) parcel at LakeView. Manu-Tronics (now known as Sanmina Corporation), a Wisconsin-based firm, was the first company to occupy a facility in the park. The complete responsiveness of WISPARK and state and local entities to their needs gave these two early-bird companies the confidence that the Pleasant Prairie cornfields would indeed become a corporate park.

Companies received incentives from the state for locating in Kenosha County. Rust-Oleum, for example, received $1 million for job training and research and development, which it applied toward the development of an environmentally friendly paint.

A total of 61 companies have located in the park since it opened in July 1988, absorbing almost 55 percent of the land. Among them are SuperValu Stores, Snap-On, and Deluxe Video Services America. Of these companies, 33 percent lease and 67 percent own their facility.

LakeView's primary market is metropolitan Chicago, not Wisconsin. Thirty-two companies have moved to LakeView from Illinois, and six have come in from other states.

WISPARK developed an incubator for small businesses at LakeView, called LakeView Center, which was recently sold to Liberty Property Trust. LakeView Center has graduated several businesses into larger facilities in the park. Unified Solutions, for example, started with 14,000 square feet (1,300 m²) in LakeView Center and has since relocated into a 215,000-square-foot (19,973-m²) facility in LakeView Corporate Park.

Lot sizes for owners and tenants range from four to 150 acres (1.6 to 60.7 ha). Rail links have been important for some of the tenants, including plastic manufacturers for which rail is a cheaper mode of transportation than trucks for the resins they use.

Once a sufficient level of activity was attained, LakeView began attracting service uses that have made it an even more attractive location for its office and industrial tenants. Among the service amenities at LakeView are a daycare facility that can accommodate 240 children, a 120-room Radisson Hotel and Conference Center, a technical college for high school students, a 250,000-square-foot (23,225-m²) outlet mall, 130,000-square-foot (12,077-m²) physical fitness facility, restaurants, and a gas station.

Experience Gained

- Its large, uninterrupted size initially made the site attractive, but this also became a disadvantage in that it made it difficult to inspire a sense of community in the park. However, as the park matured and the developer was able to attract retail and service uses, a sense of community evolved. To reinforce the community aspect of the park, WISPARK publishes and distributes a monthly newsletter on park issues and invites all LakeView tenants to quarterly round-table lunches to give them a chance to meet and socialize.

- Doing it over, the developer might ease the building setback requirements and somewhat reduce the open-space standard. Increases in land values have made obtaining sites more expensive, and the deep setback requirements increase the effective price of land for prospective tenants.

- Cooperation among public sector entities, private sector participants, and the community was essential to the success of the project.

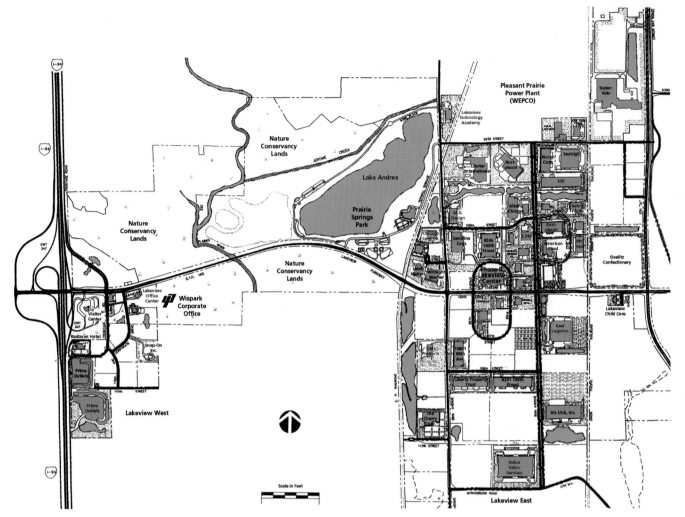

Site plan.

Project Data: LakeView Corporate Park

Land Use Information

Site Area   2,290 acres (926 ha)

Gross Building Area (GBA)

	Square Feet (m²) Completed[1]	Square Feet (m²) at Buildout[2]
Office	199,472 (18,530)	500,000 (46,450)
Manufacturing/warehouse/industrial	6,663,033 (618,995)	13,800,000 (1,282,020)
R&D	0	100,000 (9,290)
Retail	375,895 (34,920)	600,000 (55,740)
Hotel	83,000 (7,710)	100,000 (9,290)
Total	7,321,400 (680,158)	15,100,000 (1,402,790)

Number of Buildings

Completed[1]	50
At Buildout[2]	110

Land Use Plan

	Acres (ha)	Percent of Site
Office	100 (40.4)	4.4%
Industrial	1,500 (607)	65.5
Retail	70 (28.3)	3.1
Retention/landscape/roadways	195 (78.9)	8.5
Nature Conservancy land	425 (172)	18.6
Total	2,290 (926)	100.0%

Tenant Information

Occupied Net Rentable Area (NRA)   95%

Average Annual Rent

Office	$8.50–15 per square foot ($91.50–160/m²)
Warehouse/industrial	$3.75–4.50 per square foot ($40–50/m²)

Average Length of Lease   5–10 years

Typical Terms of Lease   triple net

Typical Tenant Sizes

	Square Feet (m²)
Office	10,000 (929)
Small warehouse/industrial	35,000 (3,251)
Large warehouse/industrial	200,000 (1,858)

Development Cost Information

Building construction[3]	$211,000,000
Infrastructure investment[4]	64,000,000
Total	$275,000,000

Developer/Owner

WISPARK Corporation
10211 Corporate Drive, Suite 100
Pleasant Prairie, Wisconsin 53158
262-857-4661

Engineer and Land Planner

STS Consultants
11425 West Lake Drive
Milwaukee, Wisconsin 53224
414-359-3030

Consultant

North American Realty Advisory Services
    (formerly Security Pacific Realty Advisory Services)
100 Park Avenue, 19th Floor
New York, New York 10017
212-883-0500

Development Schedule

1976–1989	Site purchased
1985	Planning started
1988	Construction started
1991	Phase I completed
2010	Projected buildout

Notes

[1] As of mid-1999.

[2] 2010.

[3] Includes the cost of constructing owner-built facilities.

[4] Includes infrastructure development spending by the developer and public entities.

Meridian Business Campus
Aurora, Illinois

CMD-Midwest assembled and acquired the land for Meridian Business Campus in the early 1970s, intending to develop a traditional industrial park. By the time sites were ready for development, however, the industrial market had changed, and, in the early 1980s, CMD retained the SWA Group to completely redesign the project.

The development strategy pursued by CMD and continued by the RREEF Funds, a San Francisco–based pension fund advisory firm that acquired the property from CMD in 1992, has combined several key principles: multiple uses, phased development, a flexible master plan, and flexible buildings designed to accommodate a variety of uses. The project's success is also due to the SWA master plan and landscape design, which have given Meridian Business Campus a high-profile image and public open space amenities (including parks and lakes) that have attracted prestigious clients and community support.

Development and Financing
CMD got its start early in the 20th century in Chicago as a pioneer developer of industrial districts—the 200-acre (80.9-ha) Central Manufacturing/Original East District (1902) and the 80-acre (32.3-ha) Pershing Road District (1916). By the late 1960s, CMD was developing industrial parks in suburban areas, and, in the early 1970s, the company purchased and consolidated several farms near the Chicago suburb of Aurora in what would become known as the I-88 Research Corridor—now home to AT&T, Amoco Research, Lucent Technologies, and the Fermi National Accelerator Laboratory, among other operations.

CMD thought that the best use of the 660 acres (267 ha) would be a traditional industrial park. A Burlington Northern Railroad line bordered the northern edge of the site; an Elgin-Joliet Eastern Railroad line bordered the western edge; and Illinois Route 59, a major trucking corridor, adjoined the eastern edge.

The company built a street, extended sewer and water service into the property, subdivided it, named the project Liberty Industrial Park, and put the industrial lots on the market in 1981. Nothing happened.

Not only was the project hampered by its distance from Chicago, but also the market had changed during the nearly ten years it had taken to bring water and sewer pipes to the site. Industrial tenants no longer needed rail access. Furthermore, Liberty Industrial Park came to the market in the midst of a recession when demand for industrial space was low—and plenty of nonrail industrial land was available. According to a 1981 study by Real Estate Research Corporation (RERC), 2,300 acres

(930.8 ha) of industrial land was potentially available within five miles (8 km) of the site.

Based on RERC's recommendations, CMD decided to differentiate its project from the competition by repositioning it as an upscale business campus that would serve light industrial/warehouse, high-tech, and office tenants. The property would be given a high-profile image that would add competitive value to the project and a new name: Meridian Business Campus

CMD hired the Sausalito, California–based SWA Group, a land planning and landscape architecture firm, to restructure the property into a campus setting. The developer wanted a flexible land plan that would accommodate multiple and flexible land uses. SWA was asked to establish an image for the campus through a plan for common area landscaping and amenities and to prepare landscaping and building design guidelines for the development of individual parcels.

Initially, CMD developed Meridian Business Campus using its own cash to develop the land and to construct the buildings. Long-term financing was obtained for each completed building upon lease-up, and this money was used to construct subsequent buildings.

Between 1985 and 1990, the project thrived. More than 1 million square feet (92,900 m²) of building space was developed, much of it speculative. But, in 1990, CMD abandoned its conservative financial strategy and, on the eve of an economic recession, overleveraged the property with a participating mortgage made by RREEF. The recession was compounded by significant overbuilding in the industrial and business park market; vacancies at Meridian Business Campus grew and new speculative buildings stood empty. By 1992, the project's cash flow was insufficient to cover the mortgage interest payments.

RREEF took over the project from CMD at the end of 1992, at the bottom of the market. Lacking a development background, the firm hired Brian L. Rieger, who had been president of CMD-Midwest, to oversee the completion of the campus. The project recovered. By 1994, the tenant-occupied buildings enjoyed a 92 percent occupancy rate, and the next phase of land improvements was underway. RREEF completed the final phase of land improvements, and, in 1998, more than 4 million square feet (371,600 m²) of space was in place. In 1999, four new buildings totaling 250,000 square feet (23,225 m²) broke ground. Duke Realty of Indianapolis acquired Meridian in February 1999.

Meridian Business Campus has succeeded through two tumultuous decades by combining multiple uses,

The 660-acre (267-ha) Meridian Business Campus accommodates office, warehouse/industrial, R&D, and retail uses.

phased development, and a flexible master plan with flexible buildings—a combination that has helped attract and retain high-quality tenants over the long term and for the long term. The outlook for Meridian Business Campus seems assured. The project is well known and respected within the market. The land planning and design elements have added value to the property far in excess of the cost of improvements. Continued strict enforcement of the design guidelines will help keep the master-planning concept intact.

Land Planning

A flat midwestern landscape of cornfields and hedgerows was the raw material from which SWA was challenged to create a landscape that would help create a sense of place, be an emblem of the region, and reveal and glorify the beauty of the native prairie.

The stormwater management system became the organizing land planning element. Instead of reserving open space on each parcel for stormwater detention purposes, the plan called for transferring the detention requirements to common areas on the site. Six lakes, ranging in size from five acres to ten acres (2 to 4 ha), were constructed, and open space was consolidated into several significant pieces around these lakes, giving the site a green backbone and Meridian's tenants and surrounding community an open-space amenity. Three of the lakes, arranged in a chain, channel runoff from a 1,500-acre (607-ha) watershed freely and safely through Meridian

Business Campus. These lakes have been integrated with a trail system that forms a linear park for the community and links the business park to a commuter-rail station and nearby residential areas.

Transferring stormwater detention requirements from the individual parcels to the centralized lakes made it possible to create a more flexible land plan. The master plan divided the property into four flexible use zones—office, light industrial/warehouse, high-tech, and retail—and called for phased development running from west to east. The initial development would be for the existing industrial market, preserving the eastern portion of the campus for office use if and when the office market matured. "Basically," says Rieger, "we saved the best land for last to get the maximum value from it."

The first 130 acres (52.6 ha) was developed south of Liberty Street, a two-lane east/west regional road. One goal of this first phase was to demonstrate the intended quality of the land planning and development of the overall campus. Liberty Street was upgraded to a four-lane, median-divided parkway, and monumental-scale signage was created. The first lake was constructed and landscaped to create a park area. Streets and intersections were landscaped.

Manufacturing and industrial uses occupy the campus's western and southern lots, while higher-profile corporate facilities line Liberty Street. The Tech Center, a multitenant complex, provides an easy and attractive transition between the warehouse and the office zones.

The landscape design provides a green backbone that has both functional and aesthetic value.

The campus's front door and main high-image road is Meridian Parkway, an east/west thoroughfare that has been richly landscaped. It serves to separate uses: office buildings on one side and high-tech and flex space on the other side. Running north/south, Commons Drive separates manufacturing and warehouse zones located west of the road from transitional and office building zones to the east. Retail uses front Route 59, the most visible edge of the campus. The lots along Route 59 were originally intended for hotel and office uses, but retail growth out from Fox Valley Shopping Center to the south reached Meridian first and the hotel market never matured.

The master plan's use zones were deliberately flexible, allowing the developer to modify them depending on market demand. If the high-tech market was booming and light industrial was not, the high-tech zone would be expanded into the light industrial zone and the light industrial zone contracted accordingly. The landscape design helped to make such shifting of zones unproblematic. For example, uniform landscape easements and berms screen parcels from the roads, allowing high-image office areas to be located near light industrial uses without downgrading the overall character of the office areas. The plan also permitted lot sizes to be changed to meet market demand and to accommodate tenant expansion needs. In 1995, for example, Time Warner wanted 40.8 acres (16.5 ha), so a 40.8-acre (16.5-ha) site was created and streets were laid out to accommodate this user's building design and future growth plans.

The campus's landscaping guidelines are fairly detailed, specifying, for example, one large tree for every 375 square feet (34.8 m²) of landscaped area, or two rows of a specified hedge shrub on the landscape easement along a parking lot. Building setbacks range from 35 feet to 70 feet (10.6 to 21.3 m). Landscape easements along streets range from a width of 25 feet (7.6 m) on culs-de-sac and secondary streets to 70 feet (21.3 m) on Commons Drive. Other landscaping elements that unify Meridian Business Campus and help create its strong identity in the marketplace include continuous four-foot-tall (1.2-m) berms that run from lot to lot and across property lines, hedge backdrops that screen parking lots and service areas, and large trees.

The design guidelines for the individual parcels succeed in creating a seamless transition from business uses to public and recreational uses, inviting the campus's employees to enjoy the outside. The public streetscapes, entries, and lake areas were all designed by SWA. The landscaping appears lush, an effect that was achieved cost-effectively by initial installations of large amounts of relatively small plant materials that over time matured into a rich landscape.

Building Design

Six of the 38 buildings that had been developed by 1999 were developed on a speculative basis. These six buildings, ranging in size from 11,000 to 92,000 square feet (1,022 to 8,546 m²)—and currently in both single-tenant and multitenant uses—are designed to be flexible enough to accommodate a wide variety of uses and to be adaptable to changes in the marketplace. A flexible building is a building that can easily accommodate changes in use, whether the need for such change comes from the operational needs of an existing tenant or from a change in tenants. A flexible building should be able to serve as a light industrial building, or a warehouse, or a service center, or a showroom, or even an office building—with just a few changes required in going from one use to another.

Light industrial firms, for example, generally place their assembly or manufacturing uses in the rear of the building and set aside a corner of the front of the building for office use. Some of the speculative buildings designed for light industrial uses at Meridian Business Campus include windows along two and sometimes even three exterior walls, a feature that makes it easy for existing tenants to expand their office-using functions or for tenants with higher office use requirements to move in.

The project's spec buildings are furnished with mechanical, power, and communications systems that can be reconfigured easily to accommodate tenant changes and expansions. The multitenant buildings provide loading docks and other facilities and services that can be shared.

Most of Meridian's flexible buildings allocate four or five parking spaces per 1,000 square feet (100 m²) of building space, rather than the 2.5 or three spaces more typical for flex or high-tech buildings in industrial

Many of the buildings at Meridian are designed to be flexible and adaptable to a shifting market.

parks. More parking spaces enable more office uses in buildings.

The spec buildings come in a wide variety of sizes, enabling Meridian to retain its tenants as they grow or contract. Engineering Systems Inc. (ESI), a forensic engineering consulting firm and laboratory, is a prime example. The company began life in 1987 with three principals and five associates, at which time it took 600 unpartitioned square feet (55.7 m²) in the multitenant

Tech Center while it was still being built out. Subsequently, ESI moved into 4,500 square feet (418 m²) in the same building, three-quarters of which was office space and one-quarter of which was a high-bay laboratory area. After a year, ESI needed additional space and expanded into an adjacent 2,000 or so square feet (185 m²). When after several years ESI outgrew its space again, it found a five-acre (2-ha) site across the street, subdivided it, and constructed an 18,623-square-foot (1,730-m²) headquar-

Three of the development's lakes have been integrated with a trail system that forms a linear park for the community and links the business park to a commuter rail station and nearby residential areas.

ters building on three acres (1.2 ha). By 1999, ESI had once again outgrown its space, and once again it leased space in the Tech Center across the street, this time as a temporary annex while it constructed additional space on its remaining 1.5 acres (0.6 ha). The last expansion was facilitated by Meridian's giving ESI permission to tunnel under the street to install a dedicated telephone line and data-link connection between the ESI annex and headquarters.

Marketing

After SWA redesigned Meridian Business Campus in the early 1980s, CMD targeted and courted the brokerage community in its marketing program. The developer also allocated a significant part of the marketing budget to advertising and set up a sales/marketing office and show-room in the Tech Center. A scale model of the campus was built to help prospective tenants and buyers visualize its development. It was felt that high-quality marketing materials were essential for establishing the image of the project.

The public and civic sectors were helpful in marketing. JVC, a *Fortune* 500 company that purchased a 12-acre (4.8-ha) site in 1990 for a 225,000-square-foot (20,902-m²) showroom/warehouse plus enough land to expand the warehouse, was contacted before closing by the city of Aurora's Economic Development Commission and the chamber of commerce—both agencies wanting to know what they could do to help the company move in. And after closing, they were quite helpful too, says a company executive.

In the late 1980s, Burlington Northern Railroad selected the northeast corner of Meridian Business Campus as the location for a new commuter train station, making the campus the only master-planned industrial and office park within the I-88 Research Corridor that is directly served by commuter rail. This unexpected dividend connected the site not only to the western suburbs but also to downtown Chicago.

By the time RREEF took over the project in late 1992, it was well established, so the marketing program was scaled back. As a proven location, Meridian Business Campus was basically selling itself.

By 1999, 120 acres (48.5 ha) remained for disposition, divisible into parcels of any size, with the largest remaining contiguous lot being 23 acres (9.3 ha). By the late 1990s, office demand had become a genuine market. In 1998, Hamilton Partners purchased land to build two 75,000-square-foot (6,967-m²), two-story office buildings. Rieger says that RREEF expects more office and R&D development and less industrial development in the early years of the current decade. In the late 1990s, the lakefront sites on the eastern edge of the property were opened for development.

One strategy the developer adopted for reserving land for a future office market was to seek high-quality interim uses that would help carry the land. In 1995, for example, the Michael Jordan Golf Company leased 30 lakefront acres (12.1 ha) in the eastern third of the property for a golf range and teaching center. When the lease expires in 2005, the office market should be strong enough to develop the parcel for office uses.

Experience Gained

- Transferring open space requirements from individual parcels to consolidated common areas and landscape easements gives a business park a focus (or a sense of place) that adds value and attracts higher-end tenants. It also means that each parcel can be developed more efficiently and densely.

- If a business park is planned to serve a variety of tenants—such as light industrial, warehouse, office, and high-tech firms—it will be able to draw from the other tenant markets when one or another of these segments suffers a downturn. In a multiuse park, some buildings should be designed specifically to be an easy and attractive transition between different use

The master plan called for transferring stormwater detention requirements for each parcel to common areas on the site, allowing for the creation of an open space amenity made up of six constructed lakes with open space consolidated around them.

Two roads—Meridian Parkway and Commons Drive—divide the campus into four separate use zones, which are deliberately flexible to enable the business park to accommodate market demand over time.

Starting with relatively small plant materials that matured over time was a cost-efficient way to achieve a lush landscape.

zones, such as between a warehouse zone and an office zone.

• Flexibility—a flexible master plan with flexible land uses and flexible buildings—is the key to retaining tenants and profitably serving the ever-changing marketplace over the long term. Flexibility can be maximized by good road planning, master-plan zoning, landscape design that makes different adjacent uses compatible, and smart phasing. The zoning system should allow changes in land uses depending on the market. Lot sizes should be adjustable to meet market demand and tenants' growth needs. The first phase that is built should strive to convey the intended image of the whole development. Phasing at Meridian Business Campus led to a retail component, a use that had not been considered in the original master plan.

• Parking for flex or warehouse buildings should be allocated at five or six spaces per 1,000 square feet

(100 m²) of building, so that the building is also marketable to office users.

• A business park needs to stand out from the crowd in order to secure long-term success. Among the elements that add value to a business park development are attractive landscaping and building design as well as amenities like parks, streams, lakes, and playing fields that serve the people who work in the park and those who live in the surrounding community.

• A business park should be designed contextually, so that it reflects the architecture of the area and the natural environment.

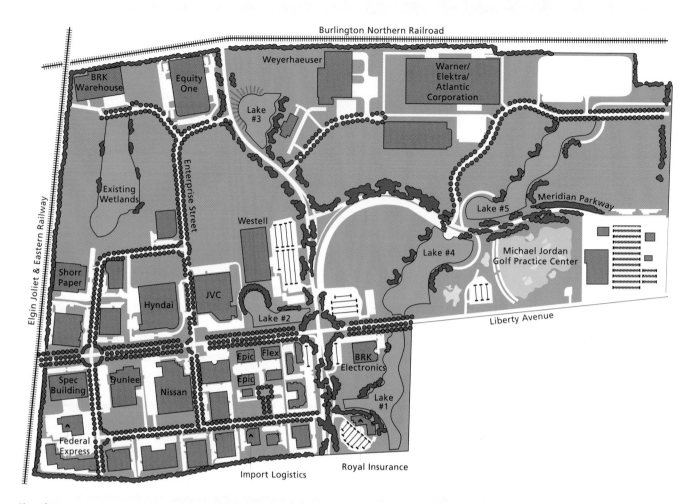

Site plan.

Project Data: Meridian Business Campus

Land Use Information

Site Area   660 acres (267 ha)

Gross Building Area (GBA)

	Square Feet (m²)
Office	487,359 (45,275)
Warehouse/industrial	3,309,605 (307,462)
R&D	115,187 (10,703)
Retail	150,216 (13,955)
Total	4,062,367 (377,393)

Number of Buildings   38

Land Use Plan

	Acres (ha)	Percent of Site
Buildings	321 (129.9)	48.6%
Lakes	53 (21.4)	8.0
Golf range	30 (12.1)	4.6
Other uses[1]	256 (103.6)	38.8
Total	660 (267.1)	100.0%

Tenant Information

Occupied net rentable area (NRA)	90%
Number of tenants	47

Developer

(1992 and earlier)
CMD-Midwest
Chicago, Illinois

(after 1992)
RREEF
101 California Street
San Francisco, California 94111
415-781-3300

Owner

Duke-Weeks Realty Corporation
600 East 96th Street, Suite 100
Indianapolis, Indiana 46240
317-808-6000

Land Planner

SWA Group
2200 Bridgeway Boulevard
Sausalito, California 94966-5904
415-332-5100

Civil Engineer

Robert H. Anderson
220 West River Drive
St. Charles, Illinois 60174
630-584-3530

Development Schedule

Early 1970s	Site assembled
Early 1980s	Project redesigned
1990	Total space reaches 1 million square feet (92,900 m²)
1992	Project foreclosed
1998	Total space reaches 4 million square feet (371,600 m²)
1999	Remaining sites opened for building

Note

[1] Includes parks, roads, parking, and undeveloped areas.

O'Hare Express Center

Chicago, Illinois

Constructed on the grounds of Chicago's O'Hare International Airport, O'Hare Express Center functions primarily as a transshipment facility at which cargo containers flown into O'Hare are received, broken down, and reassembled into pallets—which are, in turn, loaded onto trucks for delivery throughout the central United States. The containers come into O'Hare on jumbo jets. They are off-loaded at the airport's south cargo area and ferried by "tug-cars" to O'Hare Express Center over a road built on airport property for the transshipment facility and dedicated for the exclusive use of its tenants. In reverse, the process is similar. Goods trucked to O'Hare Express are put on pallets, the pallets are assembled into containers, and the containers are tugged to the south cargo ramps and loaded onto 747s for long-distance and overseas deliveries.

Goods received at O'Hare Express—which range from computer parts to clothes to the occasional racehorse or racecar—typically remain in its warehouses for fewer than 48 hours and sometimes for fewer than 24. A small amount of long-term storage is maintained for companies that wish to keep spare parts or other items available for quick shipment to their customers.

Development Process

The O'Hare Express Center is located at the southeast corner of the airport, where it fronts on two of the airport's perimeter roads. The 50-acre (20.2-ha) site is part of a 150-acre (61-ha) collateral land area that is held by the airport to buffer surrounding development. The course of a creek running through the relatively flat site had to be relocated to provide buildable pads for the project.

In the late 1980s, the city of Chicago decided to develop the site known as Parcel 19. A group of Chicago-area investors leased the site, on which they attempted—unsuccessfully—to develop office buildings. The market demand for airfreight facilities and the site's suitability for such a use eventually became apparent. Prentiss Properties took over the project in the early 1990s and brought in Michael Mullin from CenterPoint Properties as project manager, based on his experience in airfreight development projects.

By 1994, the feasibility of the project was established and CenterPoint Properties, which had become the controlling developer, began negotiations to buy out the partnership holding the Parcel 19 lease. The most significant aspect of the negotiations, according to Mullin, concerned the commitment on the part of various city agencies to having a road built inside the airport to link the proposed cargo facility to the existing South Cargo Terminal. Having access to an airfreight facility so close to the airport was an important advantage to shippers only if they could avoid having to compete with—and worry about—local traffic. (Moreover, full-size containers, which are up to 16 feet (4.8 m) wide, are not permitted on public roadways.) Getting stuck in traffic and missing a shipping facility's lockout time, typically 3:30 p.m., can seriously upset just-in-time delivery schedules, which are increasingly common. Often a driver on such a schedule who has been locked out in Chicago will have to haul the shipment to New York City for the next available jet. A further benefit of the internal road is that it allows O'Hare Express Center to set its lockout time at 4:30 p.m., giving it a major advantage in the airfreight business.

The plans for O'Hare Express were subject to review by a long list of city, state, and federal agencies. In due diligence testing, the developer discovered buried 55-gallon (230-l) drums that were leaking contaminants into the subsurface soils, a condition that necessitated review by the U.S. Environmental Protection Agency. The Federal Aviation Administration had to pass on such design issues as the height of equipment on rooftops, the reflectivity of roof finishes, tree species used in landscaping (FAA's concern is how attractive the trees are to birds), signage, and facility security. Facility security was of concern also to the city of Chicago's police and aviation departments. Security concerns required that barbed wire be installed around the new road and that staffed checkpoints be installed at both ends of the road. The project proceeded through the regulatory maze relatively smoothly and quickly, thanks in part, according to Mullin, to the active involvement of CenterPoint's development partner, the Chicago Department of Aviation, and the department commissioner, Mary Rose Loney.

Planning and Design

Six office/warehouse structures are planned for O'Hare Express for a total 945,000 square feet (87,790 m²); five of them are completed. The structures resemble large distribution warehouses with some significant variations based on the requirements of the airfreight business. The completed buildings range in size from 121,000 to 215,000 square feet (11,240 to 19,973 m²). The buildings typically are steel-frame, post-and-beam structures with precast concrete exterior walls. The typical bay is approximately 40 feet (12.2 m) wide by 40 to 48 feet (12.2 to 14.6 m) deep, providing as much unobstructed floor area as is economically possible.

The DHL building at the 50-acre (20.2-ha) O'Hare Express Center, the first privately developed facility permitted at Chicago's O'Hare International Airport. The O'Hare Express Center represents an advance in public/private partnering for airport-related industrial development.

The buildings have superflat concrete floors. The extreme flatness is achieved by using a laser screed to level the floors. Superflat floors allow warehouse operators to stack goods higher than they could on ordinary floors. The floors at O'Hare Express are poured on raised pads constructed of compacted earth, putting them at the height of a standard truck bed.

The typical ceiling height is 24 feet (7.3 m). The roofs are flat, with single-ply roofing set over a concrete deck built on metal decking. An early-suppression/fast-response sprinkler system coupled with a guarantee of rapid response by the fire department provides fire protection.

The amount of space devoted to office functions differentiates the buildings at O'Hare Express from other warehouses. In a typical warehouse project, 5 to 7 percent of the total space may be used for offices. Airfreight shipping and receiving is associated with a high level of paperwork, and to accommodate the office aspects of the transshipping business, from 16 to 26 percent of the area of each building at O'Hare Express is office space.

The large amount of space allocated for loading docks also differentiates the warehouses at O'Hare Express from other warehouses. This project needs significantly more loading space than traditional facilities because of the quick turnaround times. Forty-three loading docks are provided in Building B2, for example, amounting to one dock per 3,000 square feet (278.7 m²) of warehouse space. The O'Hare Express buildings have cross-dock loading —loading on opposite sides of the warehouse—which

allows for better use of the space and a faster turnaround of goods. The cross-dock design also makes it easier to divide up the space for multiple tenants.

With a floor/area ratio of approximately 0.25, O'Hare Express Center has a lower development density than typical warehouse projects, which have FARs ranging from 0.4 to 0.5. This lower density is a consequence of higher parking requirements as well as the requirements for truck-access facilities to serve the additional loading docks. The large amount of office space in the O'Hare Express buildings necessitates providing more parking spaces than typical warehouses would need, and 874 spaces were provided for the first four buildings.

In structure and building systems, each building in the project is like the others. At the same time, each building has been given its own identity, principally through the articulation of the office spaces attached to the warehouses and through signage and color.

Financing and Ownership

O'Hare Express Center was developed as a cooperative venture between the city of Chicago and CenterPoint Properties. The project is built on public land leased to the developer for 60 years. The city facilitated the financing of the project's $63 million development cost by issuing $55 million in tax-exempt airport revenue bonds. The city also constructed the internal road, which was paid for by the developer.

The project developer officially is CenterPoint O'Hare LLC, an Illinois limited liability company whose membership interest is owned by CenterPoint Properties Corporation (95 percent) and O'Hare Tech Center Associates LP (5 percent). The latter entity is a carryover from the original ground-lease lessee.

CenterPoint Properties, a publicly traded real estate investment trust, is the largest owner and developer of industrial property in the Chicago region. Its portfolio includes approximately 25 million square feet (2,322,500 m²) of industrial space, and its total market capitalization exceeds $1 billion. The company's activities include renovation of warehouse/industrial facilities as well as new construction, redevelopment, property management, and investment.

In contrast to the relatively easy permitting process, assembling the financing package was a complicated undertaking. Airport-owned facilities traditionally are financed with tax-exempt credit. For this project to qualify

for tax-exempt financing, its ownership had to revert to the city at the end of the 60-year ground lease.

The bond issue provided $55 million at 5 percent interest, with an initial term of 35 years that is extendable to 60 years. Principal and interest are repaid from a portion of tenant rents and are guaranteed by a letter of credit from First Chicago NBD (now BancOne). The letter of credit is backed by CenterPoint Properties. The financing is a revenue bond, not a general obligation of the city of Chicago, and the bond is not secured by the real estate. This was the first unsecured tax-exempt financing completed by a REIT, says Paul Fisher, chief financial officer of CenterPoint Properties, adding that the ability to obtain this financing hinged on the developer's strength— its experience in airfreight development, its deep client roster, and its investment-grade debt ratings.

For its part in the financing partnership, the developer agreed to take down parcels faster than originally

The center's buildings were designed with cross-dock loading—loading on opposite sides of the warehouse—to allow for better use of space and faster turnaround of goods. The cross-dock design also facilitates subdividing the space for multiple tenants.

Though similar in structure and building systems, each of the buildings at O'Hare Express Center achieves its own identity through the articulation of the office spaces attached to the warehouses and through the use of color and signage.

A secure road built inside the airport links the O'Hare Express Center directly to the existing South Cargo Terminal, providing a competitive advantage for firms locating in the center.

required, thus accelerating the start of cash flow to the city. The faster schedule also meant that jobs would be created sooner, providing another benefit to the city in return for having contributed its bonding capabilities. Also, the city could build its image as a business-friendly locale through its participation in the public/private partnership that developed O'Hare Express Center.

Leasing

The execution of the master plan for O'Hare Express Center has proceeded with varying degrees of involvement by the end users. The first building (A1), a 138,000-square-foot (12,820-m²) structure completed in 1996, was a build-to-suit for Burlington Air Express. The second (A2), a 121,000-square-foot (11,241-m²) spec building completed in 1997, was leased to its two tenants—Air Canada and DHL Worldwide Express—before completion, and modifications were made to suit the tenants. The third building (B1), a 172,000-square-foot (19,973.5-m²) structure completed in 1997, also was begun without a signed tenant. Shortly after ground breaking, Alliance Airlines, a cargo service company, leased the entire building. Alliance in turn subleases space to several smaller cargo carriers, including Iberia and Korean Air.

The fourth and fifth buildings (B2 and C1) were completed in late fall 1998. Building B2 is shared by two tenants, Alliance Airlines and British Airways. The 215,000-square-foot (20,000-m²) Building C1 is leased by the U.S. Postal Service. The final building of the master plan (C2) will replace a small existing structure in the final phase of the project.

With its prime location and private road access to O'Hare's jet ramps, the space commands rents in the range of $10 to $12 per square foot ($108–130/m²), comparing very favorably with rents of $6 to $7 ($65–75/m²) outside the airport—and less favorably with rents of $22 to $30 ($237–323/m²) at the South Cargo Terminal, which has its own jet ramps. Leases at O'Hare Express have terms of five to 15 years and are triple net

with the exception of the roof, which is maintained by the owner.

Experience Gained

- The long-term outlook for airfreight facilities as a building type appears bright. The increasing reliance of suppliers and manufacturers on just-in-time production systems should spur demand for short-term storage facilities like O'Hare Express Center. The spread of the just-in-time mentality to the retail sector adds fuel to this demand.

- Airfreight facilities based on short-term goods storage are a hybrid type of industrial building, needing more office space and more loading facilities than traditional warehouses. A project like O'Hare Express Center "can't have enough truck docks," says Mullin, and the closer and more direct the links to the jet ramps, the better.

- Public/private partnerships are a logical model for the development of airfreight facilities. Typically, airports are long on land and short on cash, and airport buffer lands are ideal for such projects. Further, given the usual complexity of the approval process for development of land adjacent to airports, the locality's active support and participation in the project can be critical. And finally, public sector participation in the financing can lower the development cost and strengthen the feasibility of the undertaking.

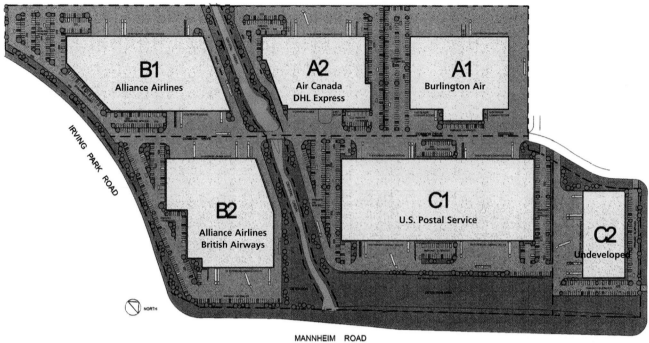

Site plan.

Project Data: O'Hare Express Center

Land Use Information

Site Area

Site Area	50 acres (20.2 ha)

Gross Building Area

	Phase I	At Buildout
	Square Feet (m²)	Square Feet (m²)
Office	129,608 (12,040.5)	235,926 (21,917.5)
Warehouse/industrial	454,393 (42,213)	709,379 (65,901)
Total	584,001 (54,253.6)	945,305 (87,818)

Number of Buildings

	Phase I	At Buildout
Number of Buildings	4	6

Parking (all surface)

	Phase I	At Buildout
Parking (all surface)	874 spaces	1,045 spaces

Land Use Plan

	Acres (ha)	Percent of Site
Buildings	22 (8.9)	44%
Paved[1] and landscaped areas	28 (11.3)	56
Total	50 (20.2)	100%

Tenant Information

Occupied Net Rentable Area (NRA)	100%
Average Annual Rent[2]	$10–12 per square foot ($108–130/m²)
Average Length of Lease	10–15 years
Typical Terms of Lease	triple net (excluding roof)
Typical Tenant Size	120,000–150,000 square feet (11,148–13,935 m²)
Typical Space in Office Uses	16–26%

Major Tenants

Building	Tenant	Warehouse Use (Square Feet/m²)	Office Use (Square Feet/m²)	Truck Docks	Site Area (Acres/ha)
A1	Burlington Air	106,000 (9,850)	32,000 (2,975)	12	6.85 (2.8)
A2	Air Canada DHL Express	92,288 (8,575)	28,683 (2,665)	15 (and 4 drive-in doors)	6.44 (2.6)
B1	Alliance Airlines	127,399 (11,840)	44,286 (4,115)	23	9.03 (3.6)
B2	Alliance Airlines British Airways	128,706 (11,960)	24,639 (2,290)	43	8.45 (3.4)
C1	U.S. Postal Service	195,000 (18,125)	20,000 (1,860)	20	17.78 (7.2)
C2	Undeveloped	–	–	–	–

Development Cost Information[3]

Site improvement	$4,050,000
Construction	47,500,000
Soft costs	11,978,000
Total	$63,528,000

Annual Operating Expenses

Total	$3.50 per square foot ($37.70/m²)

Financing

Tax-exempt revenue bonds	$55,000,000
Developer equity	8,500,000
Total	$63,500,000

Developer/Owner

CenterPoint O'Hare LLC
1808 Swift Road
Oak Brook, Illinois 60523-1501
630-586-8000

Architect

Capital Design
107 South 3rd Street
Bloomingdale, Illinois 60108
630-295-9576

Construction Manager

Prentiss O'Hare Illinois
9950 West Lawrence Avenue, Suite 105
Schiller Park, Illinois 60176

Development Schedule

1996	Site purchased
1992	Planning started
1996	Construction started
1996	Leasing started
1997	Phase I completed
1998	Phase II completed

Notes

[1]Surface parking and roads.

[2]Combined office and warehouse rents.

[3]At buildout, estimated.

Shekou Logistics Center

Shenzhen, Guangdong, China

The $12 million Shekou Logistics Center is a modern office/warehouse facility developed in the Shenzhen special economic zone, the export platform for the south China region established to attract foreign investment as part of China's economic reform and open-door policies.

The facility was developed by China Distri-Park Limited (CDP), a 50/50 joint venture of Crow Holdings International, an affiliate of the Trammell Crow group of companies, and Prudential Asset Management, an equity investment arm of the Prudential Insurance Company of America. CDP owns and manages the facility.

The project also involves several minority investment partners, including China Merchants Group, the oldest state-owned enterprise in China, which developed and owns Shekou Port; China Merchants Shekou Industrial Zone Real Estate Company, which has developed nearly 8.5 million square feet (789,650 m²) of space in Shekou, including major infrastructure projects; and China Merchants Shekou Port Service Company, a public company listed on the Shenzhen and Singapore stock exchanges, which is engaged primarily in the operation and management of Shekou Port.

The target tenants are distribution and logistics companies. Completed in April 1998, Shekou Logistics Center is the first of 20 regional distribution centers that CDP plans to develop in China over five years. It sets the tone for the company's plans to develop high-quality, modern warehouses in major markets throughout China.

Site and Development Process

The 236,624-square-foot (21,982-m²) Shekou Logistics Center sits on a five-acre (2-ha) site in Guangdong Province in southeast China. The site was selected because of its proximity to primary transportation nodes. It is 1.2 miles (2 km) from the container terminals at Shekou Port, the busiest cargo and container port in south China, and it abuts the Ping Nan Railroad, which connects Shekou Logistics Center with the national rail system. The site is 20 nautical miles (37 km) from Hong Kong, 15 miles (24 km) from Shenzhen International Airport, and 6.2 miles (10 km) from the superhighway linking Guangzhou and Shenzhen. It also is close to the major deepwater cargo and container ports of Chiwan and Yantian. Located in the midst of small foothills, the site is graded flat and is served by streets on three sides.

In early 1996, Crow Holdings International and Prudential Asset Management, the major equity investor, began discussing the possibility of developing modern

industrial buildings like Shekou Logistics Center throughout China. Partners from China and Hong Kong (at that time a British crown colony) were brought in to familiarize the development team with local regulations and to contact with local authorities. Local partners were essential for getting through the lengthy review and approval process, which included many varieties of applications, registrations, reviews, approvals, permits, and certificates covering land uses, site plans, design, fire safety, environmental impact, construction, and occupancy. Local architectural, engineering, and planning associates were retained to help smooth the review and approval process and thus avoid unnecessary delays. The international/local development team capitalized on Trammell Crow's development experience and expertise as well as on the specific local knowledge of the various associates.

Design and Construction

The two-story office/warehouse center is a reinforced concrete structure. The modern, western-style building features dock-high loading platforms, wide column spacing, and high clearance ceilings on both floors as well as space suitable for office use. One-way ramps on both floors and on two sides of the building can accommodate 45-foot (13.7-m) container trailers.

The first floor has a cross-dock configuration with a clearance height of 23 feet (7 m), while the second floor is front loading with a clearance height of 28 feet (8.6 m). A typical bay is 42.7 by 45.3 feet (13 by 13.8 m). Floor-loading capacity is 1,200 pounds per square foot (5,870 kg/m²) on the first floor and 500 pounds per square foot (2,445 kg/m²) on the second. Office space on both floors is located above the warehouse space to maximize storage space and provide an overhead view of the working area from the office area.

Shekou Logistics Center represents the latest in high-tech, high-quality industrial/warehouse space in China. Most competing projects are metal buildings with low clear heights, narrow column spacing, and at-grade loading doors, and they offer little or no space that is well suited for office use. Like most warehouse projects in China, this one differs from typical modern U.S. warehouses in several key ways. Tilt-up construction is not an option because of the lack of experienced contractors with the needed lifting equipment. Concrete floors are finished with a floating trowel rather than a laser screed. And fire protection is provided by low-tech systems rather than an ESFR system.

Shekou Logistics Center caters to exporters using the city's nearby container port. It is the first of about 20 such warehouse and distribution centers that the developer plans for major cities and seaports in China.

In China, building construction uses low-tech, labor-intensive methods that make it less expensive but more time-consuming. Requiring more than 300 people on site working 18-hour days, the construction of Shekou Logistics Center still took about 15 months, whereas a similar project in the United States would take eight to nine months.

Financing, Marketing, and Management

The Bank of China provided 50 percent of the financing for Shekou Logistics Center. Trammell Crow, Prudential, and the other investment partners put up the remaining 50 percent. CDP plans to start four or five similar facilities a year for five years, after which the company will seek a listing on a major public market in the United States or Asia.

The developer also financed the racking system inside the warehouse and the mechanical equipment needed for unloading, storage, and retrieval to enable tenants

to take full advantage of the project's modern warehouse space. The facility is bonded.

The Shekou complex was conceived as a consolidation and export center to serve manufacturers and suppliers in China (and Hong Kong) using the nearby Shekou container port. Marketing studies indicated that Hong Kong–based operators could save 20 percent in storage and transport costs by transporting goods to Shekou and storing them there. Exporting directly out of China rather than through Hong Kong (when it was a crown colony) provided big savings on shipping, storage, and customs.

In marketing the project, contacts known to Crow Holdings International were of great help, but because the target market was primarily local operations, the marketing effort required the identification of potential tenants—logistics operators/consolidators were identified as the primary market—to which a direct-mail campaign and follow-up marketing were addressed. Other marketing tools used for this project included on-site signage,

The second-floor loading docks, which are accessed by one-way ramps, can easily accommodate 45-foot (13.7-m) container trailers.

View of first-floor loading docks. Both floors have dock-high loading platforms.

advertising in Chinese- and English-language media, outsourcing to a Chinese real estate services company, various presentations, and a Web site.

Rents vary based on the ratio of office to warehouse space. Office rents average $14 per square foot ($150/m²), and warehouse rents average $9 per square foot ($97/m²). United States Consolidation, a major consolidator, leases the entire ground floor. The average length of a lease is three to five years.

CDP's basic management philosophy is to provide tenants with all the support—building services, personal contacts, and so forth—that they need to prosper. The company seeks to establish the capacity to serve its tenants wherever they will need space in China and to develop build-to-suits for them as they grow.

Experience Gained

• For a U.S. or multinational development company, finding the right partners is essential in projects abroad, especially in Asia. Securing partners with the right connections is necessary for navigating successfully through China's development process. In recruiting CDP's top executives and professional consultants, Trammell Crow sought mostly local professionals. Only a few of CDP's executives and consultants are from the United States. In staffing its regional operations, CDP also recruits locally.

• Turbulence in global money markets makes it critical for a venture like this one to be well capitalized.

• Development abroad is management-intensive. Be ready for the unexpected—it will happen. The approval process in countries like China that are undergoing a transition to a market economy can be especially arduous. Development in China is extremely difficult and time-consuming, but most things can be achieved with the right connections and a realistic timetable.

The second-floor warehouse space features a ceiling clearance height of 28 feet (8.5 m).

One-way ramps provide truck access to the second floor.

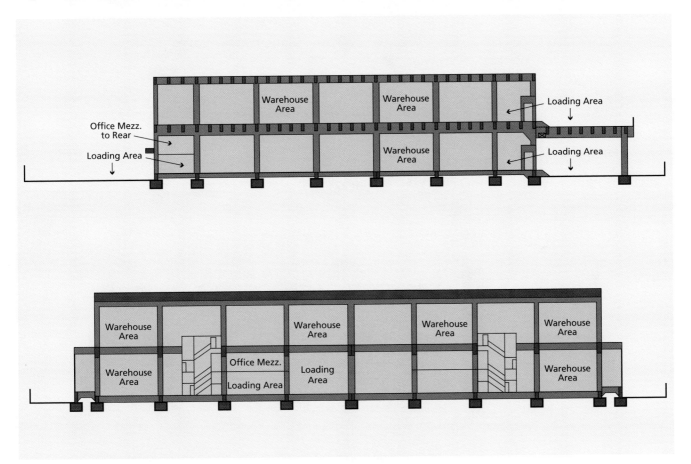

Cross section.

Second-level floor plan.

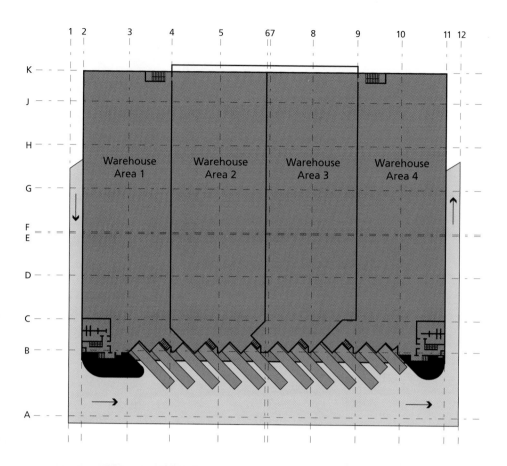

Master plan and ground-floor plan.

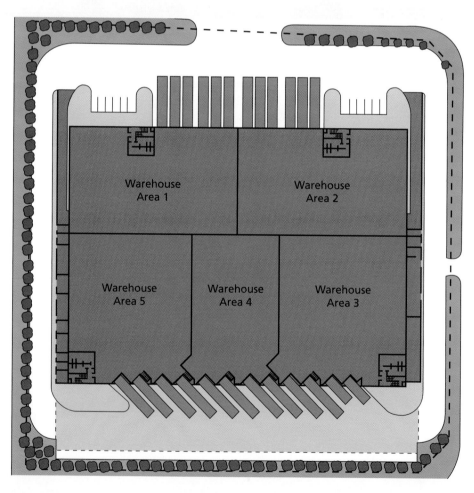

Project Data: Shekou Logistics Center

Land Use Information

Site Area	5 acres (2 ha)
Gross Building Area (GBA)	236,624 square feet (21,982 m²)
Floor/Area Ratio	1.08

Net Rentable Area (NRA)

	Square Feet (m²)
Office	10,000 (929)
Warehouse/industrial	226,000 (20,995)
Total	236,000 (21,924)

Number of Floors	2

Clear Height

	Feet (m)
First floor	23 (7)
Second floor	28 (8.5)

Bay Size	42.7 x 45.3 feet (13 x 13.8 m)
Number of Loading Platforms	36

Tenant Information

Average Annual Rent

Office	$14–15 per square foot ($150–161/m²)
Warehouse	$8.50–9.30 per square foot ($91.50–100/m²)

Average Length of Lease	3–5 years
Annual Gross Income	$3,300,000

Development Cost Information

Site Acquisition	$2,360,000

Construction Costs

Footings and foundations	$890,000
Superstructure	4,720,000
Waterproofing	222,000
Fire construction	265,000
Electrical	134,000
Elevators	60,000
Contingency and other costs	444,000
Total	$6,735,000

Soft Costs

Professional fees	$535,000
Project management	420,000
Leasing/marketing	600,000
Construction interest and fees	650,000
Office expenses and other costs	690,000
Total	$2,895,000

Total Development Cost	$11,990,000

Owner/Developer/Manager

China Distri-Park Limited
Tower II, Suite 802, Lippo Centre
89 Queensway, Admiralty
Hong Kong
011-852-2525-9180

Architecture/Engineering/Planning Associates

RMJM Hong Kong Limited
21st Floor, Pacific Plaza
410 Des Voeux Road West, Hong Kong
011-852-2548-1698

Ove Arup & Partners
56th Floor, Hopewell Centre
183 Queen's Road East, Hong Kong
011-852-2528-3031

Levett & Bailey
11th Floor, Asian House
1 Hennessey Road, Hong Kong
011-852-2823-1823

Development Schedule

11/1995	Planning started
11/1996	Site purchased
11/1996	Leasing started
1/1997	Construction started
4/1998	Project completed

Starbucks Center

Seattle, Washington

Starbucks Center occupies most of a six-block area in an established industrial district approximately one mile (1.6 km) south of Seattle's central business district. It consists of four buildings that together total 1,951,600 square feet (181,303.6 m²). The main building, containing 1,529,110 square feet (142,054 m²), is a six- to nine-story warehouse structure that was built by Sears in phases between 1912 and 1975 as a distribution center. This building has been converted to a mix of uses, including manufacturing, warehouse/storage, shipping/mailing, office, and retail. Two freestanding retail stores south of the main building—a 130,730-square-foot (12,144.8-m²) Home Depot store and a 19,200-square-foot (1,783.6-m²) Sears Auto Service Center—and a number of parking facilities make up the remainder of the project. Parking is provided in four lots (831 total spaces) and a six-level, 272,560-square-foot (25,320-m²) garage (605 spaces) that was converted from warehouse use. Begun in 1991 and planned for completion in 2001, the project has been profitable and has spurred the revitalization of the surrounding neighborhood.

Site and Development

The 17.06-acre (6.9-ha) site is within a five-minute drive of downtown Seattle and close to the region's principal land, sea, and air transportation routes. The site consists of six parcels spread over six city blocks. The two largest parcels are occupied by the main building and the Home Depot building. The narrow block east of the main building contains the main parking lot, which can be accessed directly from First Avenue South. The parcel east of Home Depot is occupied by a Sears Auto Center. The two remaining smaller parcels are used for parking. The property is level and at grade with all adjoining streets.

The Seattle distribution center that Sears opened in 1912 was the retailer's first venture outside Chicago. Over the years, Sears made several additions to the original building before vacating it in 1987 because of changes in transportation technology and retail merchandising strategies. Sears's asking price of $23 million for the property met with little buyer interest. In other cities, similar buildings were being demolished, and this one looked like a white elephant. Its sheer size deterred most prospective buyers, and its use history suggested that soil contamination could be a problem. For three years following Sears's departure, most observers doubted that a suitable use could be found for the structure, and many people were concerned about the fate of the landmark complex and the surrounding neighborhood.

In 1989, the development firm of Nitze-Stagen was looking for a renovation project to undertake in the Seattle area. In early 1990, Frank Stagen toured the Sears property and determined that it had potential based on its size and excellent location with easy access to highway, rail, and port transportation facilities. Although potential environmental problems represented a risk, the developer did not think that they were incurable. Nitze-Stagen won a bidding competition for the property and, after seven months of negotiations, secured it in December 1990 for $11.6 million. A limited partnership called First & Utah Associates was formed to develop the project.

The reuse plan involved no substantial change in uses. Nitze-Stagen would market the project mainly for distribution, industrial, and retail uses because those uses were allowed under the zoning code and because the buildings were designed to accommodate them.

The main buildings had been well maintained by Sears, so their upgrading involved mainly cosmetic repairs. The building exterior was cleaned and repainted. The facility was renamed SODO Center to reflect its location: SODO is shorthand for the neighborhood known as South of the Seattle KingDome. In early 1991, SODO Center officially opened for business. Response was good, and leasing was brisk.

Starbucks, the world's largest purveyor of specialty coffees, leased 25,000 square feet (2,322 m²) of corporate office space in 1992. It planned to stay at SODO Center only until it could develop its own campus. Starbucks wanted to build in an urban location, but it had difficulty finding a suitably large site within the city of Seattle. In the meantime, the company grew explosively, and SODO had room to accommodate this growth. Within one year of coming to SODO Center, Starbucks occupied an entire floor—130,000 square feet (12,077 m²)—in the main building. Later, the company agreed to take up to 600,000 square feet (53,740 m²), at which point Nitze-Stagen gave Starbucks the naming rights to the project for free. The project was officially renamed Starbucks Center in June 1997.

The parcel south of the main building is not located on a main arterial, and the developer thought it would be best suited for a large-format destination retailer. In the early 1990s, big-box home improvement stores were one of the fastest-growing segments of the retail industry. Home Depot, which was trying to break into the Seattle market, made an offer to locate at SODO Center. Although the site was smaller than what Home

Starbucks Center, situated on a 17-acre (6.8-ha) infill site near downtown Seattle, includes warehouse, manufacturing, office, and retail uses.

Depot typically preferred, the retailer was anxious to be in this location. Two buildings—the old Sears arcade and auto center (the auto center was relocated to the parcel east of this one)—were demolished, which left a level, full-block parcel totaling 5.38 acres (2.1 ha). Four out-parcels were acquired to improve the parking ratio, bringing the area of the site to 6.61 acres (2.67 ha). Home Depot opened for business in August 1993.

The main building's design presented a development challenge. A number of its floorplates exceeded 130,000 square feet (12,077 m²), and clearance heights were only eight to ten feet (2.4 to 3 m). Because the heavy reinforced concrete construction made it impossible to modify the structure significantly, the developer had to market the building to tenants that could live with its limitations.

Few major changes were made to the main structure. Two interior columns were removed to create a lobby in the Starbucks space, and five interior stairwells connecting the

Starbucks floors were carved out of the floorplates. The atriums created by these stairwells were topped by glass skylights. The Starbucks floors have been finished to create Class A office space. Corridors radiating from a multi-story central atrium topped by a 40- by 60-foot (12.1- by 18.2-m) skylight divide the space into work areas for individual departments. Rooms for support services are located near the middle of each floor. Private offices take up less than 5 percent of the total space, while meeting rooms constitute approximately 10 percent of the space.

The north building was converted into the Starbucks garage. High ceilings on the first and second floors made it possible to add mezzanines within the shell to create additional parking levels. Parking ramps connecting the floors were added on the west side of the building. A new structure connecting the main building and the parking garage contains passenger elevators and elevator lobbies, primarily for use by Starbucks.

The Sears Building in 1943.

The developer updated the electrical system to provide 14,000-volt, three-phase service throughout the building and also added enclosed loading docks for an existing 254,000-square-foot (23,596.6-m²) Sears store on the lower floors of the main building. Sears undertook a cosmetic renovation of its store, and other retail tenants also made their own improvements.

The main warehouse floors are basically unchanged. Large tenants, such as Olympic West Sportswear, installed their own equipment and made their own tenant improvements where needed. The developer installed floor-to-ceiling chain-link partitions along the interior column grid to subdivide the multitenant storage/warehouse floors into storage bays. The partitions can be easily relocated to suit the changing needs of tenants, and they provide adequate ventilation and security on these floors. Wide walkways/driveways running between the storage bays provide access for forklifts and loaders.

The SODO Center in the early 1990s. The developer restored the building's original clock tower to reinforce a sense of place and history in this urban neighborhood.

The only major change made to the main structure was to remove two interior columns to create a lobby in the Starbucks space and allow for the installation of a 40- by 60-foot (12.1- by 18.2-m²) skylight.

Approvals

Concerned about the loss of the Sears distribution center, which had employed 2,100 people, and welcoming the opportunity to bring a major Seattle landmark back to life, the city of Seattle gave strong support to the developer. The city generally supported the redevelopment plans, interpreted zoning and building codes with considerable flexibility, and willingly accepted innovative solutions to problems. Nevertheless, several major approval issues arose.

When Nitze-Stagen bought the property, the city had agreed that seismic work would not be needed. However, major earthquakes in Japan and California and the conversion of the main building's upper floors for high-occupancy office use by Starbucks led the city to change its opinion and require extensive seismic bracing throughout the main building. The seismic retrofit—a state-of-the-art system of vertical and diagonal steel braces that was installed while the building was fully occupied—was the project's most significant structural improvement. It cost more than $6 million and took a 65-person crew 14 months to complete. Construction was done at night to avoid disturbing tenants.

Accommodating extensive office uses has been problematical. In zones designated for general industrial uses in Seattle, offices are allowed as an accessory use up to a total of 50,000 square feet (4,645 m) per project, and a height limit of 85 feet (25.9 m) is imposed for non-industrial uses. Starbucks alone occupies much more than 50,000 square feet (4,645 m²) of office space—and, fur-

thermore, this space is located on the upper floors of the main building, which are above 85 feet (25.9 m). The amount and location of office space at Starbucks Center are issues that remain unresolved.

Environmental conditions and hazardous materials on site were not a major problem. As part of the purchase agreement, Sears agreed to reimburse Nitze-Stagen up to $3 million in cleanup costs in the first seven years of Nitze-Stagen's ownership. Nitze-Stagen spent more than $1 million on cleanup. The method of remediating the Home Depot site has not yet been approved for final certification. The store's site was where the old Sears auto center had been located. Sears had previously cleaned up the petroleum contamination, and the Home Depot store was built on top of the old auto center's footprint, effectively capping the site.

Financing

Nitze-Stagen was able, with difficulty, to obtain financing without a specific plan for the property. After several banks had been approached, Rainier Bank, a local bank, stepped forward with an $18 million construction loan to cover interior demolition, exterior cleanup, tenant improvements, leasing costs, and other development activities. The fact that Nitze-Stagen was willing to put up $11.6 million in cash to buy the property played a large role in Rainier Bank's decision.

Financing was complicated by a series of bank mergers: while the loan was being negotiated, Rainier Bank

Five interior stairwells connecting the Starbucks office floors were carved out of the floorplates.

was acquired by Los Angeles–based Security Pacific Bank; Security Pacific was acquired later by Bank of America, the owner of Seafirst Bank in Seattle. Seafirst had concerns about the proposed mix of uses and the sheer scale of the project, and was less willing to fund the project. Because delays in obtaining financing jeopardized the target date for delivering a new building to Home Depot, the original deal with Home Depot was restructured to allow the retailer to build its store and then sell it to Nitze-Stagen. Seafirst provided additional construction and permanent financing for the Starbucks expansion. Starbucks Center has been paying off all loans on schedule.

Marketing
Initial marketing focused primarily on the distribution of brochures to prospective tenants. The developer spent approximately $25,000 to produce a promotional video aimed at major prospects. Extensive free coverage in the local media was easy to obtain because of the size and unusual nature of the project. To some extent, this media attention confirmed the adage that there is no such thing as bad publicity: reports questioning the sanity of Nitze-Stagen in taking on the project and reports emphasizing the risks of the project seemed only to heighten interest.

The main building is an easily recognizable local landmark that advertises itself. Initially, the developer mounted 12-foot-tall (3.6-m) red neon *SODO* signs on all four sides of the ten-story central tower, replacing longstanding, tall, green neon *SEARS* signs and drawing complaints

from some people who said they had grown used to the green letters. The *SODO* signs dominated the entire district south of downtown and could be seen for miles.

Experience Gained
- Buying and renovating the Sears distribution center cost less than would have been required for new construction. The low upfront cost gave the developer considerable latitude in setting lease rates and booking tenants to fill the huge building.
- If a building already works, there is no need to change it. Change is not required to make a reuse project work. The uses in Starbucks Center are substantially the same as the uses that existed on the site when it was the Sears distribution center—storage, warehouse/distribution, administrative office, and retail. With the exception of the Starbucks office lease, the project turned out much as originally planned. The retail portion has done extremely well.
- It helps to be lucky. The Starbucks corporate office lease was an unanticipated windfall for this project.
- Well-located, close-in industrial districts face an underlying problem, which is that nonindustrial uses can outbid industrial and distribution activities for land and building space. The industrial/warehouse component of Starbucks Center has been profitable, but the most profitable elements have been the Starbucks corporate offices and the retail.
- One important measure of the success of Starbucks Center is its positive effects on the surrounding neighborhood. The facility's parking lots, which had been virtually empty for years, are full or nearly full much of the time. Pedestrian counts in front of the main building shot up from 10,000 per week in 1991 to 25,000 per week in 1998. Several new restaurants have opened in the neighborhood, and some of the old, run-down industrial buildings along First and Fourth avenues have been renovated.

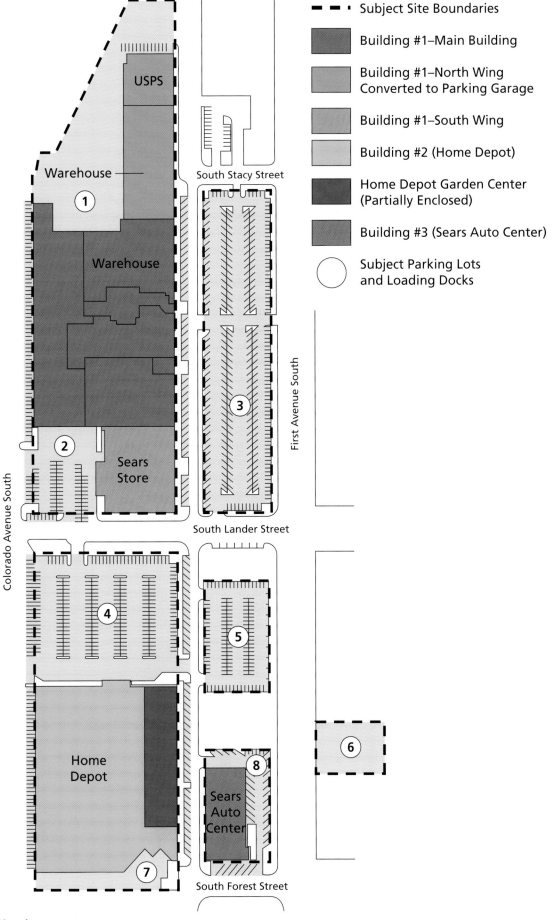

Legend:

- Subject Site Boundaries
- Building #1–Main Building
- Building #1–North Wing Converted to Parking Garage
- Building #1–South Wing
- Building #2 (Home Depot)
- Home Depot Garden Center (Partially Enclosed)
- Building #3 (Sears Auto Center)
- Subject Parking Lots and Loading Docks

USPS

Warehouse

①

Warehouse

South Stacy Street

③

First Avenue South

②

Sears Store

Colorado Avenue South

South Lander Street

④

⑤

⑥

Home Depot

⑦

⑧

Sears Auto Center

South Forest Street

Site plan.

Project Data: Starbucks Center

Land Use Information

Site Area   17.06 acres (6.9 ha)

Gross Building Area (GBA)

	Square Feet (m²) Completed	Square Feet (m²) at Buildout
Office	483,487 (45,000)	565,000 (52,500)
Warehouse/industrial	518,487 (48,200)	600,000 (55,800)
Retail	451,705 (42,000)	451,705 (42,000)
Other	497,921 (46,300)	436,408 (40,600)
Total	1,951,600 (181,400)	2,053,113 (190,800)

Number of Buildings   4

Parking

Structured	605 spaces
Surface	831 spaces
Total	1,436 spaces

Land Use Plan

	Acres (ha)	Percent of Site
Buildings	8.7 (3.5)	50.9%
Parking structures	1.0 (.4)	5.9
Paved areas	6.9 (2.8)	40.4
Landscaped areas	0.5 (.2)	2.9
Total	17.1 (6.9)	100.0%

Office/Industrial Tenant Information

Occupied Net Rentable Area (NRA)   95%

Average Annual Rent

Office	$4–6 per square foot ($43–65/m²)
Warehouse/industrial	$4–10 per square foot ($43–108/m²)

Average Length of Lease   month to month; up to 3 years

Typical Terms of Lease   triple net

Typical Tenant Size

Office	400,000 square feet (37,175 m²)
Warehouse/industrial	5,000 square feet (465 m²)

Development Cost Information

	Projected[1]	Actual[2]
Acquisition	$13,600,000	$13,600,000
Hard Costs		
Facade rehabilitation	$705,000	$705,000
Street improvements	144,000	144,000
Roof replacement	220,000	220,000
Elevators	467,000	467,000
Life safety	570,000	570,000
Sears Auto Center building	1,329,500	1,329,500
Home Depot building	7,571,500	7,571,500
Environmental remediation	1,150,100	1,114,000
Electrical	1,250,000	1,250,000
Docks	390,000	390,000
Security	123,200	123,200
Construction supervision	1,405,000	1,405,000
Building shell upgrades	1,648,100	1,550,800
Tenant improvements	33,058,300	22,475,000
Building systems	12,638,500	12,638,500
Building amenities	3,922,500	3,922,500
Seismic upgrade	6,000,000	6,000,000
Total	$72,592,700	$61,876,000
Soft Costs		
Architecture/engineering	$338,300	$338,000
Legal	289,000	288,800
Leasing commissions	1,708,100	1,638,100
Other costs	11,862,600	11,862,600
Total	$14,198,000	$14,127,500
Total Development Cost	$100,390,700	$89,603,500

Developer

Nitze-Stagen & Company

2401 Utah Avenue, South

Seattle, Washington 98134

Notes

[1] Projected as of December 31, 1997.

[2] Actual costs through December 31, 1997.

Architects

NBBJ-West
111 South Jackson Street
Seattle, Washington 98104

Lance Mueller & Associates
130 Lakeside Avenue, Suite 250
Seattle, Washington 98122

Olson-Sundberg Architects
108 First Avenue, South
Seattle, Washington 98120

Land Planner

Hillis Clark Martin & Peterson
1221 2nd Avenue, Suite 500
Seattle, Washington 98101

Consultant

Engineers Northwest
6869 Woodlawn Avenue, NE
Seattle, Washington 98115

Development Schedule

12/1990	Site purchased
1/1991	Planning started
1991	Construction started
1991	Leasing started
8/1992	Phase I completed
2001	Completion expected

Subic Bay Freeport

Bataan Province, Republic of the Philippines

In 1992, the Subic Bay U.S. naval base was converted to the Subic Bay Freeport (SBF), commonly referred to as Subic, which is designated as a special economic zone whose purpose is to attract investment. The United States had turned the 10,127-acre (4,100-ha) site over to the Philippine government after the withdrawal of its military forces from the Philippines. The site's excellent infrastructure, its strategic location on the Pacific Rim, the community's quality of life, and economic incentives offered by the Subic Bay Metropolitan Authority (SBMA) —the public agency created to develop the site—have attracted domestic and foreign companies.

Considerable infrastructure was inherited from the U.S. Navy, and SBMA has added to it. Subic offers a deepwater pier, an airport, a 12-megawatt power plant and a new 118-megawatt power plant, water and sewage treatment facilities, almost 2,000 housing units, modern telecommunications infrastructure, and a 49-mile (80-km) network of roads. In addition, about 4,700 acres (1,900 ha) of pristine forest on the site make Subic a popular tourist destination. Key land uses at Subic include a central business district, an industrial park, a technology park, and a nature reserve.

A global transpark—a business and industrial park featuring advanced multimodal transportation facilities —is under development to take advantage of the SBF's access to multiple modes of transportation: air, sea, and highway. Subic has attracted investment totaling more than $2.3 billion from such tenants as FedEx, AT&T, Volvo Penta, Acer, Hitachi, and Enron.

Site and History

Subic is located 68 miles (110 km) northwest of Manila on the island of Luzon, the largest island in the Philippines. Olongapo, the city just outside Subic, has a population of 200,000. Subic's location on the Pacific Rim makes it ideal for shipping and airfreight operations. By air, the free port is only two hours from Hong Kong, three hours from Bangkok, 3.25 hours from Singapore, and four hours from Tokyo.

Subic has a natural deepwater harbor surrounded by protective mountains. Spain used the port as an outpost in the 19th century. After the Spanish-American War, U.S. forces maintained a presence in Subic until the base was seized by the Japanese during World War II. U.S. forces regained control of the base after the war and remained there after Philippine independence as a lessee under the 1947 Military Bases Agreement. Subic Bay became the largest U.S. military port outside the United States and

a major military staging area during the Korean and Vietnam wars. In 1991, the Philippine Senate rejected the renewal of the Military Bases Agreement, and U.S. military forces withdrew from the Philippines in 1992.

The departure of these forces had a major impact on the local and national economies. The Subic Bay naval base had employed 43,000 residents of the surrounding community in skilled and service jobs, and the Philippine government received substantial revenue from the lease agreement with the United States. But the base closures also offered a unique development opportunity. In 1992, the Philippine government created the Bases Conversion Development Authority (BCDA) to guide the conversion of three former U.S. military bases—the Subic Bay naval base, Clark Field air base, and Camp John Hay— to special economic zones.

The special economic zones were designed to attract domestic and foreign investment. Among the investment incentives offered to businesses that locate within the Subic special economic zone are tax- and duty-free imports, unrestricted foreign investment, no foreign exchange controls, and exemption from all local and national taxes. The only charge on businesses in Subic is a 5 percent corporate tax on gross income. Money generated from the corporate tax covers SBMA's expenses, and the excess revenue goes to the national government.

The SBMA was established as the operating and implementing arm of the BCDA. Richard Gordon, a former mayor of Olongapo, became its first chair and served until replaced by Felicito C. Payumo in 1998. An influential leader known for his salesmanship, Gordon is generally credited with having developed the early vision of the free port.

The SBMA has a chair and a 15-member board of directors, all appointed by the president of the Philippines. Eight board members represent the business and investment sector, and they serve a three-year term. Board members representing the public sector serve a six-year term.

Development

The SBMA strategy is to use the site's infrastructure and strategic location and the area's skilled, English-speaking labor force to attract investment and economic development. Subic's Pacific Rim location and its status as a free port make it a prime site for a global transpark, which in concept is the provision of a 21st century setting— multimodal transportation, advanced telecommunications, and links to suppliers and customers far and near—in support of global manufacturing and distribution oper-

The SBMA's waterfront office was formerly headquarters for the U.S. Navy's top brass. The SBMA created a one-stop shop for businesses seeking to establish operations at Subic: the availability of on-site branch offices of the departments of immigration, customs, and internal revenue means that investors need not go to Manila to deal with those government agencies.

ations. A number of regions and countries—including North Carolina, Thailand, Germany, Brazil, Panama, and South Africa—are working on plans for developing global transparks. When a network of such parks has been created, global transparks will likely become a necessary location for many competitive industrial operations.

With an eye to developing the regional economy, the SBMA joined with the Clark Development Corporation, the development authority for the former U.S. military base at Clark Field to the northeast of Subic. The two authorities recently finished the engineering plans for a 56-mile (90-km), six-lane highway to link the two development zones. The highway will open up tracts of flat and developable land, and should attract businesses that can use both the deepwater port at Subic and a new air cargo hub and distribution center at Clark Field. This growth corridor's easy access to global markets via shipping and airfreight facilities will, it is envisioned, make it competitive with the industrial and manufactur-

ing centers of metropolitan Manila and other Pacific Rim locations.

The SBMA is also developing Subic as a tourist destination. Tourism and industrial uses might seem to conflict, but Subic as a tourist attraction benefits from the fact that the U.S. military left large tracts of pristine forests virtually untouched—while much of the Philippines has been deforested. Subic's forests, white beaches, and clear water draw more than 100,000 tourists a week during the peak summer season.

For business tenants, the ease of doing business at Subic and its security precautions are major draws. The SBMA created an on-site, one-stop shop for businesses seeking to establish operations at Subic. Branch offices of the departments of immigration, customs, and internal revenue relieve investors of the need to go to Manila to conduct business with these government agencies. Security is a concern of many foreigners working in the Philippines. Subic addresses this concern in a variety of ways.

The new passenger terminal at Subic Bay's airport can handle 700 people per hour. The airport has state-of-the-art navigational and communications equipment that makes it capable of accommodating 17 wide-bodied and three 747 jets at one time. The airport serves as the Asian hub for FedEx.

The SBMA maintains its own police force. A controlled-access fence surrounds the zone. Subic operates its own hospital, fire department, and 911 service. While the availability of such security services may be the norm in most industrialized countries, this level of security sets Subic apart from its competition in the Philippines.

The project's key development sites—the Central Area, the Subic Bay Industrial Park (SBIP), and the Subic Technopark—are developing under separate plans. The SBMA is working toward the creation of an overall master plan that will unify development planning for all the areas.

The Central Area is Subic's central business district, the portion of the site on which office, hotel, retail, and entertainment uses are concentrated. Encompassing 447 acres (181 ha), the Central Area is where the U.S. Navy had its administrative offices, commissary, and housing. A recent master plan for the Central Area that was funded by the World Bank and designed by Kenzo Tange Associates concentrates initial development—office, commercial, and resort hotel—along the waterfront.

Subic Bay Industrial Park is a joint development of the SBMA and United Development Corporation of Taiwan. The target market is nonpolluting light to medium industries. SBIP's first major tenant was Acer, a computer manufacturing company based in Taiwan. Acer currently occupies three factory buildings at SBIP and employs more than 1,000 people.

Subic Technopark is being developed by the Subic Technopark Corporation (STEP), a joint venture of the SBMA, the Japanese International Development Organization (JAIDO), and several other Japanese entities. STEP targets nonpolluting, high-tech, high-value-added industries, most of which have come from Japan. STEP develops the land and leases parcels to developers for terms up to 50 years. It has also developed space for lease. The site is hilly and adjacent to the protected forest, conditions that have made developing the site challenging. Infrastructure for the technopark is now in place, but STEP's poor timing in entering the market—at the onset

of the Asian economic crisis in the late 1990s—resulted in a sluggish start.

The supply of developable land at Subic is limited, despite the site's large size. The topography and the designation of much of the land as conservation areas make only 20 percent of the land suitable for development. Furthermore, high-rise construction is generally uneconomic, because the poor bearing capacity of the soil makes the cost of building foundations prohibitive. Maintenance of its environmental standards to ensure that development does not occur at the expense of the natural areas is an important ongoing issue for the SBMA.

The SBMA's long-term strategy for overcoming its limited supply of land is to expand the area enjoying freeport status to encompass 130,910 acres (53,000 ha) around Subic, without changing the boundaries of Subic. Businesses in the expansion area would enjoy the economic advantages of a free port, such as duty-free imports, and could also take advantage of Subic's shipping, airfreight, and communications facilities. When the superhighway linking Subic and Clark Field is built, more land will be opened for development and the area will become established as a key economic hub in the Philippines.

Infrastructure

The extensive infrastructure left by the U.S. military—including power plant, water and sewerage treatment facilities, deepwater pier, airport, and roads—provided an excellent foundation for making the transition from military to industrial use. The military also left many buildings that could be easily adapted for use as offices, hotels, housing, stores, schools, warehouses, and factories.

The SBMA built a 118-megawatt power plant under a build/operate/transfer program to complement the 12-megawatt plant left by the U.S. Navy. The new power plant serves Subic while supplying excess power to the national grid. Throughout the Philippines, inadequate power supply and frequent power brownouts have been chronic problems. At Subic, power supply generally is more dependable than elsewhere, but occasional brown-outs—and higher-than-expected costs for power, water, and sewer services—have become a point of contention with many investors. The SBMA under Gordon promised tenants 100 percent uninterrupted power, and the current administration is tasked with easing investor tensions and making good on the promise.

The water and sewerage facilities left by the U.S. military have been adequate so far for tenant needs. Subic is using a $40 million loan from the World Bank to tap new water sources for future development.

The SBMA improved the telecommunications infrastructure by replacing the telephone trunk lines with fiber-optic cables and a digital switching system that is capable of handling 100,000 lines. Subic is the only place in the Philippines with direct satellite, fiber-optic, and microwave communication connections.

With an 8,858-foot (2,700-m) runway and state-of-the-art navigational and communications equipment, Subic's airport can accommodate 17 wide-bodied and three 747 jets at one time. A new passenger terminal built by the SBMA can handle 700 people per hour. In 1998, almost 100,000 incoming/outgoing passengers passed through the airport on more than 1,000 international and nearly 6,000 domestic flights. A $1.6 million transponder landing system—the first of its kind in Asia—was just put into operation, allowing planes to land during severe weather conditions. One of Subic's largest tenants is FedEx, which has made Subic its Asian regional hub.

With docking facilities for up to 70 ships, the deep-water pier at Subic can accommodate supertankers. The 101-acre (41-ha) port area includes a fixed pier, a movable pier, a cold storage facility, 22 warehouses, and a container yard. A master plan for the port is being prepared by the Japan International Cooperating Agency under a technical assistance program. Within ten years, the SBMA plans to develop the port to a full-scale container terminal with automated container-handling systems and new cranes. The SBMA hopes that the port's improved infrastructure and easy access to major shipping lanes will allow it to compete directly with Manila.

Many buildings that were part of the military base have been reused or converted to other uses. Military offices were made into SBMA headquarters, ammunition bunkers were turned into warehouses, and the base commissary has become a duty-free shopping facility. Many of Subic's tenants have been able to move into existing buildings instead of constructing new facilities and thus to start operations with minimal delay.

Almost 2,000 military houses have been converted to rental housing for executives working in the Subic Bay Freeport or to weekend vacation homes. Roughly 3,000 people reside within Subic. A small community of waterfront luxury houses was built near the naval magazine to house the participants at the APEC (Asia-Pacific Economic Cooperation) summit held at Subic in November 1996.

Once used as housing for U.S. Navy personnel, these buildings have been converted into hotels and casinos by Legend International, a Malaysian resort development firm.

A newly constructed $76 million yacht club, just one of Subic's many tourist draws, hosts the annual President's Cup Regatta.

These houses were sold after the conference. More residential development is planned for the marina area and Redondo Peninsula, a 9,386-acre (3,800-ha) tract of land on the opposite side of the bay from the SBF that will be connected by marine transit to the SBF.

Tourism

Attracting the tourist trade is an integral part of the development strategy for Subic. Among the diverse attractions

Subic Bay's 101-acre (41-ha) port includes a fixed pier, a movable pier, a cold storage facility, 22 warehouses, and a container yard. The deepwater pier has docking facilities for 70 ships and can accommodate supertankers.

drawing visitors to Subic are casinos, duty-free shopping, yachting, golfing, water sports, restaurants, special events, and the natural environment. The Asian economic crisis of the late 1990s slowed the tourist trade—especially duty-free shopping—but Subic remains a major destination for foreign and domestic tourists.

Legend International, a Malaysian resort development firm, has completed three hotels offering 600 rooms at Subic. The firm's Crown Peak hotel/casino is a conversion of the former base's bachelor officer quarters. Its Legenda and Subic International hotels also have casinos, and they cater to Malaysian and Taiwanese travelers. Subic's $76 million yacht club—host of the annual President's Cup Regatta, a sailing race that attracts competitors from other Asian countries—is the centerpiece of the marina. The SBMA has plans to develop waterfront villas and a commercial center in the marina area.

Subic's forest, covering about 4,700 acres (1,900 ha) provides habitat for hundreds of plant and animal species, including the world's smallest and largest bats, and is an ideal environment for ecotourism. The SBMA uses some of the revenue it generates to protect the forest from illegal logging and poaching. Subic Bay offers a rich marine environment, including several shipwrecks, that attracts scuba divers from around the world. Realizing that the area's beautiful scenery greatly contributes to the quality of life at Subic, the SBMA is careful to balance development and environmental concerns. Subic's natural amenities give the development an advantage over competing industrial areas in the Philippines, many of which are located in congested and polluted urban areas.

Experience Gained

- To compete in a global market, a project needs to offer more than facilities that merely beat the domestic competition. The SBMA inherited excellent facilities from the U.S. Navy but continued to upgrade the power, water, airport, shipping, and telecommunications infrastructure to maintain its global competitiveness.

The rich tropical ecosystems of Subic Bay provide recreational opportunities that attract tourists.

- Providing a stable business environment is the key to future success for Subic. When Philippine president Joseph Estrada appointed a successor to Gordon as SBMA chair, political tensions flared and a two-month standoff ensued when Gordon refused to step down. The widely publicized turmoil taught the SBMA a hard lesson; for two months, tourism came to a standstill, infrastructure improvements halted, and investors questioned the future stability of the freeport. The crisis eventually ended without the loss of any investors, but the SBMA learned that Subic's tenants will not long put up with domestic political squabbles.
- Large-scale developments need to retain the flexibility to evolve over time. In the early years of development at Subic, tourism and duty-free shopping were emphasized. This strategy worked well, but SBMA executives think in retrospect that promoting industrial development early might have been a better strategy. Now that industrial development is underway, the SBMA has begun to focus its efforts on office development.
- Creating a development authority can be a challenge. The task of establishing its powers, procedures, and responsibilities takes time and engenders conflict. National government authorities, desirous of obtaining more revenue from Subic, currently are reexamining the powers of the SBMA.
- The symbiotic relationship between development and the preservation of the environment—the beautiful scenery draws tourists and attracts investors while the revenue generated by development helps protect and preserve Subic's natural areas—has made important contributions to Subic's success.

Warehouse space at Subic Bay Freeport.

Bibliography
and Index

Bibliography

Data Sources: General Economics and Demographics

CACI
1100 North Glebe Road
Arlington, VA 22201
(800) 292-2224
www.demographics.caci.com

Claritas
5375 Mira Sorrento Place, Suite 400
San Diego, CA 92121
(800) 866-6510
www.claritas.com

Demographicsnow.com
SSRC, LLC
131 North Glassell Street, Suite 200
Orange, California 92866
(714) 516-2400
www.Demographicsnow.com

DevelopmentAlliance.com
Published by the International Economic Development Council and
    Conway Data, Inc.
www.DevelopmentAlliance.com

U.S. Department of Commerce
Bureau of Economic Analysis
Washington, DC 20230
www.bea.doc.gov

U.S. Department of Commerce
Census Bureau
Washington, DC 20233
(301) 457-4608
www.census.gov

U.S. Department of Labor
Bureau of Labor Statistics
Washington, DC 20212
(202) 606-5886
www.bls.gov

Woods & Poole Economics
1794 Columbia Road, N.W., Suite 4
Washington, DC 20009
(800) 786-1915
www.woodsandpoole.com

Data Sources: Local and Regional Real Estate Markets

CB Richard Ellis
Pacific Corporate Towers
200 North Sepulveda Boulevard, Suite 300
El Segundo, CA 90245
(310) 563-8600
www.cbrichardelllis.com

Colliers International
4 State Street, 3rd Floor
Boston, MA 02109
(617) 772-0221
www.colliers.com

CoStar Group
2 Bethesda Metro Center
Bethesda, MD 20814
(301) 215-8300
www.costargroup.com

Cushman & Wakefield
51 West 52nd Street
New York, NY 10019
(212) 841-7500
www.cushmanwakefield.com

F. W. Dodge
24 Hartwell Avenue
Lexington, MA 02173
(800) 591-4462
www.mag.fwdodge.com

Grubb & Ellis
2215 Sanders Road
Northbrook, IL 60062
(847) 753-7500
www.grubb-ellis.com

Insignia/ESG
200 Park Avenue
New York, NY 10166
(212) 984-8033
www.insigniaesg.com

Jones Lang LaSalle
200 East Randolph Drive
Chicago, IL 60601
(312) 782-5800
www.joneslanglasalle.com

Lend Lease Real Estate Investments
787 Seventh Avenue
New York, NY 10019
(212) 554-1600
www.lendleaserei.com

PricewaterhouseCoopers
1301 Avenue of the Americas
New York, NY 10019
(212) 520-2666
www.pw.com

Real Estate Research Corporation
980 North Michigan Avenue, Suite 1675
Chicago, IL 60611
www.rerc.com

REIS
5 West 37th Street
New York, NY 10018
(212) 921-1122
www.reis.com

Society of Industrial and Office REALTORS®
700 11th Street, N.W., Suite 510
Washington, DC 20001-4511
(202) 737-1150
www.sior.com

The Staubach Company
15501 Dallas Parkway, Suite 400
Addison, TX 75001
(972) 361-5000
www.staubach.com

TCN
2419 Coit Road, Suite A
Plano, TX 75075
(972) 769-8701
www.tcnre.com

Torto Wheaton Research
200 High Street
Boston, MA 02110
(617) 912-5200
www.tortowheatonresearch.com

ULI–the Urban Land Institute
1025 Thomas Jefferson Street, N.W., Suite 500 West
Washington, DC 20007-5201
www.uli.org

Journals

Buildings: The Facilities Construction and Management Magazine. Stamats Communications, Inc., 427 Sixth Avenue, SE, Cedar Rapids, IA 52406; Phone: (319) 364-6167; Fax: (319) 364-4278. www.buildings.com.

Commercial Investment Real Estate. CCIM Institute, 430 North Michigan Avenue, Chicago, IL 60611-4092; Phone: (800) 621-7027; Fax: (800) 839-2387. www.ccim.com.

Corporate Real Estate Executive. NACORE International, 440 Columbia Drive, Suite 100, West Palm Beach, FL 33409; Phone: (800) 726-8111; Fax: (561) 697-4853. www.nacore.com.

Development. National Association of Industrial and Office Properties, 2201 Cooperative Way, Herndon, VA 20171-3034; Phone: (703) 904-7100; Fax: (703) 904-7942. www.naiop.com.

Facility Management Journal. International Facility Management Association, One East Greenway Plaza, Suite 1100, Houston, TX 77046-0194; Phone: (713) 623-4362; Fax: (713) 623-6124. www.ifma.org.

Plants, Sites and Parks. Cahners Business Information, 7025 Albert Pick Road, Suite 200, Greensboro, NC 27409; Phone: (336) 605-1099; Fax: (336) 605-3800. www.bizsites.com.

Site Selection. Conway Data, Inc., 35 Technology Parkway, Suite 150, Norcross, GA 30092; Phone: (770) 446-6996; Fax: (770) 263-8825. www.siteselection.com.

Urban Land. ULI–the Urban Land Institute, 1025 Thomas Jefferson Street, N.W., Suite 500 West, Washington, DC 20007-5201; Phone: (202) 624-7105; Fax: (202) 624-7140. www.uli.org.

WERCsheet. Warehousing Education and Research Council, 1100 Jorie Boulevard, Suite 170, Oak Brook, IL 60523-4413; Phone: (630) 990-0001; Fax: (301) 459-1522. www.werc.org.

Organizations

American Industrial Real Estate Association
700 South Flower Street, Suite 600
Los Angeles, CA 90017
Phone: (213) 687-8777
Fax: (213) 687-8616
www.airea.com

Association of University Related Research Parks
1730 K Street, N.W., Suite 700
Washington, DC 20006
Phone: (202) 828-4167
Fax: (202) 223-4745
www.aurrp.org

Building Owners and Managers Association International
1201 New York Avenue, N.W., Suite 300
Washington, DC 20005
Phone: (202) 408-2662
Fax: (202) 371-0181
www.boma.org

CCIM Institute
430 North Michigan Avenue
Chicago, IL 60611-4090
Phone: (800) 621-7027
Fax: (800) 839-2387
www.ccim.com

Council of Logistics Management
2805 Butterfield Road, Suite 200
Oak Brook, IL 60523
Phone: (630) 574-0985
Fax: (630) 574-0989
www.clm1.org

Institute of Real Estate Management®
430 North Michigan Avenue
Chicago, IL 60611-4090
Phone: (312) 329-6000
Fax: (321) 329-6039
www.irem.org

International Development Research Council*
35 Technology Parkway, Suite 150
Norcross, GA 30092
Phone: (770) 446-8955
Fax: (770) 263-8825
www.idrc.org

International Facility Management Association
One East Greenway Plaza, Suite 1100
Houston, TX 77046-0194
Phone: (713) 623-4362
Fax: (713) 623-6124
www.ifma.org

International Society of Logistics
8100 Professional Place, Suite 211
Hyattsville, MD 20785
Phone: (301) 459-8446
Fax: (301) 459-1522
www.sole.org

NACORE International*
440 Columbia Drive, Suite 100
West Palm Beach, FL 33409
Phone: (800) 726-8111
Fax: (561) 697-4853
www.nacore.com

National Association of Industrial and Office Properties
2201 Cooperative Way
Herndon, VA 20171-3034
Phone: (703) 904-7100
Fax: (703) 904-7942
www.naiop.com

Society of Industrial and Office REALTORS®
700 11th Street, N.W., Suite 510
Washington, DC 20001
Phone: (202) 737-1150
Fax: (202) 737-8796
www.sior.com

ULI–the Urban Land Institute
1025 Thomas Jefferson Street, N.W., Suite 500 West
Washington, DC 20007-5201
Phone: (202) 624-7105
Fax: (202) 624-7140
www.uli.org

UK Science Park Association
Aston Science Park, Love Lane
Birmingham B7 4BJ
United Kingdom
Phone: 44 (01) 121 359-0981
Fax: 44 (01) 121 359-0981
www.ukspa.org.uk

Warehousing Education and Research Council
1100 Jorie Boulevard, Suite 170
Oak Brook, IL 60523-4413
Phone: (630) 990-0001
Fax: (630) 990-0256
www.werc.org

*As of mid-2001, plans were to combine IDRC and NACORE into one organization.

Index

sis, 42; debt coverage ratio (DCR), 43; development budget, 39–42, **40**, *40, 40–41;* discounted cash flow (DCF) analysis, 39, **44,** *45,* 48; infrastructure costs, **47**; internal rate of return, 42, **43, 49**; key ratios, 42–43, **46**; net present value, 42, **43,** 49; pro forma statement, 42, *42;* return on cost (ROC), 46; sensitivity analysis, 46, **46,** 49; in underwriting process, 60

Financial Institutions Reform, Recovery, and Enforcement Act of 1989 (FIRREA), 89

Financing, 51–97; analysis of business park development, 61–70; analysis of industrial park development, 70–76; build-to-own development, 77, 80–81, 82; capitalization for industrial development, 52–55, *53;* characteristics of lending sources, *88;* closing requirements for permanent and interim loans, **94–95;** comparison of construction loans with permanent loans, *90;* construction financing, 87–90; debt, 51, 52, *52;* equity, 51, 52, *52;* equity investors' requirements, 76–82; fees for loans, 88; general requirements for loan submission package, **94;** interest rates, 88; interim, 90; joint venture build-to-own analysis, 82, *84–85;* lenders' requirements, 59–76; minimizing risk of lenders, 96; ownership forms, *54–55,* 55–58; package, 93–97; permanent, 90–93; predevelopment, 83–87; recourse loans, 60; REITs, 58–59; for research parks, 7; by seller, 86–87; sources of, *53;* of stages of development, 83–93; timetable for, 97; trends, 297; turnkey development, 77, *78–79. See also specific business parks*

Fire protection, 115, **132–33,** 137, 146, 189. *See also specific business parks and facilities*

First Industrial Realty Trust, 190

First Services, 190

First & Utah Associates, **260**

Fisher, Paul, **250**

Fixed-rate mortgages, 91

Flex facilities, **128**

Flex space, 138–39; defined, 3

Flex Tech (Chantilly, Virginia), *96*

Flexibility: building design, 5; industrial buildings, **131;** master plans, 4; R&D buildings, 140; warehouse/distribution facilities, 134

Flexible leases, **166**

Floorplates. *See* Size and shape of buildings

Focus Park (Brussels, Belgium) marketing plan, *153*

Foothill Ranch Business Park (Lake Forest, California), *104*

Foreign investors, 92–93, *93*

Foreign trade zone (FTZ), 137–38, **138, 296**

Fort Worth Alliance Airport, **198,** *199, 200*

Fred Hutchinson Cancer Research Center (Seattle, Washington), *102*

■

Gateway Business Park (South San Francisco, California), **216–21,** *217, 218, 219, 220, 221*

GE Capital, 89

Genentech, **216**

General contractors, 19

General Motors Acceptance Corporation (GMAC), 89

General Motors plant (St. Louis, Missouri), **282–83,** *283*

General purpose zone (GPZ), **138**

Geographic information system (GIS), **25**

Geometric requirements for roadways, 108

Geotechnical engineers, 18

Germany: Gewerbepark Regensburg, *224, 225, 226, 227*

Gewerbepark Regensburg (Regensburg, Germany), **222–27,** *223, 224, 225, 226, 227*

Gewerbeparks (logistics parks), 5

Glass, 135, 137, 138

Global TransPark (GTP), **268, 269, 296**

Goose Island (Chicago, Illinois), **10–11,** *11, 132*

Gordon, Richard, **268, 273**

Grading subcontractors, 28, 112–13

Graham Webb International (Carlsbad, California), *125, 145*

Green buildings, 124, **126–27,** 297

Gross leases, 165

Gross metropolitan product (GMP) and industrial warehouse analysis, 34

Ground leases, 87

Growth trends, 24

Grubb & Ellis, 30

GTE Communications Network (Dallas, Texas), *162*

Guard services, 190

■

Habitat Goose Island (Chicago, Illinois), **11**

Hanover, New Jersey, warehouse, *12*

Harman, Athena Z., 178

Harte Hanks Building (Valencia, California), **228–33,** *229, 230, 231, 232, 233*

Heavy industry, 12; reuse of buildings, 144–46

Height of buildings, **132;** manufacturing/assembly facilities, 136; warehouse/distribution facilities, 134; Web hosting facilities, 142

Hewlett-Packard facility (Bergamo, Italy), *133*

High-tech firms, 289; leasing to, **166;** technology parks for, 6

Highlands Industrial Park (Dallas, Texas): feasibility hypotheticals, 23; financial feasibility, **47–49,** *48. See also* Tradeport Distribution Center (Dallas, Texas) feasibility hypothetical

Highway Capacity Manual (Transportation Research Board), 108

Hillwood, **198–203**

Home Depot (Seattle, Washington), **260, 261, 264**

"Hot turnover," **192–93**

Hughes Aircraft Co. R&D facility (California), **168**

Hunt Midwest Real Estate Development, **276–78**

Huntwood Business Center (Haywood, California), *83*

HVAC systems: green buildings, 126–27; industrial buildings, **132;** renovation, 146; warehouse/distribution facilities, 134; Web hosting facilities, 142; wireless management of, **187.** *See also specific business parks and facilities*

■

Identity of project, 152–54

IDI Services Group, *101, 178, 179*

Illinois Environmental Protection Agency, **10**

Illustrative plans, 100

Impact fees for development, 27

In-house leasing agents, 164

Incentives for development, 24

Incubator parks, 6, 147

Individual direct ownership, *54–55,* 55–56

Industrial buildings: comparison of types of, **128;** design of, 124–47, *125;* key considerations for developers, **130–33;** location of, **130;** positioning of, 103; site plan of, **130–31;** size and shape of, **131–32.** *See also* Warehouse/distribution facilities; *specific buildings*

Industrial parks: definition of, 9; lenders'/investors' analysis of development, 70–76; site selection for, 27; types of facilities, 5. *See also specific industrial parks*

Industrial restricted (IR) zoning designation, 13

Industrial Vacancy Index of the U.S. (CB Richard Ellis), 30

Infrastructure, 24; costs, **47;** Global TransPark (GTP) system, **296**

Institute of Transportation Engineers' *Trip Generation,* 105

Institutional buildings, reuse of, 144–46

Insurance, 171, 179, 193. *See also* Life insurance companies

Intech Park (Indianapolis, Indiana), *4, 4*

Intelligent building systems, 127, **136**

Interest rates, 88

Interim financing, 90; closing requirements for, **94–95**

Internal rate of return (IRR), 42, **43, 49**

Internet: access, **136, 141;** advertising via, 159; and distribution patterns,